CONSUMER INSIGHT

MARKET RESEARCH IN PRACTICE SERIES

Published in association with The Market Research Society
Consultant Editors: David Barr and Robin J Birn

Kogan Page has joined forces with The Market Research Society (MRS) to publish this unique series which is designed specifically to cover the latest developments in market research thinking and practice. Taking a practical, action-oriented approach, and focused on established 'need to know' subjects, the series will reflect the role of market research in the international business environment. This series will concentrate on developing practical texts on:

- how to use, act on and follow up research;
- research techniques and best practice.

Great effort has been made to ensure that each title is international in both content and approach and where appropriate, European, US and international case studies have been used comparatively to ensure that each title provides readers with models for research relevant to their own countries.

Overall the series will produce a body of work that will enhance international awareness of the MRS and improve knowledge of its Code of Conduct and guidelines on best practice in market research.

Other titles in the series:

Market Research in Practice: A guide to the basics, Paul Hague, Nick Hague and Carol-Ann Morgan

Market Intelligence: How and why organizations use market research, Martin Callingham

The Effective Use of Market Research, Robin J Birn

Questionnaire Design, Ian Brace

Forthcoming titles:

Business to Business Market Research

To obtain further information, please contact the publisher at the address below:

Kogan Page Ltd
120 Pentonville Road
London N1 9JN
Tel: 020 7278 0433
www.kogan-page.co.uk

MRS MARKET RESEARCH IN PRACTICE

CONSUMER INSIGHT

HOW TO USE DATA AND MARKET RESEARCH TO GET CLOSER TO YOUR CUSTOMER

MERLIN STONE, ALISON BOND
& BRYAN FOSS

KOGAN
PAGE
London & Sterling, VA

Dedication

To my wife and daughters, Ofra, Maya and Talya – Merlin Stone

To my parents, Roy and Jacqueline Bond – Alison Bond

To my wife and children, Carol, Simon and Helen and to our extended family – Bryan Foss

Publisher's note

Every possible effort has been made to ensure that the information contained in this book is accurate at the time of going to press, and the publishers and authors cannot accept responsibility for any errors or omissions, however caused. No responsibility for loss or damage occasioned to any person acting, or refraining from action, as a result of the material in this publication can be accepted by the editor, the publisher or any of the authors.

First published in Great Britain and the United States in 2004 by Kogan Page Limited

120 Pentonville Road
London N1 9JN
United Kingdom
www.kogan-page.co.uk

22883 Quicksilver Drive
Sterling VA 20166-2012
USA

ISBN 0 7494 4292 1

British Library Cataloguing-in-Publication Data

A CIP record for this book is available from the British Library.

Library of Congress Cataloging-in-Publication Data

Consumer insight: how to use data and market research to get closer to your customer/Merlin Stone ... [et al.].
p. cm. – (Market research in practice series)
Includes index.
ISBN 0-7494-4292-1
1. Customer relations – Management. 2. Marketing research. 3. Database marketing. I. Stone, Merlin, 1948- II. Series.
HF5415.5.C6625 2004
658.8'34--dc22

2004014622

Typeset by Datamatics Technologies Ltd, Mumbai, India
Printed and bound in Great Britain by Creative Print and Design (Wales), Ebbw Vale

Contents

The Market Research Society

With over 8,000 members in more than 50 countries, The Market Research Society (MRS) is the world's largest international membership organization for professional researchers and others engaged in (or interested in) market, social and opinion research.

It has a diverse membership of individual researchers within agencies, independent consultancies, client-side organizations, and the academic community – at all levels of seniority and in all job functions.

All MRS members agree to comply with the MRS Code of Conduct (see Appendix), which is supported by the Codeline advisory service and a range of specialist guidelines on best practice.

MRS offers various qualifications and membership grades, as well as training and professional development resources to support these. It is the official awarding body in the UK for vocational qualifications in market research.

MRS is a major supplier of publications and information services, conferences and seminars, and many other meeting and networking opportunities for researchers.

MRS is 'the voice of the profession' in its media relations and public affairs activities on behalf of professional research practitioners, and aims to achieve the most favourable climate of opinion and legislative environment for research.

The Market Research Society (Limited by Guarantee) Company Number 518685

Company Information: Registered office and business address:
15 Northburgh Street, London EC1V OJR
Telephone: 020 7490 4911
Fax: 020 7490 0608
e-mail: info@marketresearch.org.uk
Web site: www.mrs.org.uk

The editorial board

CONSULTANT EDITORS

David Barr has been Director General of the Market Research Society since July 1997. He previously spent over 25 years in business information services and publishing. He has held management positions with Xerox Publishing Group, the British Tourist Authority and Reed International plc. His experience of market research is therefore all on the client side, having commissioned many projects for NPD and M&A purposes. A graduate of Glasgow and Sheffield Universities, David Barr is a Member of the Chartered Management Institute and a Fellow of the Royal Society of Arts.

Robin J Birn has been a marketing and market research practitioner for over 25 years. In 1985 Robin set up Strategy, Research and Action Ltd, which is now the largest international market research company for the map, atlas and travel guide sector, and the book industry. He is a Fellow of the Market Research Society and is also the editor of *The International Handbook of Market Research Techniques*.

ADVISORY MEMBERS

Martin Callingham was formerly Group Market Research Director at Whitbread, where he ran the Market Research department for 20 years and was a non-executive director of the company's German restaurant chain for more than 10 years. Martin has also played his part in the market research world. Apart from being on many committees of the MRS, of which he is a Fellow, he was Chairman of the Association of Users of Research Agencies (AURA), has been a council member of ESOMAR, and has presented widely, winning the David Winton Award in 2001 at the MRS Conference.

Nigel Culkin is a Fellow of the Market Research Society and member of its Professional Advisory Board. He has been a full member since 1982. He has been in academia since 1991 and is currently Deputy Director, Commercial Development at the University of Hertfordshire, where he is responsible for activities that develop a culture of entrepreneurism and innovation among staff and students. He is Chair of the University's, Film Industry Research Group (FiRG), supervisor to a number of research students and regular contributor to the media on the creative industries.

Professor Merlin Stone is Business Research Leader with IBM's Business Consulting Services, where he works on business research, consulting and marketing with IBM's clients, partners and universities. He runs the IBM Marketing Transformation Group, a network of clients, marketing agencies, consultancies and business partners, focusing on changing marketing. He is a director of QCi Ltd., an OgilvyOne company of the Database Group Ltd, Digital Data Analysis Ltd, The Halo Works Ltd and Nowell Stone Ltd. Merlin is IBM Professor of Relationship Marketing at Bristol Business School. He has written many articles and 25 books on marketing and customer service, including *Up Close and Personal: CRM @ Work*, *Customer Relationship Marketing*, *Successful Customer Relationship Marketing*, *CRM in Financial Services* and *The Customer Management Scorecard*, all published by Kogan Page, and *The Definitive Guide to Direct and Interactive Marketing*, published by Financial Times-Pitman. He is a Founder Fellow of the Institute of Direct Marketing and a Fellow of the Chartered Institute of Marketing.

Paul Szwarc began his career as a market researcher at the Co-operative Wholesale Society (CWS) Ltd in Manchester in 1975. Since then he has worked at Burke Market Research (Canada), American Express Europe, IPSOS RSL, International Masters Publishers Ltd and PSI Global prior to joining the Network Research board as a director in October 2000. Over the past few years Paul has specialized on the consumer financial sector, directing multi-country projects on customer loyalty and retention, new product/service development, and employee satisfaction in the UK, European and North American markets. Paul is a full member of the Market Research Society. He has presented papers at a number of MRS and ESOMAR seminars and training courses.

List of contributors

Julie Abbott is a Marketing Consultant and co-founder of the Sorath Partnership, specializing in Strategic Marketing and Knowledge Value.

David Bearman is CRM Manager of Boots, where he is responsible for its Advantage Card loyalty scheme.

Stephan A Butscher is a Partner with Simon, Kucher & Partners, Strategy & Marketing Consultants, specializing in price optimization and developing growth strategies for international companies.

Paul Crick is a Managing Consultant at IBM Business Consulting Services. He specializes in consumer marketing.

David Gilbert is Professor of Marketing in the School of Management at the University of Surrey. He specializes in marketing in the service sector and is the author of leading books on retailing and tourism.

Bryan Hassett is Managing Director of Digital Data Analysis Limited, specialists in customer insight and knowledge management.

Martin Hickley is a Senior Consultant with Customer Essential. He has worked for many years in the financial services and automotive industries. He specializes in Data Protection and CRM database design and use.

Jennifer Kirkby is Principal of White Waves. She has worked on many CRM projects and was until recently CRM Research Director for Garter.

Paul McDaid is an Insurance Solutions Architect with IBM. He has worked on many of IBM's most advanced data warehouse projects in financial services.

Tess Moffett is a Senior Consultant with IBM Business Consulting Services. She specializes in marketing and customer facing processes in the retail sector.

Douglas Morrison is a Senior Consultant with IBM Business Consulting Services Australia. He has been involved with many of IBM's most innovative CRM projects in airlines and financial services.

Clive Nancarrow is Professor of Marketing Research at Bristol Business School. He worked for 16 years in the market research industry and is still actively involved in many market research projects.

Nick Orsman is Management Partner and Head of Consultancy, OgilvyOne Consulting, London.

Mark Patron is a database-marketing consultant. Previously he was Managing Director of Claritas, and an Executive Vice President of VNU Marketing Information Europe BV.

Sharon Rees is Director, TNS Financial & Professional Services, specializing in Customer Commitment and Retention.

David Selby is an Advanced Analytics Consultant, with IBM Business Consulting Services. He specializes in real-time, data mining and other analytics solutions for CRM, supply chain and fraud detection.

Ronèl Schoeman currently heads the analysis team at The Database Group, where she is responsible for leading innovative projects with major clients in many industries.

Dr Alan Tapp is a Senior Lecturer in Marketing at Bristol Business School, University of the West of England. He is the author of the UK's best-selling direct marketing text.

Steve Wills is Managing Director of Strategic Research, an agency that specializes in the integration of insight from multiple sources.

Neil Woodcock is Chairman of QCi Ltd, owners of CMAT(tm) and specialists in helping companies improve profitability through better customer management.

Foreword

Consumer insight is a great term. It implies a depth of understanding of consumers. More than that, it implies sensible use of this understanding - to help consumers fulfil their needs. It also implies wisdom - organizations using understanding so that their position is as they want it to be, eg meeting customer or stakeholder needs, profitable, within budget, secure, or ethical.

Insight doesn't just happen, as this book shows. It's the result of different disciplines - particularly market research and customer database analysis - being combined and used to manage consumers, and to allow consumers to manage themselves because the insight has been used to develop ways to allow them to do it. In a world of Internet and mobile telephony, insight is often instant - or nearly so. The consumer calls you or logs on to your site, and tells you something, and you change what you offer them, based on the information they have just given.

Of course, not all insight is like this. Many marketers would argue that the most important consumer insights of all are to do with your brand, or with your overall offer or proposition. Others would argue that in addition, you must use consumer insight to work out whether your overall marketing effort is effective (doing what it should be doing) or efficient (doing it economically).

Of course, consumer insight supports all these areas - from changes in marketing strategies to improving interactions with individual consumers. Good consumer insight is the foundation of good customer relationship management. It's the foundation of any strategy to change how your operation relates to its market, such as e-business on demand strategies. This book is about business to consumer markets, but we at IBM can testify to the importance of understanding our business customers - insight has been a major area of investment for our global marketing community. The way we understand our customers and their needs has been responsible for our massive shift into solutions and consulting, which now account for the majority of our business. Perhaps most importantly of all, the work we do in IBM Business Consulting Services is dominated by projects in which insight into our clients' customers is the foundation stone.

This book is an introductory book, so it cannot give you 'everything you need to know about consumer insight'. But it covers nearly all the main issues, the issues we work on with our clients. It is the first book to map out fully the consumer insight territory. It's a great introduction for the many new recruits into insight - whether as clients, consultants or marketing service agencies. For more senior folk, it is full of ideas about how you can improve your consumer insight. It also explores some of the more difficult areas, like partnering and outsourcing, two of the areas we are asked about most often.

So whether you are just starting to reconsider how you understand your customers, or whether this is an issue that has been a top priority for years, this book is a great journey guide.

We wish you luck, and more importantly, better insight.

Gavin Potter
Customer Intelligence Partner,
IBM Business Consulting Services

Rod Street
CRM Partner,
IBM Business Consulting Services

Acknowledgements

The list of those I have to thank grows every year and is finally too long to include particular names. It includes anyone who has ever contributed to my thinking or publications (this book is a good example), the many companies that have allowed me to dig into them, and even paid me to do so, the senior professionals who have mentored me, my fellow directors of the various companies I am involved with for their desire to work with me, the academics who have encouraged me over the years and tolerated my intolerance of some academic ways, the professional institutes that have listened to me - and even those who haven't, the many publications, publishers and conference organisers who have disseminated my work and most importantly of all, my close colleagues at IBM who have ensured that I can continue to irritate people productively.

Merlin Stone

Thanks to Trevor Millard, my husband and business partner at ABA Research Ltd. His hard work allows me to focus on breaking new ground. The many discussions and debates with James Burkhardt at VNU Business Publications have sharpened some of the ideas in the book. Abigail Tierney of IBM has helped me fully realise the Halo concept, while Richard Lees of The Database Group provided valuable input into the early development of the Halo concept.

Alison Bond

Thanks to all those that continually encourage me, including my worldwide network of IBM colleagues, client contacts, IBM alliance partners, academics, professional body members, and not least, my mentors and mentees (you know who you are).

Bryan Foss

Introduction

Merlin Stone, Bryan Foss, Alison Bond and Steve Wills

INTRODUCTION

This is not just another book about market research, or about customer relationship management – although it has much say about both. It uses the term 'insight' advisedly. The term is not used just because it has become a fashion to name the person in charge of a newly merged market research and customer database department the 'customer insight manager'. 'Insight' is considered by some companies just a new name for market research, perhaps enhanced by information from a customer database, or the other way round.

Consumer insight has two forms. Firstly, there are Insights (plural) – flashes of inspiration, or penetrating discoveries that can lead to specific opportunities. Market research or customer databases can deliver these, and often do. However, much bigger than this, and central to what companies need today, is Insight (singular), defined as 'the ability to perceive clearly or deeply', a deep, embedded knowledge about our consumers and our markets that helps structure our thinking and decision making. Everyone involved in marketing needs this form of Insight. In a customer-focused organization (as many claim to be), it is something that almost everyone should have.

This type of insight is not just about having some pieces of a jigsaw, but all the pieces, and joined up to produce a quantified picture that all, from senior management to those who actually manage consumers, can see. It comes not just from market research. It comes from many pieces of research, combined with data from database(s), financial and planning data, market and competitor intelligence, and feedback from sales and customer service staff, including customer complaints. It comes from having a passion for expressing marketing situations in real numbers, and from trying to understand these numbers. It is a picture built from any and all sources that may be available – in a coherent format that addresses anomalies and apparent contradictions, and gives appropriate weight to all of them. The following case study shows how important this insight it, and how it results from combining evidence from customer databases and market research.

USING INSIGHT TO ATTACK

Tesco is the UK's largest retailer. Data from its loyalty card scheme, Clubcard, revealed that families with babies who shopped for childcare products at Tesco spent much more than similar families who did not buy these products from Tesco, although they bought similar amounts of other products. Tesco's market research revealed that non-baby product buyers trusted the Tesco brand less for baby products than for the other products that they bought at Tesco. These customers preferred to take their baby business to Boots, the leading retailer of healthcare products, despite it often charging up to 20 per cent more. Tesco therefore decided to modify its positioning towards mother and baby customers, partly by setting up the Tesco Baby Club. This and a number of other initiatives led to Tesco gaining share rapidly from Boots, and it now sells as much in childcare as its nearest two competitors, Boots and Mothercare.[1]

Few companies have this kind of Insight. Consumer goods companies have historically built insight-hungry cultures. Most of their insight comes from market research rather than consumer databases. They have fewer sources, so it is easier for them to build a complete picture. In many other industries, particularly those with direct contact with their end-consumers, so much information is available from so many sources (with databases often predominant) that creating a 'joined up' picture is much harder. Few companies have a formal structure that brings all these sources together.

What 'insight' includes

'Insight' combines several ideas. It includes 'classic' areas, such as knowing who consumers are, what they do, where they are, what they buy, what they would like to buy, what media they are exposed to and what media they choose to view, listen to or read. It also includes more psychological areas – what consumers think and feel, what their objectives and strategies are, and how these influence how they behave. Many of these are not conscious behaviours or thoughts on the part of consumers. Most are affected, perhaps even conditioned, by various external factors, from the state of the economy and society, to the way a brand is marketed. Consumers are not born wanting to buy a particular brand!

We also include areas that customer service (and latterly marketing) people focus on – such as the experience that the organization and its competitors gives to consumers. We include their feelings about the experience, and whether they indicated what they think about it, through complaints or compliments, or through requests for further information, or indeed whether they have unresolved problems. Perhaps most importantly of all, we include some idea of whether the organization has delivered against any promises made to customers (for instance through branding, product descriptions or marketing communications), and whether it has fulfilled the role in their life that consumers have allocated to it. Finally, it includes whether the organization is gathering and using customer insight properly – both in the legal sense but also in the sense of allowing customers to delineate where their privacy begins and consumer insight should end.

Process is included

This description of what we include in insight merely describes the insight organizations want to achieve. However, this book also covers the management of consumer insight – that is to say, the process by which organizations decide what consumer insight they need to have, then try to gain it, and then use it. For knowledge without a proper process to manage it can be expensive and even obstructive to the purposes of the organization. However, it is not just a question of whether or not the organization has a process. Rather, it is the quality of the process that counts. This process includes deciding what consumer insight it needs and what it does not need. It also includes how it aims to use insight and what operational processes are needed to make sure that it does use insight – either when the organization or its business partners are interacting with consumers, or when it is planning what to do with consumers. The many studies we have undertaken demonstrate that this is the main problem in this area that faces most larger organizations.[2]

We applaud companies that want to manage insight well – but we know it is not easy. Most organizations expect to have problems in managing consumer insight. This is partly because consumers are human, independent beings who are not in our control, but whose welfare is, or at least should be, important.

THE PROFESSIONAL DOMAIN OF CONSUMER INSIGHT

Professionally, the domain of consumer insight stretches from market research into database marketing, into customer service, into any function that deals directly with consumers - and into some that do not, but still have a strong interest in how consumers are managed, such as supply chain management. This book aims primarily to explain to market researchers how consumer insight is used in what used to be called direct marketing or even direct mail, then database marketing (a term still used by some, perhaps with 'customer' tagged on at the beginning), and in its latest forms customer relationship management or customer experience management. We use the term 'database marketing' a lot in this book. This is partly because while there is controversy about whether consumers want a relationship with suppliers or can successfully be managed in one, there is broad consensus among marketers that when you manage consumers using a database containing details about individual consumers, it greatly changes what you *can* do with them.

The relationship between market research and database marketing is often troubled. Database marketers need research to make their work effective. They also generate information that is useful to market researchers. However, sometimes market researchers feel threatened by database marketers, rather than encouraged to work with them. Much can be gained by using the information that database marketing generates. This includes how many and which customers a company has, how they are contacted, who responds and how, what they buy as a result, and so on. Knowing what to do with the numbers that normally result from a direct marketing campaign is a researcher's skill. The marriage between database marketing and market research can produce consumer insight without a single market research project being commissioned.

In this book, where market research is covered, it is generally from the database marketer's perspective. This is because this book has been written specifically for the Market Research Society's series, for market research practitioners and users, and more generally for marketers who want an introduction to how companies try to understand customers. Its aim is to explain to the market research community how organizations that have consumer databases use them for marketing. This includes how a database marketer uses market research to complement insights derived from the consumer database. Several other books in this series give researchers all they should know about market research. So, when we refer to the kinds of things your organization can do with customer data, we are not addressing the specialist database marketer, but rather the market researcher or marketers in general.

MANAGING CONSUMER INSIGHT

Most market researchers (other than in those few companies where consumer insight is properly organized and managed) have every reason to be confused by the inroads knowledge from customer databases has made into 'their' territory. However, this is an adversarial perspective. Both share a strong interest in consumer insight, in gaining it and acting upon it. The book is about the former – the 'acting on it' is of course the justification and the focus of books on marketing and customer relationship management. However, market researchers may well have been confused by the many transformations that database marketing has gone through, certainly in the 20 or so years that the authors have been involved with it. Fashions have come and gone. They are often linked with the great waves of technology that break upon the marketer's shore, particularly those associated with the ability to manage large customer databases, and with the technology used to interface with consumers – from advanced systems for producing direct mail, to telemarketing systems, and now the Internet and mobile telephony.

People too have come and gone. Direct mail or direct response marketing was born, like market research, in the 19th century. It looks very different in the 21st century, though many of the lessons learnt in earlier decades still apply. Perhaps just as importantly, the disciplines of database marketing have evolved as their application has spread from the world of mail order into utilities, financial services, retailing and business to business marketing. Today, mobile telephones, digital interactive television and the Internet have taken their place alongside direct mail, the sales force, ordinary telephony, stores and branches as important marketing media or channels. As a result, consumer insight arises from many sources. It must also be fed back to many channels, if consumers are to feel that they are being managed as they should be, using *their* information, irrespective of the channel they first used to contact a company.

CUSTOMERS AND CONSUMERS

This book focuses on final consumers, not on all customers. Given the word length restriction of the series (a good discipline that ensures that the authors communicate the absolute essentials), we cannot cover everything we would like. Because most market research is about individual consumers, citizens, patients or donors as customers, rather than organizations or companies as customers, this book focuses on consumers. The distinction is convenient, because database marketing and market research both differ in the two domains. So we have excluded organizational customers from this book. Focusing just on individual consumers makes it easier for us to write this book and for readers to read. We do not need to qualify statements constantly by saying 'In business markets, however ... '.

Of course, individual and organizational customers are not completely different. In most countries there are millions of small businesses, whose buying decisions are researched using consumer research techniques, and where database marketing techniques are virtually the same as in consumer markets. In many product and service categories, buyers decide using both business and personal criteria , as they do for financial services, travel, cars, even housing. For our purposes, the distinction is really between the techniques used to research markets or market segments where there are typically thousands, often millions, of consumers, as opposed to those where the number of customers is much smaller.

This means that database and direct marketers who read this book may be a little confused by the use of the word 'consumer' in phrases where they would normally expect to see the word 'customer'. We use the term 'consumer' wherever we can, to keep the focus clear. It is also grammatically correct, as many individuals who are the subject of this book are not customers of the organization but potential customers, or 'prospects'. Occasionally, a phrase we use would sound odd if we used 'consumer'. Thus, we have retained 'customer relationship management' (abbreviated it as CRM), 'customer satisfaction' and 'customer service'. With such phrases, using the word 'consumer' might make readers think we imply something other than the normal meaning.

KEEPING CONSUMERS AND STAKEHOLDERS HAPPY – FROM RESEARCH, THROUGH MEASUREMENT, TO MANAGEMENT

Organizations need consumer insight for much more than supporting specific marketing or service decisions. Consumer insight is an essential part of a mechanism that tells the organization whether it is meeting its consumers' needs while meeting the needs of other stakeholders. These include owners (such as shareholders), business partners (such as distributors and marketing service suppliers) and staff – particularly those who have to manage consumers, in stores or branches, contact centres, and leisure and transport facilities. This use of consumer insight is very important. Perhaps the best example is customer satisfaction surveys, but we also include measurement of the effectiveness of marketing campaigns and other initiatives.

This area is controversial because despite all the science of market research and customer database analysis, consumer insight is rarely used properly in this area. So rather than bury this discussion in the body of the book, we decided that we needed to air it at the beginning. This gives organizations something else to worry about – whether marketing and customer service are doing their job properly or whether they need transforming. Much in the planning of marketing and management has not changed for years, although the rapid evolution of information and communications technology has changed many areas. The authors are engaged in a programme of research and consulting in an area we have defined as 'marketing transformation'. Much of the work that we are doing relates to changes in how customers are managed, and in particular how insights into customers are developed and used.

Measuring customer satisfaction has become very big business. Many market research companies make much of their profit from it. Staff measurement and motivation systems are increasingly based on customer satisfaction targets. Despite this, surveys show declining customer satisfaction in most markets. Setting targets and measuring customer satisfaction do not make customers any happier, or more likely to repurchase. Much so-called consumer insight purports to tell organizations what their consumers want, but only tells them what they have said – very different. This may be because if an organization focuses only on what consumers say about its products or services, this can stifle its creativity and limit innovation. Setting staff targets using information based on what consumers are saying they want can make the situation worse. Organizations are driven in the direction of their targets and measures. This is fine if the measures and targets are something that the people in the business and its stakeholders and consumers truly want, but this is rare. Customers may say they want to be answered more quickly in call centres. However, they might give much higher priority to better value for money. They might be happy to make compromises in terms of ease of access by telephone. The success of low-cost airlines demonstrates this.

The targets and measures being set in larger companies and public service organizations have become increasingly complex and controlling in the last few years. 'If you can measure it you can manage it' has spread like a cancer. This led to large-scale customer satisfaction surveys, targets and league tables – and a fall in customer loyalty and overall satisfaction. The focus has been on winning the league rather than offering customers the products or services they want. This focus has become internal, leading staff and the entire organization away from first considering the customer.

League tables and metrics induce stress. They focus mainly on cost reduction and control. Neither motivate staff. They stifle innovation and bold thinking, vital for success. Retention of good staff gets harder. Negative staff behaviour spreads. Perhaps the best example is replying quickly to complaints rather than resolving them. Organizations have targets for so many areas that are nothing to do with the organization's original intent. For a target to move a business the direction its customers would really like, targets should relate to things customers and staff both want, to the real reasons customers buy its products or services, not to transactional factors whose only justification for inclusion is that they are easy to measure.

In many health service organizations, the strategic intent is far removed from where it should be. A health service's reason for being is about helping new humans be born, keeping people as healthy as possible, and where this fails, healing and sustaining them and in the end, helping them die with dignity and minimum pain. For many health workers, measures are not related to any of these. Rather, measures are process and transaction-based, counting beds, people on trolleys, queue lengths, waiting times and costs to serve, all important in achieving efficiencies, but not delivering the service people need.

Wherever there is a disconnect between the internal measures and the real reason a company or organization exists, there is stress, because staff know they are not doing what they should really be doing. Short-term thinking dominates because the organization is only trying to hit the next target. Consumers are unhappy because they can feel the organization's pain every time they deal with it.

Head or halo?

The answer to this apparent conundrum is to ensure that the consumer insight process helps to change how we think about consumers, staff and our organizations, rather than supports a counterproductive way of thinking about them. Marketers need to think about why they are doing the things they are doing, and why their organization exists. Once this has been defined, they should redefine what they measure. This may mean disposing of many internal measures, put in place to manage and control people. We call these the 'head' measures. Marketers tend to be hyper-rational. Their actions and measures relate to things like:

- profiling and targeting;
- cost per contact and response rates;
- conversion rates and cross/up-sell ratios;
- campaign return on investment (RoI) and value of the customer to the company.

We argue that they should be replaced, or at least balanced, by measures relating to what the business or organization aims to do for its customers. We call these 'halo' measures, and they can be measured, but differently. We define the 'halo' as follows:

- It is what customers see when the organization is as they want it to be.
- It is what staff and suppliers are proud to have when the organization is as customers want it to be.
- It shines in every communication with customers.
- It makes customers welcome the organization's communications and treat them seriously.
- It makes them opt in to the organization's communications, not opt out.
- It appears when the organization creates its future around its customers' needs, and its communication supports this.

The reason is that while consumers might want to cost minimize or just get the best return, depending on the product or service category, they might just want to feel happy, interested, safe, reassured or insulated from shocks. They might even want their suppliers to be their guardian angel (for the category).

A clear halo definition enables an organization to assess the effectiveness of its actions in relation to its stakeholders' expectations. Defining the organization's halo and structuring its objectives around this halo is the departure point for such transformation. It gives a clear, unambiguous destination for an entire organization. Put simply, if the organization wants people to have a good day, then the measurement needs to relate to whether its consumers had a good day, not whether staff picked up the phone quickly! If the organization aims to bring benefits to consumers (a standard marketing objective), its measurements should affirm its desire to do so, and ensure that it is on course for this aim. It is not a vision statement, but a measurable affirmation of the aim of the organization. The measurement attached to it should be visible to all in the organization.

Each person should be able to see where his or her part of the effort to meet the measurable affirmation is, and how close he or she is coming to their goal.

This argument has clear implications for consumer insight. The main one is that if the organization uses performance measurement techniques that are based upon consumer insights but that exclude insight into whether consumers really got what they wanted, then they are likely to be unwittingly driving the organization in the wrong direction. At a technical level, it means that any interpretation of consumer insight that does not use insights into whether consumers got what they wanted is likely to be misleading.

THE HALO AT WORK IN INSURANCE

Motor insurance Company A bought a smaller insurance Company B. The management of the combined operation wanted to know why Company B was performing less well under its new owners. Company A always made good profits, whereas Company B only made moderate profits, despite being known as an excellent employer and having a good share of markets known to be more profitable. Company A had focused on reducing costs in Company B, whose sales levels and profits were falling. Across both companies, complaints were rising, staff turnover was above 50 per cent in some key areas and their public profile was being dented by media stories concerning the quality of their service when claims were made and vehicles repaired. The halo process was used to discover whether the reasons for the above were related to the direction in which staff were facing.

It turned out that staff in both companies were focused on very small areas of the business. This focus was intense and heavily targeted. The transactional focus of all the measures meant that the company was being managed by numbers and not a vision. The staff vision was now simply of the company making lots of money. Not surprisingly this was the focus that customers felt when they made a claim. All staff jobs were divided into small parts, where each individual delivered only a small part of the overall service. This allowed the company to set targets for virtually every transaction, but no one could see the big picture.

Research using the halo process allowed the company to put the disparate pieces of information together and show how it felt to be a customer receiving service from such a fragmented company. Once the company saw the result of breaking its staff's roles into such small pieces and setting each area of the business in competition with other areas, it was left with a choice. It could take action and join the pieces together again by re-targeting on bigger measures (what the customers wanted) and taking out some of the harmful transactional ones, or stay as it was.

The validity of this approach was confirmed when an insurance company got very bad publicity about the quality of work from one of its own repair centres. It was targeting its repair shops on the speed of the repair. It had taken it as a given that the quality of the repair would be up to standard, but the need to meet time targets prevailed over the quality of the repair. Staff were bonused on repairing quickly. Clearly targeting needed to change to encourage safe repairs. If this business had been using good customer insight techniques, allowing it to understand what its customer really wanted, this problem could have been avoided.

A similar problem surfaced through a research study carried out by the authors.[3] When a customer buys auto insurance there is a myth that everyone only wants to buy the cheapest, and that price drives the decision. This might be true of those who have never claimed, but once individuals have claimed, whether on their own or someone else's insurance, the service received when claiming becomes much more important. One of the key factors is the provision of a replacement car while the claimant's car is being mended or replaced. To save money, many insurers do not give a replacement car as standard. Some offer it as a paid-for extra. However this is often not discussed with consumers, as it takes the premium above a price point and highly targeted sales people do not want to jeopardize the sale. One insurance company that practised the add-on price, and found that sales agents did not offer it, discovered that its claim complaint levels were rising, to such an extent that the agents handling claims had unprecedented call volumes. The majority of complaints came from claimants left with no replacement car. The company needed to modify how it motivated its agents so that they sold what customers really needed, rather than just on price.

INSIGHT AND KNOWLEDGE MANAGEMENT

Consumer insight is part of what organizations know. Knowledge comes in two forms, explicit and tacit. Explicit knowledge is recorded, in manuals, documents, databases, intranets and so on. Tacit knowledge is in people's heads. It is based on learning, skills and experience. Much of the focus on knowledge management comes from recognition that so much of any business's knowledge base is tacit – and therefore, as an asset it is not 'fixed'. If an individual with vital knowledge leaves the organization, that knowledge is lost.

This idea of tacit and explicit knowledge leads to four forms of communication:

- **explicit to explicit** (such as IT data transfers);
- **tacit to explicit** (formally recording what people know);
- **explicit to tacit** (getting stored knowledge into people's heads such that it can be applied);
- **tacit to tacit** (helping people to communicate directly to share knowledge and experience).

The main difference between consumer insight and mainstream knowledge management is in the emphasis on these forms of communication. The emphasis of much knowledge management work is on making tacit knowledge explicit, helping organizations to capture and secure as an asset knowledge in the heads of their people. With consumer insight, the emphasis is the other way round. Most information is explicit already – in the form of research reports, statistics, and presentations – and the issue is that of making it tacit. The goal is to communicate it widely and to get it into the heads of all those who should be using it.

The effectiveness of communicating insights depends on many factors. Just a few factors account for most of this.[4] The four main factors are resources, skills, organization and planning. After these, success depends on factors such as measuring the impact of Insight, and actively helping with implementation of recommendations. In other words, the keys to success are 90 per cent structural and process, with only the 'icing on the cake' coming from creativity and presentational techniques. Put simply, if you plan to communicate insight effectively, and have the resources, organization and primary skills to do it, then it will happen.

CONSUMER INSIGHT AND MARKETING TRANSFORMATION

The agenda of marketing transformation includes everything from merging marketing with other functions, or abolishing or outsourcing marketing, to marketing taking over accountability for new areas. It includes destroying the boundaries between marketing, sales, service, human resources, operations, logistics and so on. It includes making radical changes to marketing strategies, processes, organization, targets and so on. Transformation requires answering strategic questions. For example, how can your marketing be twice as effective at half the cost? How can you accelerate your marketing activities so you can do everything at four times the speed and half the cost without sacrificing quality? How can you learn more quickly and effectively what your customers need and reorganize your resources to meet these needs? However, it also involves dealing with more tactical issues, such as the cost-effectiveness and quality of specific marketing activities.

Some organizations have already made big changes. Gone are the separate customer database and market research departments, merged into a customer insight department. Gone are the separate departments managing individual channels, such as mail, call centres or the e-channel, to be replaced by a team managing delivery channels. Brand is no longer the preserve of the brand manager and the advertising agency – it is a shared accountability. Gone is the idea of a five-year business plan and a two-year marketing plan, with the current year's plan unchanged for the whole year. Feedback from the market now arrives in hours, even minutes, and policies can be changed in days, even hours. This acceleration of the feedback loop from consumers into real time has put new pressures on marketing managers – they need to understand more quickly in order to react coherently. The development of much improved standards covering everything from customer data to electronic interaction has also facilitated outsourcing of many marketing tasks – even systems for managing the sales force have been available on an applications service provision basis for some time. While the debate about the strengths and weaknesses of outsourcing for different marketing activities continues to range, very few large marketing departments do not outsource some aspects of their activity.

In marketing effectiveness, a similar story emerges. In the last two decades we have taken great leaps forward in gathering, analysing and interpreting data from marketing, sales and service. For most companies marketing spend is between 3 and 10 per cent of turnover, so the sums of money involved are not small. For most companies, marketing is a strategic investment rather than a support cost. This means that getting it right influences the organization's long-term competitiveness and prosperity. However, it is hard to optimize it. It is hard to identify impact and value, especially where it comes to longer term/strategic benefits. The costs can usually be identified readily, but benefits are more often uncertain. Marketing is a competitive business, so inevitably there are winners and losers. It seems that much marketing spend is 'wasted', whether measured financially or in terms discussed above – it focuses on the head, not the halo.

The problem is compounded by problems of definition. For example, should we consider all customer-facing investment and activity, or just specific areas such as advertising and promotion? There is an important distinction between efficiency and effectiveness – a spend can be efficiently executed but yet be ineffective judged against strategic goals, and these in turn might be poorly articulated (and ignore what the consumer wants), so efficiency alone is not enough. Problems of definition and measurement are compounded by today's environment (new models, channels, new technologies) facing the customer and in the back office (new types of relationship, and even new consumer behaviour). The use of mobile phones by young people is a good example.

This is all the more reason for organizations to need to focus strongly on marketing effectiveness, and to admit the possibility that this focus may necessitate a radical rather than incremental change in how marketing money is spent, involving a redefinition of what the organization is trying to do for consumers. An explicit drive by management to improve marketing effectiveness pays in several ways. The first is by eliminating wasted spending. In our work we often see savings of 15–30 per cent of total marketing spend. More importantly, aligning investment behind an organization's main priorities shows that 40–50 per cent of total spend needs to be reallocated. This usually comes as a result of a comprehensive review of effectiveness.

The gains made by reallocation can be conserved in two ways. First, organizations need to develop the capability to sustain improvements in performance in the market. Second and perhaps more importantly, they need to build a foundation for transformation in the market. In many cases this is done by establishing the essential measurement conditions for consumer insight to lead the organization, but it may also lead to changes in the way supply chains are managed, to reduce costs all the way through to the consumer, so consumers get what they want, and cost-effectively too! Of course, achieving absolute effectiveness is impossible, but the basics can be achieved. This means putting the right analytical effort into tracking the effectiveness of large investments, into sustained improvement, and into being smarter than the competition.

This approach demands that marketing works as a reinforcing system of activities that lead to customers getting what they really want, not just their transactional requirement. An essential prerequisite is true consumer insight – what do consumers really want, and how do they go about trying to get it? In some areas it would be better to spend more to achieve greater effectiveness (accompanied by greater cuts or switches elsewhere). Proportionate cuts and stiff targets across the board rarely produce the best outcome. Priority-based budgeting helps to re-base the budget, but care has to be taken that the resultant 'portfolio of spend' is balanced and aligned strategically to what consumers want.

One example of success is e-enablement (for example, Web-based marketing as practised by low-cost airlines and book retailers), where consumers control the process, decide what they want and buy it. There are also many examples of situations in which up-to-date and accurate consumer insight data is given to call centre or branch staff when the customer calls in (inbound marketing). Sales (and customer satisfaction) levels escalate. The proportion of contacts (compared with outbound marketing, when the supplier contacts existing customers) that results in both qualified prospects and sales can increase 20 or 40 times. This is because consumers are being offered something they want as opposed to something they don't want!

Is this transformation? Well, the work that needs to go into cleaning and analysing data and making it available via computers to the staff members handling customer calls, into training and motivating staff to want to meet customers' needs and to being sensitive to the immediate reason for their calls, into devising compensation systems that do not lead staff to push at the wrong time, *is* transformational. It requires changing marketing emphasis and breaking down functional barriers (between marketing and service, for example). It requires consumer-focused marketing to have a strong influence on branches and call centres, and on Web sites. It affects product design as well, as organizations discover much more quickly what their current customers really want, now. The gain is transformational too – it is not trivial.

However, you must determine whether and what you need to transform. Transformation costs money and takes much management thought, time and effort. It must start at the top too. If your competitors get more value per consumer than you do because they are using consumer insight to meet their consumers' needs, they may be under less pressure to recruit new customers. They know, better than you, which customers yield greater value if their needs are met, so they can be more selective about whom they recruit. They can concentrate their marketing on attracting potentially more valuable customers, leaving you with the rest. Over the years, the value of your customer base will decline relative to theirs. You will find it hard to meet your consumers' needs while making a profit. That's insidious! However, this situation can be changed by a change of focus and attitude, particularly at the top of a business, if this change of attitude relates to a move towards something that customers really want from the business or organization, or away from something they do not. The idea of pounding the numbers to squeeze out an extra half of one percent return is fading, as consumers wise up to smart communication and want a real benefit from the product or service being offered.

The implications of this for marketing, customer insight and market research are clear. We can learn from success and failure in customer relationship management (see Chapter 4). Here, companies are more likely to succeed if they understand that they are changing their model of consumer management, and so must use change management techniques and have people dedicated to managing change. This applies to marketing in general and to managing efficiency, effectiveness and consumer insight. If this change is not managed well, you will probably gain little insight and fail to understand how changing the relationship between you and your consumers can improve your business. You have a choice about how to use consumer insight. You can use it just to get slightly better at what you do now, or you can use it to transform your marketing and customer service. This book shows you how to do both, but we would prefer it if you took the transformational option and learnt from the getting-slightly-better one.

ORGANIZATION OF THIS BOOK

Chapter 1 considers why we need different kinds of consumer insight in a world where many organizations use database marketing techniques. It introduces the reader to the world of database marketing. It investigates the kinds of policy decisions that depend on it, for different kinds of organizations (not just companies) in different situations (direct to consumer, intermediated), with different perspectives (strategic to tactical) for different policy areas (such as different types of marketing mix decisions).

Chapter 2 explains how consumer databases are used, and what kinds of companies use them, for what purpose.

Chapter 3 explains how database marketing and customer care use consumer insight for their day-to-day operations of planning and running campaigns.

Chapter 4 examines the idea of different models of consumer management, from situations in which individual named consumers are managed in a very explicit and overt fashion, to situations where consumers are managed by intermediaries on behalf of a supplier, and where suppliers prefer to manage consumers on an anonymous basis, focusing on other aspects of the marketing mix, such as brand, product, price, media advertising and distribution channels. It probes how consumer insight is used in these different models. It then explores in more detail the customer relationship management model (CRM).

Chapter 5 explores the relationship between consumer insight as derived and used in database marketing, and CRM and consumer insight as developed in market research. It investigates how consumers give data during an organization's transactions with them, how data can be acquired from other sources, how data is built up during the consumer's relationship (if any) with the organization, and how market research can add depth to this data. Chapter 4 also considers how we get the information into a form that we can use for consumer insight, and whether to analyse and understand consumers in general or in groups, or to manage particular consumers so as to meet their needs more effectively.

Chapter 6 investigates how consumer insight is developed as a result of analysis of consumer data. Having lots of data in a usable form is one thing; analysing it to make sense of is another. This chapter covers topics such as statistical analysis and profiling. It also suggests how market research can add value to this process, by for example probing more deeply the needs and behaviour of groups that have been identified by profiling. This chapter also explores how other methods of analysis in marketing, service and other functions (for example, as applied to other aspects of the marketing mix, such as communications media, products, pricing and channels, or as applied to other problems, such as risk) need to be modified to take into account the consumer dimension. This chapter also covers an advanced topic within analysis - data mining. This approach for extracting insights from large amounts of consumer data is becoming increasingly common.

Chapter 7 examines two very important aspects of consumer insight's use in marketing - in customer retention and customer development.

Chapter 8 explores what happens when two organizations wish to share consumer insights. It then explores how customer loyalty schemes work when data sharing is involved.

Chapter 9 considers the many legal, political and social issues associated with consumer insight. These include data protection, compliance with sector regulations (as for financial services or telecommunications) privacy, intrusiveness, social exclusion, risk management and security.

Chapter 10 explores the effect of information and communications technology on the processes by which customer information is gathered, stored, updated, analysed and used, for every purpose from marketing and service planning to interacting with individual consumers.

Chapter 11 suggests different ways to organize and manage consumer insight. This is not just about organizational structure, but rather about how to make use of consumer insight in practice - including issues of speed and quality of deployment. It also covers issues of rules and rights that need to observed between departments, between suppliers and intermediaries, between companies and data providers, if the arrangement is to work well. It also explores how you can identify where you are in consumer insight terms, where to go and how to get there. It explores how change management and programme management disciplines can help. It also explores the investments required and business case issues.

NOTES

1 For details on this, see Humby, C and Hunt, T with Philips, T (2003) *Scoring Points*, Kogan Page, London, chapter 12.
2 See, for example, Stone, M, Woodcock, N and Foss, B (2002) *The Customer Management Scorecard*, Kogan Page, London, especially chapters 11, 12, 22 and 31.
3 Bond, A and Stone, M (2004) *Consumer Research Study into the Motor Insurance Market*, Bristol Business School.
4 Wills, S and Williams P (2004) Insight as a strategic asset: the opportunity and the stark reality, paper presented at Market Research Society Conference 2004.

1 What is database marketing?

Merlin Stone, Alison Bond, Bryan Foss and Mark Patron

INTRODUCTION

In this chapter, we describe the discipline of database marketing– direct contact with individual consumers. We show that its strengths lie in using consumer insight to support targeting, measurement and testing, so as to find the best method of managing consumers. We show that its focus is not just on the acquisition of new consumers, but on keeping consumers, and developing their value.

Database marketing is now an essential part of marketing in many industries. The main principle of database marketing is that at least part of the communication organizations have with their consumers is direct – to named consumers. From this simple principle has grown a whole new discipline. However, it has not grown that quickly. The seeds of database marketing as we use it today were sown in the 19th century by the US mail order industry, which served so well the needs of remote farmers, ranchers, settlers and new townships.

Database marketing can be summed up as essentially:

- **Targeted:** reaching the consumer in an appropriate manner for them, to prompt a response.
- **Direct:** the communications go directly between the organization and the consumer, with no intermediary. Consumers can generally feel, touch, see or hear the communication to them as individuals.
- **Marketing:** it helps meets consumers' needs and the organization's profit, sales and other objectives.

Database marketing has three further important characteristics:

- It is based on **direct** responses. Database marketing communications invite consumers to respond – by mail, telephone, Internet, redeemable retail vouchers and so on. The response may range from enquiry and giving information to ordering. This opportunity for monitoring feedback is critical to database marketing.
- Database marketing is **measurable**. In any database marketing campaign, responses are measured, evaluated and analysed. Responses can be through any medium – telephone, mail, Internet hits or whatever. Measuring responses leads to accountability. All costs can be related to response. Return on investment can be calculated. Traditional advertising relies mainly on market research techniques based on samples to measure effectiveness, although for some campaigns sales results can be accurately measured (for example, if the campaign is run in test areas only). Database marketers use transaction data to measure. This is one reason database marketing has been called scientific advertising. Database marketers conduct their tests in controlled environments. While environments do change, database marketing is as near to a science as marketing achieves.
- Database marketing usually requires the organization to build and maintain a database of consumers and prospects. This gives it better understanding of the market and can give it competitive advantage.

Technical definition

Database marketing is the planned implementation, recording, analysis and tracking of consumers' direct response behaviour over time to derive future marketing strategies, for developing long-term consumer loyalty and ensuring continued business growth. Let's consider this definition in more detail:

1. **Planning marketing activity.** All database marketing should form part of a controlled marketing strategy, which has been produced as a result of market and competitor analysis and in relation to achievable objectives.
2. **Targeting consumers.** Consumer information should be stored and capable of manipulation and retrieval from the consumer database, to contact existing consumers. Analysis of this also helps the organization to identify characteristics of future consumers.
3. **Measuring your marketing activity.** The results of database marketing should be measured, to tell you what works and what does not.

4. **Tracking.** This involves monitoring consumers' responses over time, for as long as the relationship with them lasts. This allows the organization to measure their value, and understand how much of it results from how it marketed to them.
5. **Consumer behaviour.** Tracking the spending patterns and general behaviour of consumers can help the organization establish which products are popular and which are not. This can help it determine future products and strategy.
6. **Future strategies.** One aim of marketing is to maximize the value of the organization's consumers to it. The previous steps will ensure it has the information to plan effective and efficient marketing to achieve this aim.
7. **Developing long-term loyalty.** By targeting the right consumers, offering them what they want, and encouraging them to take more of your products, an organization can protect its consumer base. Its consumers will be more likely to stay with it for longer.
8. **Encouraging profitable growth.** This is achieved by increasing the number of loyal and valuable consumers the organization has, and limiting the number of consumers with low value and/or high risk. This increases turnover and profit, which can be re-invested to ensure service and product standards are maintained and that consumers stay happy.

So database marketing is a continuing process of acquiring new consumers, continuing to satisfy existing consumers, and developing all consumers so as to achieve greater loyalty and increased purchasing. Here is an example. Increased loyalty is needed in the highly competitive airline industry to guarantee future re-purchase and provides a much needed unique selling proposition (USP) as consumers have increased choices. Scheduled airlines compete with other scheduled airlines for premium business travellers and with low-cost airlines for budget flyers (who now include many business flyers). For premium business travellers, database marketing is used to identify the most valuable consumers, who are rewarded, to motivate them to continue flying and to buy more premium tickets. Rewards include access to silver and gold business lounges, free points and free flights.

CHANNELS FOR MANAGING CONSUMERS DIRECTLY

A variety of channels are used to manage named consumers directly. They include:

- mail;
- face to face – retail/branches, rarely a sales force;
- Internet/e-mail;
- interactive digital television;
- fixed-line telephone;
- mobile telephone.

Notice that some of these (mail and retail/branch) can be used as a communication channel as well as a distribution channel for physical products, and all can be used as both for information-based products such as financial services. Note too that many businesses work, at least partially, through intermediaries – wholesalers, retailers, dealers and distributors. Much marketing effort is spent on moving the product along the channel. Here there are two communication challenges: marketing to the trade, and marketing to final consumers. In trade marketing, branding was the most powerful tool for 'pulling products through the channel'. However using database marketing, it is possible to mount targeted sales promotion campaigns to encourage consumers to visit retail outlets or dealerships. This is one way manufacturers deal with increasing retailer power and fragmenting media. To reach the consumer directly, local door drops can be used to motivate the consumer to visit the nearest outlet for the product, rather than another product.

Many packaged consumer goods companies use targeted household mailings or leaflet drops. Hair care companies and grocery product relaunches (for tea bags, washing powder and the like) often use door drops and free newspaper distribution to hit postcodes with their messages, perhaps with product samples attached. Some intermediaries have developed this further and send personalized vouchers and money-off coupons, which are scannable and trackable in-store. Car manufacturers use similar techniques, often combined with local radio, to persuade individuals to visit their local dealership. These manufacturers also collect consumer information for planning. Manufacturers of consumer durables, such as washing machines and dishwashers, collate warranty and guarantee card information, and store this information on a database for marketing of other products and repeat products after a certain time. They also sponsor lifestyle questionnaires, and market to people expressing an interest in their product or category.

There are many ways in which consumer data can be collected and added to the database, even when the organization deals with consumers through retailers. They include:

- money off coupons and other offers in the media;

- warranty guarantee cards;
- consumer satisfaction questionnaires;
- loyalty cards and schemes;
- deals with credit card or store card marketers to access their consumers;
- lifestyle surveys;
- e-mail addresses captured on the Web site.

However, when brand awareness is raised by media advertising, database marketing response rates rise, especially when the overall marketing campaign is so well integrated that consumers recognize the communication as being part of a wider campaign from the same company. Database marketing works best as part of an overall communication strategy. Combining several types of marketing communication exposes consumers to the message more times in more ways, so they are more likely to respond to the offer.

HOW DATABASE MARKETING WORKS

- **It converts interest into sales.** Database marketing does so by being, as its name suggests, direct. The message and call to action must be clear to be responsive. The call to action, often perceived as unsightly by brand advertisers, does not usually reduce the creative impact of the advertisement. Brand image is important to long-term preferences, but response can be vital to short- and long-term sales and loyalty building.
- **It can deliver prospects.** If the advertisement can get the consumer to respond, the sender can begin the process of capturing consumer information.
- **It reinforces brand image.** Database marketing can convey general branding messages, while at the same time building goodwill, reinforcing purchase decisions, or saying thank you. These are all ways to reinforce branding and future sales and to encourage word of mouth advertising, the cheapest and most effective way to acquire new consumers.
- **It creates interaction with consumers.** Mass marketing tends to consist of a one-way flow of messages, with results measured by sales and market research. An essential component of database marketing is the response mechanism. This ensures that the message has been received. The more consumer information flows back to the organization, the better targeted, more relevant and more personalized its messages to its consumers can become.

- **It is measurable and accountable.** As the pressure on advertising budgets increases, so does the need to measure the effectiveness of contacts. Database marketing produces measurable results that can prove that spend is producing results.

Database marketing is as near a science as marketing can hope to be. It allows controlled experiments and tests, where one type of contact acts as a control to represent the current situation or the norm. The other acts as the test for different approaches. This allows you to measure the effect of the changes and identify stronger formats, messages, offers and lists.

PLANNING YOUR DATABASE MARKETING ACTIVITY

There are three key areas to consider in planning what campaigns to run with your consumers:

- **acquisition** – recruiting new consumers;
- **database management** – storing and manipulating consumer information;
- **retention and development** – consumer care/loyalty and other programmes to keep and develop existing consumers.

Acquisition marketing

This involves:

- Deciding what kinds of consumers you want – your target market.
- Finding out who they are, how many of them are there and where they are – this is assessing the market opportunity.
- Understanding what motivates them – using market research and feedback to identify your key selling points and USP if you have one.
- Determining which media to use to talk to them. What media do they consume? What papers do they buy, when do they have time to think about your proposition?
- Developing communication and executing campaigns – what tone of voice to use, which paper and formats are cost-effective and appropriate, when is the best time to communicate with them, when do sales have to come in by.

- Converting prospects to consumers – the sale. What information supports this conversion, whether it takes place remotely, by letter or through a contact centre? How should sales staff be trained to do this? What material should be sent to the consumer to achieve and confirm the sale?

Database management

This involves:

- Obtaining relevant consumer information – who are the best consumers, what attributes do they have, how many prospects are available like them?
- Storing the information in a usable, retrievable and secure format.
- Enhancing this information over time – making sure systems feed into the database so it is kept up to date.
- Analysis of the information to identify consumers – when and what they last bought, their value, the segment they belong to, products held.
- Selection of target segments of consumers for campaigns – certain segments may warrant different actions for different reasons.
- Recording sales and response – it is important to know what works and what does not.
- Evaluating, measurement and future business planning – for strategies to maximize the value of the database.

Retention and development

This involves:

- Giving consumers service and product quality that meets their needs.
- Building loyalty over time.
- Maximizing the length and value of the relationship with consumers.
- Communicating to them regularly at the right time (that is right for them!).
- Deepening the relationship with consumers by encouraging them to buy different types of product, to upgrade and renew.
- Monitoring profitability.

FUTURE VALUE OF CONSUMERS

If a consumer's transaction data is accumulated for a long enough period, you can calculate the future value of the consumer. This can be used for several purposes, such as:

- Making campaign decisions which both generate a profit and increase future consumer value. Recent buyers are nearly always among the most frequent responders to additional offers.
- Setting levels of investment in consumer acquisition and reactivation.
- Monitoring future business prospects. An increasingly valuable list indicates a solidly growing business, while a list whose value is deteriorating indicates a business with a problematic future.
- By knowing who are its best consumers – who has the largest future value, their acquisition source (how they were acquired – direct mail, phone with a special offer and so on) – the organization can acquire more of the same. By matching their characteristics (where they live, age, income and so on) with the rest of the population, it can target others with the same attributes. This is smart acquisition.

APPLICATIONS OF THE CONSUMER DATABASE

Consumer databases can be used in:

- testing an offer or medium – keeping it and finding patterns;
- modelling the expected performance of potential consumers for the offer, using these results;
- analysing the financial implications of promotion to different types of consumers;
- targeting narrowly defined market segments with specialized offers;
- defining programmes for reactivating lapsed consumers;
- evaluating sources of the most valuable consumers, for targeting of new ones;
- determining the optimal frequency of promotions;
- quantifying the number of consumers likely to buy new products or services and researching their needs;
- testing new products or services;
- measuring marketing effectiveness across several distribution channels – provided each can be tracked accurately;
- identifying groups of consumers who are, or will become, loyal if communicated with through a programme.

WHAT A CONSUMER DATABASE IS AND WHY WE NEED IT

Database marketing depends on insights from consumer information. Managing a relationship with consumers over many contacts would simply be impossible were it not for recent developments in information technology - particularly telecommunications and database management. Database marketing relies on creating a bank of information about individual consumers (taken from orders, enquiries, consumer service contacts, research questionnaires, external lists). This information is then used to analyse consumers' buying and enquiry patterns. This analysis, combined with the opportunity offered by the database to contact individual consumers through a variety of media, allows you to achieve a number of different objectives, such as:

- designing products to meet the needs of identified consumers;
- targeting the marketing of products and services more accurately;
- promoting the benefits of brand loyalty to consumers at risk from competition;
- identifying consumers most likely to buy new products and services;
- increasing sales effectiveness;
- supporting low-cost alternatives to traditional sales methods;
- making the marketing function more accountable;
- improving the link between advertising and sales promotion, product management and sales channels;
- improving consumer care, by making all relevant information available at the point of contact between your company and its consumers, at any place or time, during service delivery;
- coordinating different aspects of marketing as they affect individual consumers.

HOW A DATABASE IS USED

1. Each actual or potential consumer is identified as a record on the database.
2. Each consumer record contains information on:
   - identification and access (eg name, address, telephone number);
   - other consumers associated with this consumer (in the family, business, etc);
   - consumer needs and characteristics (demographic and psychographic information about consumers);

- campaign communications (whether the consumer has been exposed to particular campaigns);
- consumer's past responses to communications that form part of the campaigns;
- consumer satisfaction;
- channel and media preferences;
- potential future value of consumers;
- past transactions of consumers (with the organization and possibly with competitors).

3. This information is used to identify likely purchasers of particular products and how they should be approached.
4. The information is available to the organization during the process of each communication with the consumer – which may have been initiated by the organization or the consumer. This enables the organization to decide how to respond to the consumer's needs.
5. The database is used to record responses of consumers to the marketing initiatives (eg marketing communications or sales campaigns).
6. The information is also available for marketing planning. This enables the organization to decide:
   - which target markets or segments are appropriate for each product or service;
   - what marketing mix (price, marketing communications, distribution channel, etc) is appropriate for each product in each target market.
7. If the organization is selling many different products to each consumer, the database is used to ensure that the approach to the consumer is coordinated (for example that campaigns for different products do not clash) and consistent, and handled in a way that meets consumers' expectations about how data is managed. Any staff in contact with the consumer, in any channel, can see relevant information about the consumer.
8. The database might eventually replace large-scale quantitative market research for existing consumers, although research will still be required for new products and markets, or for changes to the organization's relationship with consumers. Marketing campaigns are devised so that consumers' responses provide the information that is needed, possibly through questionnaires included in mailings or telemarketing campaigns.
9. Systematic processes are developed to handle some key functions of marketing management, in particular analysis and project planning. Analysis must be systematized if it is to handle the vast volume of information generated by database marketing. It ensures that marketing

opportunities and threats are identified more or less automatically, and that ways of capturing these opportunities and neutralizing these threats are also recommended. It makes higher-quality information on marketing performance available to senior management, allowing it to allocate marketing resources more effectively. It also allows management to identify situations in which direct or interactive marketing is failing. Project planning approaches are used to tighten up the management of campaigns, as database marketing involves a larger number of suppliers and much more complex actions than traditional advertising campaigns.

FACTORS THAT HAVE HELPED DATABASE MARKETING GROW SO FAST

The growth of database marketing has been facilitated by the powerful processing capability and immense storage capacity of today's computers, and the way telecommunications technology is being harnessed to make consumer and market data available to the wide variety of staff involved in marketing and sales efforts.

Enabling technologies are developing fast. Most technologies, such as those that determine data processing power and speed, memory and storage, are improving at least tenfold every 10 years. Speed of access (reading, writing) to stored data is growing more slowly. Communications technology, once slow to evolve, is accelerating. Software, once a barrier, is now easier to use and more reliable. Application packages (such as telemarketing) are more functional and flexible, and capable of customization. Application development products have accelerated programmer productivity. End-user computing has created experience and even expertise in handling computers throughout organizations. PC-based systems are available for the small user. Consumers are using additional media (e.g. mobile telephony, interactive television) that allow them to be managed as individuals, and more importantly, to manage their relationships with suppliers.

Many tried and tested database packages are available for all types and sizes of computing systems. These have been used as the foundation to develop the specific packages required, which include:

- comprehensive consumer databases;
- selection management – helping to select which consumers to target;
- telemarketing (inbound – call receiving, and outbound – active calling of consumers);
- mail fulfilment systems;

- Internet site management systems, to allow consumers to manage their relationship with the organization;
- data analysis and consumer profiling;
- systems to connect different channels and media.

Suppliers of underlying database software have made it much easier for systems professionals to adapt this software to their own specific marketing use, by marketing a wide range of programming 'tools'. Nowadays, even where consumers are managed in many locations across the world, systems are available to facilitate this. Companies that experience problems in developing or implementing database marketing systems do so because of management problems, such as:

- Lack of agreement about coverage and application of the database, and the related problem of over-specifying the first version of the system, so that it costs too much, takes too long to develop, and does not deliver benefits early enough.
- Lack of understanding that marketing databases only succeed if they are put to use and modified by practical experience – the data will grow, and along with it the knowledge of how to use it, once it is applied. This has been learned over the last 10 years, before which it was common to over-specify the database at the outset, making it more complex and difficult to use than necessary.
- Lack of attention paid to users' needs – for understanding, training and support during implementation.

These problems are common in all areas of business system development. They often occur because of failure to consult with other companies who have been through the experience. A particular risk is falling into the hands of consultants who over-specify the system because it enlarges their budget. Fortunately, in many countries, there are now enough training courses and professional groups where marketing managers can exchange experiences and avoid these obvious mistakes.

THE STRENGTHS OF DATABASE MARKETING

The use of the consumer database builds on the solid foundations of database marketing, as follows:

- It is **measurable**. Responses to campaigns are measured, allowing effectiveness of different approaches to be checked.

- It is **testable**. The effectiveness of different elements of the approach – the product, the communications medium, the offer (how the product is packaged to appeal to the consumer), the target market, and so on – can be tested. Tests can be carried out quickly, so rapid action can be taken on the results. Test results can be used to forecast sales more precisely, helping manage inventory more effectively.
- It is **selective**. Campaigns can be focused accurately, because communication is with specific consumers, and can be attuned to their expected value (for instance, more expensive and frequent communications to higher-value consumers).
- Communications to each consumer can be **personalized**, using details relevant only to them, drawn from the database.
- It is **flexible** – campaigns can be timed to have their effect exactly when required.

HOW A DATABASE WORKS

The information on a consumer database has to come from somewhere. Database marketing involves 'learning by doing' – the process itself provides most of the marketing information it needs. This is because contacts ask for responses. Each response contains information – at least, it should do. It is up to the user to make sure that this information is of value. For example, if a consumer responds by calling a toll-free number, he or she might be asked questions that qualify the lead for the product or service that is the subject of the campaign, and that give data that will help in planning future campaigns. In this way, database marketing builds up a store of information about individual consumers. It needs to be held in the most effective way. Unless it can be turned into profit, it is no use. So the database marketing system is crucial for organizing the information and making it available.

Some databases hold consumer details but are not marketing databases. Some are operations databases, used for order processing (order taking, delivery, invoicing and so on) or after-sales service. They record what consumers paid, and what they paid for, rather than helping to predict what they might like next! Some data may be derived from marketing databases, used for analysis purposes only.

Data design

Computers work best with information that is well organized to start with. That is why there is a strong emphasis on the structured collection of data. For example, telemarketing scripts must be designed to get the maximum amount of high-quality information possible from consumers, in a structured form. This allows it to be added to the database without too much further processing. The same applies to the design of forms to be completed by consumers. Structured information gathering is essential. Unless this discipline is observed from the beginning, problems will emerge later on. Thus, it may be useful to know the type of educational qualification obtained by consumers. So it might be sensible to allocate fields on the database for this information (where the consumer studied, type of course, result, data) and collect it in a structured way. However, there is no general formula stating exactly which data should be included in the database. Each database is tailored to the needs of its users. However, it is important to avoid the mistake of designing it on the basis of past requirements.

Sources of data

There are two types of data source, internal and external. **Internal or proprietary data** is data the organization already holds about consumers, usually arising out of its transactions with them. The database marketing system should use most of the information the organization has about consumers. This data is one of the company's most valuable assets. **External data** is data sourced from outside, for example by renting a list, or by exchanging data with another company.

Data is often organized into lists. A list is the simplest form of marketing database. It is a set of names and how to contact them (addresses, telephone numbers). A list may be bought or rented for use in campaigns or in database building. Good list buying is key to many successful campaigns. Alternatively it might be drawn from the database for a particular campaign. Careful list selection is the key to high response at low cost.

Internal data

Internal data include:

- consumer files;
- order records;
- service reports, complaints, etc;
- merchandise return records;
- sales force records;
- consumer satisfaction data;
- application forms (eg for credit, insurance);
- responses to promotions;

- risk/credit data (have they paid on time?);
- market research;
- enquiries;
- warranty cards.

External data

External data include compiled and direct response lists from sources outside the company. Also included are classificatory data (such as census and postcode data, data from credit reference agencies and their derivations), which can enhance other external and internal data.

Data selection

You should decide which data to put on the database according to its cost and its potential to make the organization money, typically by helping to answer the following questions:

- Who are or will be the organization's consumers, and how can it contact them?
- What will they buy from the organization or its competitors? How can they be motivated to buy more from the organization?
- Will they maintain a dialogue with the company, and which medium do they prefer to do it through?
- How can they be retained? Do they have any propensity to be loyal to suppliers in the market sector?
- Where can others like them be found?
- When are they most receptive to communications, and when are they most likely to buy from the organization?

Types of information on the database

These might include:

- **Consumer or prospect:** that is, information on how to access consumers (address, telephone number) and on the nature and general behaviour of consumers (psychographic and behavioural data).
- **Transaction:** information on commercial transactions between the organization and the consumer, such as orders and returns.
- **Contact planning and execution data:** information on what campaigns (tests and roll-outs) have been launched, who has responded to them, what the final results have been, in terms of contacts, sales and profits, and also service contacts and their results.

- **Product:** information on which products have been involved in promotion, who has bought them, when and from where.
- **Geodemographics:** about the areas where consumers live and the social or business category they belong to.

These types of data are considered in more detail below.

Consumer data

If the organization is marketing to consumers, it might hold these items about consumers on its database:

- first name;
- last name;
- title;
- salutation;
- name of spouse;
- address (in meaningful data format);
- gender;
- age;
- income;
- marital status;
- number of children;
- names of children;
- length of residence in current abode;
- type of abode and tenure;
- whether recent or anticipated home mover;
- telephone number;
- special markers (VIP consumer, do not promote, shareholder, frequent complainer);
- responses to questionnaires;
- consumer service history;
- geodemographic coding.

Transaction data

Past transactions are one of the most important indicators of likely future transactions. The use of frequency, recency, amount and category (FRAC) data in database marketing is based on years of experience of finding that these variables dominate most explanations of buying behaviour for existing products. The transaction data must include enough detail to allow FRAC information to be extracted for each consumer. It is tempting to summarize past purchasing history, but in summarizing it, vital FRAC detail might be lost. So the details of each purchase for each consumer must be logged. This includes not only the obvious 'identifying' details (who bought or returned what, when, how), but also the associated marketing data (at what price, from which promotion).

Transaction data is usually more effective as a basis for selection for promotions than geodemographic variables, based on electoral, census, credit and other third-party data. However, the widespread availability of geodemographic data that can be matched to individual consumer data means that a consumer products company with limited or no transaction data available can start with a campaign based mainly on geodemographic data. This will normally be organized in a national file based on the electoral roll, enhanced with postal coding and possibly telephone numbers. Census information will usually be used to enhance the file further and provide some of the basis for demographic classification. If you are in this position, your key objective is to learn very quickly which consumers respond the best, and focus future promotions on them, as promoting to national files is very expensive. To do this, you should start with a test, and find out which kinds of consumer respond the best, 'score' them, and focus future promotions on consumers with good scores.

In Internet marketing, new types of consumer data are available. Here are a few examples:

- cookies sent or installed;
- Web passwords;
- Web user login;
- e-mail – outbound promotions;
- e-mail – outbound promotion – response;
- e-mail – inbound;
- Web site visit;
- pages viewed (Web log file data);
- ads/promotions served;
- ads/promotions – response;
- Web user input – orders;
- Web user input – information requests;
- Web user input – questionnaire data;
- Web user input – call back request;
- Web user input – text chat question;
- referring or source site.

The main problem with this data is the sheer volume. Many sites might be generating several gigabytes, even terabytes of data a day. Yet the

Table 1.1 *Clickstream data types and uses*

Data type	Usefulness
How people get to a site	Helps understand quality of marketing campaigns and links from search engines
The most popular pages	Allows marketers to modify pages to meet consumer likes and dislikes
Where browsers leave a site	Shows which pages are seen as closing pages, and whether they are the expected ones
How they navigate through the site	Shows whether people are taking the expected route and if not, why not
The percentage of visits that lead to an enquiry or sign up to an account	Shows the success of the offering and its presentation
How much time visitors spend at a site	Shows whether spending more time at the site generates value
Which country visitors are visiting from	Shows appeal across borders
Which browser they are using	Shows whether use of different browsers (which see screens in different ways) is affecting consumers' reaction to screens
How successful are banner and advertising campaigns	Shows whether consumers are clicking through company's banner ads on other sites and whether they leaving company's site via other banner ads

resources to analyse this data usually comprise one or two analysts at most. Clickstream data types and uses are described in Table 1.1.

Scoring

Consumers are given a score by identifying their characteristics and correlating them with their likelihood to respond, buy or whatever. This makes it possible to create a 'scoring module' or 'directory' for selecting target consumers from any larger file. Scores are usually derived from tests. This is based on the idea that when a consumer is identified as belonging to a particular group, it can usually be assumed that the consumer has the same likelihood as other members of the group of buying a particular product. The score given a consumer in relation to a given product is determined by analysis of all the consumer's characteristics, and assessment of whether those characteristics, when they appear in whole groups of consumers, make those consumers likely to buy.

Once the characteristics that are important have been identified, a scoring method can be devised, to be applied instantly by the computer. This score indicates the likelihood that the consumer will buy. This information is combined with campaign objectives to determine a priority for the response.

The campaign should create transaction data fairly quickly. This transaction data is likely to dominate the selection criteria, but geodemographic data may continue to be useful. The emergence of companies offering comprehensive data services (list validation, data pooling, matching to other files) means that few new users of database marketing have to start from scratch.

Product data

In a one-product company, this raises no problem - each transaction is either a sale or a return. In companies with very wide product ranges, product classification may be a problem, and a numbering system to suit the requirements of database marketing may have to be adopted. Such a system must allow like products to be grouped easily.

Contact planning and execution data

Documentation of past and present promotions in some detail (right down to which consumers were subject to them, and the media and contact strategy used) is essential if the organization is to measure the effectiveness of its promotions and if its promotional planning is to benefit from analysis of the past. The same applies to details of inbound contacts (contacts arising from consumers - whether stimulated by the organization or initiated by the consumer) - and service contacts.

Holding the data

Some data must be accessed quickly (for instance, data on consumers who have recently received promotions, who have complained or have an immediate need). Other data can be accessible with a longer delay, and some might never be entered into the computer database. Care must be taken about which data is kept for quick access, or the system will drown in useless information. So another characteristic of database marketing systems is the constant check kept on which information is useful, and which data are 'nice to know', but not very useful. This latter data can be archived and retrieved if necessary. However, due to rapid advances in computer storage and retrieval technology, this problem is not as serious as it used to be.

DATA QUALITY AND MAINTENANCE

Databases do not stay fresh. They becomes stale, as the contacts on which they are based recede into the past. So special exercises are required to check and update data. Maintenance of the database is very important. Databases get out of date quickly. People change addresses and jobs. Errors in fulfilment records (created when a consumer responds and/or buys) occur, through commission and omission. This is why audits must be undertaken. A data audit takes a sample of consumer records, and analyses when the different data items were entered, what their quality is, and how accurate they are. Accuracy may be checked by comparing the data with a source that is known to be accurate, or asking the consumer (or consumer contact staff) to confirm accuracy.

Data quality is measured by the results of the last audit. Quality checks can be carried out via testing. Questionnaire mailing is an effective but costly way of improving data quality, so questionnaires are usually combined with another promotional initiative. The quality of the data drawn from the database depends mainly on how up to date the source data is, and whether it contains the detail needed to access the right individuals (names, addresses, telephone numbers, job titles).

If data on consumers' contacts with the company is not entered on its database, it might suffer in two ways. First, it might approach the same consumer on successive days (or worse, on the same day) with different messages (or the same message delivered twice). This cannot completely be avoided – a consumer might read an advertisement and receive a mail shot on the same day – but ensuring different direct approaches are co-ordinated can reduce wastefulness.

Second, without a history of contact, the organization will have no idea where the consumer is in the 'buying cycle'. This information is needed to determine when it should write, telephone or schedule a sales visit.

Data quality depends partly on consumer contact staff (sales, telemarketing, retail branch and so on) understanding the value of high-quality information and the importance of their feedback in improving its quality. Every opportunity should be taken to improve data quality, during every contact with consumers. These contacts might be with sales staff, over the telephone, in showrooms and dealer outlets, on service calls, in shops and at exhibitions, by return of guarantees, via competitions and through past consumer records. Lists can be traded with relevant businesses to help here. But the advantage of using the organization's own database is that it consists of people who:

- have done and are doing business with the organization;
- trust it;
- will therefore respond better to it.

External lists

These are often classified into responsive and compiled. Mail or telephone responsive lists consist of anyone who uses the post or telephone for transactions that could be carried out in some other way, for example, mail-order consumers. Compiled lists are those compiled to cover particular kinds of people (such as conference attendees, product buyers or small businesses). Lists can be sourced from list brokers who often act as agents for list owners. They may also be sourced from directories and by research.

MERGING AND PURGING DATA

Merging external data with proprietary data, or merging data from different proprietary sources, can be a problem. Special computer programs are normally used to 'deduplicate' data sources. Many companies prefer to use external suppliers to do this work. The need for deduplication arises when an individual or company is listed in different ways in different databases (or even in the same one). If the different databases are combined, consumers may be listed more than once. The databases or lists must be 'deduplicated' against each other, so that duplicate records are removed, while valuable data (which may be spread over more than one record of the same consumer) is not lost. Deduplication can be computerized. However, some human intervention may be necessary, as the computer can only deduplicate within certain tolerances. Depending on how important deduplication is, the computer may be asked to list entries where duplicate entry is suspected, for manual correction. However, you should bear in mind that the law of diminishing returns applies here, so the costs of further deduplication should be weighed against its benefits. These benefits are savings in costs of duplicated contacts, and avoiding alienating consumers by contacting them more than once for the same reason.

Software is available to carry out the following:

- the filing of all consumers and prospects together with their relevant data (eg type and date of purchasing activity);
- merging of bought or rented lists with in-house lists;

- identification and purging of duplicates;
- matching and merging of data that relate to the same consumer;
- postcoding of addresses, for ease of access to census data, accuracy of targeting and easier sorting for postal rebates;
- validation of names against relevant official or national standard files, or telephone company directories, to ensure that prospective consumers are actually resident at the stated address.

Investment in merge/purge software is often required. The investment is well worth it, and pays dividends in terms of reduced marketing costs, increased revenue and enhanced consumer satisfaction. A bureau can do this, but if you find you have to use a bureau too often, you should consider acquiring the software. However, remember that it needs more than software – it also needs expertise and time. If you do not have those, stick with the bureau.

DOING IT YOURSELF OR OUTSOURCING

Many companies prefer to outsource their consumer database management. Even companies that have their own very large consumer databases may outsource some aspects of consumer data management (such as for new ventures or additional channels), because they want to focus on using the outputs from the database properly rather than actually managing it, and in new areas of business setting up and managing a database can consume a lot of management time and resources.

USING A DATABASE IN PRACTICE

The case study is a complete study of how database marketing works in a simple, small company situation.

SILVERMINDS

This case study describes how a mail-order company, SilverMinds Direct, improved its revenues by over 5 per cent through better segmentation of its 250,000-customer database. This case study shows how, using a single channel (direct mail), a company can use some of the most basic ideas of segmentation – recency, frequency and monetary value or RFM, to improve profits. (RFM is another version of FRAC.)

It shows how a small company with limited analysis and statistical resources was able to extract greater value from its marketing database by RFM segmentation and analysis. The study describes the methodology, rationale and results of SilverMinds' RFM segmentation project, plus some of the other applications of the segmentation strategy. The project gave a return on investment (RoI) of over 20 times.

SilverMinds Direct Ltd is a special interest catalogue company, which markets nostalgic and special interest music (jazz, country, classical and so on) to consumers on its 250,000-person database. SilverMinds is a good example of the shift over the last 10 years in the UK mail-order market from 'big book' agency catalogues to specialist catalogues. SilverMinds' target market is the growing 50 plus grey market. Customer acquisition is mainly through media advertising and direct mail. The company test marketed in 1999, launched in 2000 and had by 2003 revenues of over £5 million. Most revenue is from the sales of CDs.

In 2002 SilverMinds looked at how it could get more value from its most valuable asset – its customer database. Its revenues are mainly generated by mailings to existing customers. SilverMinds considered improving its customer database mailing performance by better data mining and statistical modelling. This can be expensive for smaller companies because it requires scarce analytical and statistical skills. It decided that the benefit of the improved targeting might not justify the cost of the analytical work and its implementation, so a simpler route was chosen. Rather than building predictive models for each of its 15 annual mailings, it chose a more general segmentation route that could be used across all mailings as well as for other applications. The costs could then be spread across many different applications. RFM segmentation was chosen due to its simplicity and ease of use, in the hope that it would deliver the required economic incremental gain, or more financial benefit than cost.

RFM is closely related to another important direct marketing concept, lifetime value. Lifetime value is the expected net profit a consumer will contribute to a business over the period of time he or she remains a customer. Because of the link to lifetime value, RFM techniques can be used as a proxy for the future profitability of a business. High RFM consumers represent future business potential because these consumers are more likely to buy again and have a high lifetime value. Low RFM consumers represent less of a business opportunity, low lifetime value, and highlight that something needs to be done to increase their value.

One of the most straightforward RFM segmentation methods involves assigning a score 1 to 5 for recency, frequency and monetary value to each record on the customer database. The recency coding was 1 = over 24 months, 2 = 19–24 months, 3 = 13–18 months, 4 = 7–12 months and 5 = 0–6 months. This matched SilverMinds' existing recency bandings used for mailing selections. It was considered important not to throw away previous mailing results, but rather use the new segmentation as an enhancement to the existing selection methodology. For frequency, one-time buyers were coded 1, two-time buyers 2, and so on up to 5 for 5 or more. The score for monetary value was assigned by splitting the database into quintiles, best 20 per cent total spend, next 20 per cent and so on. The end result was that each customer record was assigned one of 125 RFM scores from 1,1,1 to 5,5,5.

The company chose the following project development path to give the quickest wins and return on investment.

1. RFM score the customer database as described above.
2. Analyse consumer mailings to find where RFM scores would give the greatest discrimination and enhance mailing selections, for example cut off at 3,2,4 records rather than 18 months recency.
3. Enhance 1,1,1 records with variables derived from existing variables on the database, for example type of music purchased, or consumer age derived from age of music bought. A geodemographic system could also be checked for economic incremental gain.
4. Carry out RFM migration studies: for example, analyse how the 5,5,5 best consumers deteriorate to see what can be done to retain their profitability. This analysis could provide a basis of future consumer contact frequency decisions. Another example is tracking the development and lifetime value of customers recruited via direct versus those from 'off the page' advertisements, to measure acceptable customer acquisition costs for different media. Typically direct-mail recruited customers have higher lifetime value and so should be given a higher allowable recruitment cost.
5. Determine which activities attract high-value consumers and focus on them.

The 250,000 customer records on the database were RFM scored and the following results were found.

Recency versus frequency

The one-time buyers are fairly evenly spaced by recency, reflecting the steady growth of the business. Analysis showed that there were few consumers who had bought more than twice who had not bought for over 12 or 18 months. Looking at the 0–6 months buyers, or recency = 5, there was a big drop off between one and two times buyers, but a lower drop between two and three times and thereafter. Once a consumer had bought twice he or she was more likely to stay loyal and go on to purchase three or more times. This highlights the often-underestimated importance of a consumer's second purchase. The best tactics to get a second order were to mail first-time buyers early and often.

Frequency versus monetary value

As expected, monetary value increased with frequency of purchase. The typical consumer development path was that a one-time buyer started in one of the bottom three quintiles for monetary value. This split of first-time buyers into three monetary spend levels was later found to be significant. With their second purchase, the consumer typically moved to the second highest 20 per cent monetary value. By their fourth purchase the consumers were in the best 20 per cent monetary value group.

Recency versus monetary value

There was a distinct polarization in the customer database. The highest total spend consumers tended to be the most recent, and conversely lowest spend consumers the least recent. There were few over 24–month high-value consumers (R = 1, M = 5). Similarly there were relatively few low-value most recent consumers (R = 5, M = 1). High monetary spend implies a recent purchase or greater mail responsiveness. The mailing analysis and results later validated this finding. It was found that borderline mailing selections could be improved by only mailing the higher spend consumers.

RFM scoring mailing results

SilverMinds' computer bureau coded a number of the monthly consumer mailings and the responses. SilverMinds' existing mailing segmentation was already quite efficient, based on recency and frequency. Each mailing would typically involve over a dozen different manual selections. For example a selection might be consumers who had bought 18–24 months ago and had bought over three times. With 250,000 customers on the database, each of the 125 RFM codes or cells had an average of 2,000 customers. When mailing responses were low, many individual RFM codes had less than 40 responses in each cell. These results were treated with caution, due to statistical unreliability. However, if the results were combined with other RFM codes, for example results for RFM codes 1,1,1 to 1,1,5 codes were collapsed or combined together, then the statistical reliability was less of an issue. Examining each RFM dimension one at a time enhanced the statistical significance of small samples to a reliable level.

A clear pattern emerged from the analysis. The response was much better for the RFM cells where monetary spend was high. An explanation for this for first-time buyers could be that high-spend buyers were more committed or had been direct-mail recruited, or both. The important thing is that the RFM analysis enabled this to be discovered easily. Analysis of the mailing showed that if the worst performing 15 per cent of the mailing, or 20,000 records, were not mailed, and the next best 20,000 records that did not fall into the original mailing selection were mailed in their place, this would result in about £25,000 more sales. RFM codes to be dropped from the mailing selections were records just inside the previous mailing recency and frequency criteria that were in the bottom monetary cells. Similarly the RFM codes to be added to the mailing selection were just outside the recency and frequency criteria and in the top money cells.

Note that up to this point nothing had actually been done except analysing the RFM coding of the database and mailing results. Simple spreadsheets had enabled data exploration to uncover potential value in the customer database. This demonstrates how profiling and data analysis can enable a lot of learning relatively quickly and for little cost.

Validation

The analysis results were validated by initially mailing 50 per cent of the additional selections based on RFM scores and omitting 50 per cent of the RFM codes to be dropped. The results were close to projected: the RFM selections gave a median result, half of the other selections were better and half worse.

Limitations of RFM

RFM does not provide information about the profitability, the potential of a customer or prospect, and what offer or communications the customer responded to. Most database analysis suffers from the inherent weakness that you do not know what you do not know. It is only possible to analyse the variables on the database, and they are not necessarily the most pertinent or relevant ones. Database marketers tend to overuse demographic and RFM or transactional/ behavioural segmentation because the data is available. These variables then become the answer to everything. In other words 'if you only have a hammer, everything looks like a nail'. Demographics and behaviour, including RFM, account for perhaps 40 to 60 per cent of the explanation of a purchase. Demographics can tell, for example, that a person can afford to buy a product or is in the right age group to remember a particular musician. The rest of the explanation is based on buyers' attitudes, motivations and needs. While the customer database can give maybe up to half of the consumer attitudes and needs profile, for example five-year-plus customers are brand loyal, further research is required to truly understand and define what is really going on.

Conclusions

By RFM coding the customer database a greater understanding of the database was gained. RFM segmentation is a relatively cost-effective, quick and easy to use way to improve analysis and profiling of a customer database. RFM is a good 'lens' through which to analyse a database; it can help discover a lot of useful, previously hidden knowledge and potential in the database. The RFM coding could be used to enhance and refine mailing selections without having to throw away previous results and learning, thereby squeezing more value from the customer database through greater discrimination of selections, giving better control of campaigns. RFM segmentation helps give an understanding of who are the best consumers in the database, what behaviours they exhibit that make them the best consumers, and what behaviours the worst consumers exhibit. Once this is known, it is possible to plan a strategy for getting more of the best consumers and avoiding the worst. A good segmentation strategy can provide a framework for the organization to make more money. By improving customer acquisition, retention, up-selling and cross-selling activities, different types of consumers can be managed differently. This enables allocation of different resources and investment levels to different consumer segments so as to deliver superior value to distinct groups of consumers. Because RFM segmentation is relatively straightforward to implement but fairly universal in its potential application, it can grow and develop with the company's needs. This case study demonstrates the benefits and return on investment simple RFM segmentation can generate.

CONCLUSION

In this chapter, we have described the basics of database marketing. We have shown that, based on the relatively simple ideas of direct marketing, database marketing has grown into a complex professional discipline. In the next chapter, we explain how database marketing is used.

2 Using the database

Merlin Stone, Alison Bond and Bryan Foss

APPLICATIONS OF DATABASE MARKETING

Consumer database applications can be split into two categories, consumer applications and management applications. A third category – dialogue applications – is effectively a combination of the two, and forms the basis of many approaches to consumer relationship management (CRM), covered in Chapter 4.

Consumer applications

Consumer applications are uses of the database that involve the creation and maintenance of contacts and relationships with consumers. The main consumer applications of a marketing database are:

- direct mail (using the system to select consumers to receive relevant mailings);
- response handling and fulfilment (using the system to record consumers' responses and manage the next step in the contact strategy – fulfilment);
- telemarketing (using the telephone to manage consumers, by contacting them or allowing them to contact the company, recording the results of the dialogue and initiating the required next contact);
- dealer, distributor or agent management systems (providing data to them, helping them meet their consumers' needs better, monitoring their performance in so doing);

- club or user group marketing (creating an 'inner circle' of consumers, who receive special additional benefits in return for their loyalty);
- customer relationship management (CRM) – managing consumers throughout their period with the organization, to mutual benefit;
- consumer promotions (such as coupon distribution and redemption);
- credit card management (using the system to recruit credit card consumers, record their transactions, invoice them and promote to them);
- targeted branding (using the system to deliver branding messages to individuals identified as either specially receptive to them or at risk from competitive actions);
- data marketing (selling or renting the consumer data on the system);
- any other dialogue application that involves a sustained series of communications with a target market.

Management applications

Management applications are those that change the way marketing management plans, implements and assesses its marketing activities. They include:

- campaign and relationship planning (selecting consumers with specific needs and identifying the kind of offers to which they will respond, and how they should be managed over time);
- campaign coordination (ensuring that campaigns fit into a logical sequence and lead to the establishment of a sensible dialogue with consumers, rather than clashing and sending inconsistent messages);
- project management (managing the delivery of communications and CRM projects);
- campaign performance and marketing mix productivity analysis (identifying which elements of the mix are best for managing different kinds of consumers, and which campaigns are most successful);
- campaign monitoring (providing interim data on campaign performance, so remedial actions can be taken where necessary).

Dialogue applications

A dialogue is defined as a structured series of contacts – involving the company contacting the consumer and the consumer responding – giving information, making purchases and so on. A dialogue is more effective than a monologue – a one-way series of contacts with no response, or than a single conversation (a one-off promotional contact). In a dialogue, the consumer is asked questions such as, 'When do you intend to buy?', 'When will you next need help?' and 'What other products might interest you?' The database system is effectively programmed to analyse these responses, and the outcome of the analysis is the triggering of future contacts - of a type and timing the consumer wants. This is how an organization develops a dialogue with its consumers. The aim of this dialogue is to:

- move the consumers towards purchase;
- keep them satisfied after the purchase;
- ensure they buy additional or replacement products later on.

The database system is essential in ensuring that the right communication reaches the right consumer at the right time. It is used to select initial contacts, to analyse the consumer response pattern and to plan the follow up. Your aim should be to develop contact strategies and dialogue applications that suit all the target consumers and prospects, and to have management applications that ensure that this can be done properly.

STRATEGIC ISSUES

The first step is to turn your consumer information into a consumer database. For example, if the organization sells to consumers directly (for example, via a field sales force), it is likely to have a reasonably high quality consumer file already, and possibly several, containing details about its consumers. There will almost certainly be a transactions file, showing which consumers have bought what and when. Many companies have many such files or databases, one for each business unit, channel and/or product. These need to be turned into a marketing database. Remember, a marketing database contains more than just consumer records - it also holds details of:

- the marketing and sales campaigns the organization runs;
- the resulting contacts with consumers;
- the outcomes of these contacts.

The transactions file might contain useful source data on frequency, recency, amount and category. It might not be stored in the right way for it to be used to target consumers and find out what purchasing histories are associated with high potential for future purchases. Other information that indicates likely consumer needs (organizational, psychographic and the like) might not have been collected methodically or at all. The database might need to be enhanced through imported or questionnaire data.

If the organization has no direct contact with consumers, there are three main options in database and application development, which can be pursued simultaneously:

- compile, through list purchasing, testing and research, a database of those likely to be buyers of the organization's products;
- create marketing applications that by themselves generate the data through direct contacts, often through 'plastic' (credit cards, club membership, promotional entitlement records/cards), clubs, and so on;
- switch (partially or wholly) to channels of distribution that do involve direct contact.

With indirect sales, critical transactions data (on frequency, recency, amount and category, or FRAC) will not be available, except through consumer questionnaires, or if the organization's bargaining position is strong enough to enable it extract the data from third parties such as automotive suppliers, or if it can buy it, perhaps from a retailer running a loyalty card.

If transactions data are not available, other data need to be found that indicate consumer propensity to buy the organization's products. It might be possible to source this data from a lifestyle data supplier. Otherwise, a questionnaire might be the best approach. The problem of getting the right data is often compounded by the fact that companies often go into database marketing at times of strategic uncertainty. They may not be sure which products they will be marketing to whom over the next few years. This means that it is not easy to determine which data will be needed. If this is your situation, your best strategy may be to start a programme of testing the importance of different variables in explaining buying behaviour for different kinds of products, combined with data reduction (see below) and profiling wherever possible, to simplify the data set, which could otherwise get out of hand.

Data acquisition and development

A data acquisition and development strategy is needed. This strategy determines:

- which data are needed to support marketing strategies;

- how sources of data are to be identified, qualified and tested (including different questionnaire programmes);
- how the data are to be maintained, archived and disposed of when no longer needed.

This strategy is needed whether or not the organization started with a consumer file, and whether the aim is to sell more to existing consumers or to recruit more consumers.

Data reduction

Data reduction is the science of finding a few variables to explain a complex set of data. This is done by statistical techniques. For example, you might use a long questionnaire to find out whether consumers are satisfied with their relationship with the organization, and use statistical techniques to find out which questions account for most of the difference between consumers. Or you might wish to segment consumers for targeting purposes. Again, you might use a questionnaire on buying attitudes and behaviour, and find which questions enable you to divide consumers most neatly into different groups. Data reduction is important because unless it is used, masses of data could be collected that prove very unwieldy to use.

There are many data sources available. It is important to keep informed about what lists and databases are available. Although the golden rule is that the organization's own data is best of all, there is always room to enhance it - particularly if the organization is moving into new areas (such as recruitment of a different kind of consumer, or launch of a radically new product). If you are considering a questionnaire, note that the costs of entering it onto the system and analysing it to provide segmentation mean that care should be taken not to acquire high volumes of information when low volumes would do. An alternative is to build a partnership with non-competing companies to share the information and cost (see Chapter 8).

Profiling consumers

Some database marketing users are investing in profiling approaches, to give convenient measures of consumer characteristics and susceptibilities. The idea is to develop (usually from an analysis of existing data) one or more profiles (for instance, of a type of consumer the company would like more of). Credit scoring is the 'home' of this kind of work - where it is used to develop profiles of consumers that are definitely not wanted!

The benefit of this approach is that it provides score cards or directories which can then be applied to any file, provided that the latter contains the variables the scoring technique uses. For example, in credit scoring these variables include income levels, home ownership and credit card history. This reduces the volume of testing required and increases the response rates of campaigns. However, campaigns may be required just to bring in the right data.

Maintaining the database

Best practice is that the database should be largely self-maintaining through the applications run on it. But the paradox is that databases that are easiest to update may be the least valuable. If all competitors are in monthly direct dialogue with their consumers (as they are in the credit card market), data on monthly purchasing patterns and repayments is plentiful. Competitive advantage will come not from having data but from turning it into a form that can be used for marketing purposes. Dialogue applications - ones in which the organization is informing and selling to consumers, and they are responding with information and orders - provide the best data, but are the most expensive to create and manage. If dialogue is intermittent and conducted through third parties (as in selling cars or domestic appliances), building a database is hard work, involving questionnaires, promotional programmes and so forth. Heavy investment in hand-raising promotion (that is, promotion intended to get potential customers to identify themselves) may be required. Once built, the database can be used to understand replacement cycles and to target promotions more effectively.

Making applications work

In most large companies, the users of the consumer database are not just database marketing users. The database is used by marketing analysts, sales managers, retail planners, brand managers and so on. The marketing applications they need could be any combination of those mentioned earlier. Developing the applications plan means aligning database plans with strategic marketing plans. If there are a large number of consumers who buy moderate amounts from the organization but not enough to justify a field sales call, the first applications that are likely to be needed are direct mail and telemarketing. On the other hand, if the organization wants to use the system to gather information about consumers buying its products through retailers, then the first applications needed might be high-volume low-cost coupon processing and questionnaire management.

WHO USES THE CONSUMER DATABASE – AND HOW

Consumer databases were once mainly established and developed only by a database marketing department. The database would be used to carry out tactical sales promotions, provide higher-quality leads for a sales force, or support an in-house credit or loyalty card operation. Or it might grow directly from sales force activity, or through the work of a consumer service department. Today, virtually every function that has anything to do with consumers can use the consumer database. Database marketing tends to progress in waves, with particular industries making rapid progress and then undergoing periods of rapid consolidation. Here are some of the industries at the forefront.

Power and water utilities, fixed and mobile telecommunications suppliers

The utilities satisfy some of the basic needs of consumers and organizations - heat, light, power, water and communications. Their use of databases ranges from bill inserts explaining the nature and benefits of the service being provided, through targeting high-value users for offers and loyalty programmes, to equipment and maintenance service marketing. The original utilities benefit from strong coverage of potential markets - they started with operational databases of practically every household and business in their area. Their strength as marketing entities derives from their regular billing arrangements. However, some utilities have added significantly to their operations. In the UK Centrica, formerly just a gas utility, now sells financial services, telecommunications and auto recovery and repair services, as well other energy-related products and services. Its database is one of the largest and deepest in the UK. Pressure to allow more direct debiting and less frequent communication with consumers may reduce the strength of the dialogue utilities have with their consumers. Paradoxically, direct debiting has been treated by some as a consumer loyalty exercise, because it locks in consumers. However, it results in less attention being paid to the supplier, so utilities have developed aggressive programmes of mailings and telemarketing to defend and develop their consumer base.

Financial services

This sector presents some of the greatest opportunities for database marketing, and has always been one of the biggest users. The underlying growth rate of this sector, relative to the economy, seems assured, notwithstanding short-term problems. The factors driving this include:

- rising incomes (which generate larger absolute amounts of saving);
- more discretion about what to spend, where, and the consumer desire to find easy ways to do it;
- increasing longevity and earlier retirement (and the need to fund a longer retirement - with government less keen to fund it);
- uncertain involvement of the state in providing for other eventualities such as sickness and education;
- the risk of longer periods of unemployment;
- awareness (stimulated by suppliers, media comment, government and personal experience) of the need for improved management of personal financial affairs.

Owing to the wide competition in the market to satisfy the needs for the above, the search for different ways of developing and then managing relationships with consumers other than through the branch network continues. In fact financial products are available without the presence of a high street branch from many direct-only companies, using direct mail, telephone and the Internet. However, many new brands do not make much profit and often act as fighting brands for their owners, which use their databases to manage consumers profitably through more conventional channels. Many companies have accepted the idea of present and future consumer value as a key variable in the acquisition equation. Once the consumer is acquired, the central objective is to sell more than just the initial product - a common fault in earlier financial services marketing. Now, these companies are aiming to keep consumers longer and raise their average number of 'relationships per consumer' - a piece of jargon which puts the focus not on the number of different products sold to each consumer, but on whether each product relationship endures. This is because switching and early cancellation are endemic in the sector.

Leisure and travel services

The leisure and travel services sector includes all suppliers of personal transport (rail, air, coach, shipping, car hire and so on), of accommodation (hotels, timeshare and the like), of packaged and tailor-made holidays, travel agents, motoring organizations, leisure operators (bingo, gambling clubs, betting shops, theme parks, and the like), theatres and cinemas. With so much information potentially (and actually, in some cases) available to suppliers about consumer behaviour and preferences, the value of a long-term relationship with consumers is well appreciated and exploited through a continuing dialogue, and marketing strategies are often based on consumer relationships (such as frequent flyer programmes and special sea cruises for previous consumers). This category looks very robust for the long term, although it has suffered in the short term due to recession and world events like terrorism. The average size of companies is growing through mergers and take-overs. There are also good cross-selling opportunities within this sector. However, the low-cost airline model has threatened the use of database techniques, as these airlines rely on a strongly product-oriented business model, in which the main aim is to sell by the cheapest channel at the best price. Here, the interactive component (selling first by call centre, then via the Internet) has come to the fore.

Non-profit and public institutions

These include public sector organizations (such as local authorities, educational establishments, government agencies), charities, political parties, professional and trade associations and other pressure groups. Charities are heavy users of direct mail, and understand the characteristics of more generous givers and their tendency to give to several different charities – hence list exchanging between them. Trade unions use database techniques to organize elections. The same applies to many professional bodies and societies. Educational institutions use databases of past students (alumni) to raise money as public funding tightens. Many institutions have introduced 'affinity group credit cards' as an additional service to their members. The credit and transaction fees they raise add to their funds, while the database operations are usually facilities-managed by the credit card providers. Governments are considering ways of using database techniques – whether in disseminating information, such as people's rights, or in tax collection (such as profiling of likely fraudsters or late payers). E-government is a common phrase. It refers to improving citizen access to government information and services. However, many governments have discovered that database marketing techniques must be complemented by a change in attitudes to relationships between government and citizen – one that is less directive and more responsive, not just in terms of communication but also in terms of the whole public proposition to consumers.

Marketers of physical products

This includes all companies who have a physical product to sell, such as household durables, cars, home improvement products and fast-moving consumer goods, such as food. They have the following attributes. First, the processes of manufacturing and physical distribution increase the time and costs involved in adjusting supply to demand. Stocks are present in the system, and this creates a strong pressure to find consumers for them. However well these companies forecast demand, there will always be this pressure.

Second is the presence (in many cases) of retailers or distributors between supplier and consumer, with their own merchandise selection and marketing policies and (in some cases) a strong hold on consumers and consumer information.

These suppliers were slow to awaken to the opportunities of database marketing. One exception to this is the motor industry, which uses it to *sustain dialogue after purchase*, and for prospecting. Domestic appliance manufacturers have for long tussled with the question of how to maintain a cost-effective dialogue with consumers when replacement for a given appliance is typically once every 7–10 years. They usually resort to retail display and occasional media bursts. But most computer suppliers have been working on developing consumer loyalty using database marketing techniques. An enhanced ability to segment and access particular groups of consumers will help them solve this problem.

Fast moving (grocery) consumer goods are a source of much controversy in database marketing circles. Some hold that the contribution of database marketing is bound to be limited. However, some families may well be spending hundreds of pounds a year on products from a given manufacturer. If cross-product branding is nurtured, these consumers become good prospects for database marketing. Their lifetime value is greater than that for many financial products. The potential competitive pay-off to successful database marketing in this area, where the only alternative is massive media spend, is clearly great, and has been realized by leading US companies, such as Heinz and Procter & Gamble. They have large databases and are sending personalized coupons to their consumers. These are giving such suppliers a good indication of which of their consumers are highest value and therefore worth investing in to keep. Meanwhile, the tactical promotional use of database marketing is receiving more attention from companies in this sector. Many promotions currently being mounted are single product promotions that yield consumer lists as a by-product. Many are toll-free telephone campaigns. Mobile telephony has worked very well for promotions by these companies.

Here are some examples of incentives to call in (and to buy the product in the first place, of course):

- to find out if the consumer has won the prize described on the pack;

- to answer questions on the product, receive a coupon and perhaps a prize;
- to listen to a commercial, receive a coupon and a free gift;
- to listen to a pop star's promotional message for a record;
- to have any problems resolved (the Careline approach).

Product retailers

Retail marketing used to be considered very different from the marketing of most of the above sectors. Now, they are converging, and database marketing is helping create this convergence. Retailers play a key role in financial transactions, representing the destination of most cash. Retailers are used at least as frequently as banks (and some provide a wide range of financial services). They are providers of a service (halfway between leisure and work), but they are also product marketers in their own right, as some of them now have strong brands of their own. The main difference between product marketers and multiple retailers is the sheer volume of data about consumer needs that they can collect because of frequent and direct contact. This makes them prime candidates for database marketing. Most large retailers have developed their marketing resources and skills quickly. This is partly because of competitive pressure that is internal to the sector, visible in the many mergers, take-overs, extensions of product lines and regional extensions of operations. Retail management is now much more aware of the lifetime values of consumers and of how database marketing can provide ways of keeping consumers. The retail credit card and loyalty schemes give them a strong weapon in their competitive armoury. Retailers already realize the tactical value of these techniques, and some understand their strategic value – as evidenced by the success of loyalty schemes such as the Tesco Clubcard (see Chapter 8). Members of these schemes are targeted for promotions aimed at getting them to visit more often, broaden their buying range, and introduce new members to the scheme.

Mail-order houses

Mail-order houses are one of the largest users of direct mail. Their databases are now used for agent recruitment, promotions and also third-party promotions. The use of specialized catalogues is becoming widespread. The question these companies must ask themselves is what their role will be when everyone else becomes a database marketer! In some cases, the answer has been to help a product retailer go into mail order.

THE DEMAND FOR DATABASE MARKETING

The demand for database marketing will continue to be driven by these factors:

- **Increased fragmentation** of consumer markets, partly as a result of more use of database marketing, allowing consumers with specific needs to be managed more easily, whetting their appetitive for more. This leads to increased ability on the part of suppliers to meet the needs of small groups of consumers, which puts pressure on non-users of database marketing to start using these approaches, causing existing users to improve their use, and so on. In many consumer markets, companies find it necessary not only to target their communications more precisely and manage relationships with consumers more 'personally', but also to plan their business using the ever more detailed information accumulated about their consumers, and the ever more sophisticated tools available for them to do this planning.
- **Increased awareness** of the absolute and competitive benefits of using computer and communications technology to manage consumers. In many markets, companies are keeping a watchful eye on their competitors' attempts to implement particular facets of CRM.
- In all markets, increased emphasis on '**getting closer to the consumer**'. Many supposedly marketing-oriented companies have been chastened by their marketing experiences. Thinking that the information provided by market research gave them good understanding of their consumers, they found that their consumers' loyalty was less strong than they supposed, or that they were wrong about the kind of consumers they had.
- In many businesses, the presence of an **increasing band of professionals** with database marketing or similar backgrounds. These managers are demanding that their companies seize the best that database marketing has to offer, not just in marketing communications, but in all marketing.
- In many public sector organizations, **greater sensitivity to needs of 'customers'** (patients, users, consumers, ratepayers and the like). This is emerging not only in the 'attitude' training being undertaken by many organizations, but also in the kinds of information technology being installed to give better service to 'consumers'. Some of them are actively looking to improve communication with their 'consumers'. Government pressures have added fuel to this fire, sometimes in the form of tough regulations governing how consumers should be managed.

- In charities, political organizations and pressure groups, increased **striving to influence people** and reach them first and/or more effectively.

THE SUPPLY OF DATABASE MARKETING SERVICES

The above trends spell radically increased opportunities for companies serving the database marketing market. The leading-edge suppliers in this market form a new group of specialist companies, which work to turn the most advanced technology and marketing concepts into usable marketing systems. The 'supply-side' factors encouraging increased use of database marketing include further advances in computing and telecommunications, making it easier and cheaper to hold more complex information about individual consumers or users, to analyse it more comprehensively, accurately and quickly, and to transform analysis into policy. Relationships with consumers can be managed more professionally, using the information held on the database or generated during each step in the relationship.

Another factor is relative increases in costs of more labour or media-intensive modes of marketing, and relative weakness in performance. In the United States, the lack of national broadcast and printed media and relative cheapness of database marketing media (post and telephone) may have been factors in the dramatically higher usage of the latter for marketing purposes than in the UK.

Many suppliers are broadening out the range of services supplied. Database marketing agencies offer fulfilment and database services. Database bureaux offer mailing and fulfilment services. Many offer Internet-based services. With this rapidly developing supply of services, no company that needs to stay in touch with its consumers has the excuse that it does not know how to use database marketing.

CONCLUSION

In this chapter, we have explained the main uses of database marketing. In the next chapter, we explain how database marketing uses consumer insight. We also introduce the notion of customer care and how it uses data.

3 How customer care and database marketing use customer insight

Merlin Stone, Alison Bond and Bryan Foss

DATABASE MARKETING AND CUSTOMER CARE

Database marketers tend to focus strongly on interactions between their organization and its consumers. These interactions are normally at their most intense when consumer and organization are exchanging information, communicating about a possible or actual purchase, or about a service issue. While the classic disciplines of marketing, such as product design, branding and advertising focus more on the consumer's broad relationship with the supplier and product, database marketing can lead to too narrow a focus. It is almost as if the only consumer insight that matters is the insight needed to help the organization sell more.

While the ideas of database marketing were developing, a different set of ideas emerged from the world of customer service. Often, the customer service function was left 'holding the baby', dealing with mistakes caused by the narrow, rational or 'head' focus of database marketing. The idea of 'customer care' emerged.[1] This focused on consumers as individuals, throughout the cycle of awareness of need to use of the product, with the aim of developing and using insights into how they felt about the product and associated service. In this chapter, we describe how these two disciplines, customer care and database marketing, use consumer insight as a prelude to the more comprehensive view advocated in customer relationship management (CRM).

THE MEANING OF CUSTOMER CARE

Caring for customers is a simple idea. It means looking after customers and meeting their needs. In a world where most suppliers need to meet their customers' needs, the experience of many customers is not very happy. When customers do have poor experiences, rather than tell the supplier, they often allow the situation to fester. They infect other customers with their attitudes, creating a snowball effect. Meanwhile, the supplier carries on in blissful ignorance, until its overall success starts to falter.

Why do so many suppliers fail in customer care? Why have so many suppliers not worked out how to improve their standards of customer care? Why have so few implemented improved standards? One reason is that customer care is not the only way of meeting customer needs. A well laid-out store, a high-quality, well-designed new product, a well-planned Web site, a well-structured telemarketing conversation, a properly targeted and designed direct-mail letter - all are ways of looking after consumers and meeting their needs. A special feature of customer care is that it relates to how consumers are treated by supplier staff, or by the systems that manage the consumer automatically. The following case study shows the relationship between delivery of good-quality customer care and the data and systems that underpin it.

EPSOM AND EWELL

Located to the southwest of London, Epsom and Ewell Borough Council provides its citizens with a wide range of public services, from community centres and healthcare to planning, recreation and waste management. Delivering high-quality service consistently was a struggle. Each council service was run by up to 40 separate teams. It was difficult for citizens to reach the right individual, and there was minimal interdepartmental communication. Up to 20 per cent of callers hung up before they were connected. If the appropriate departmental individual was unavailable, service collapsed. For example, if a citizen called to arrange collection of outsized waste but could not reach the council, at best he or she might deliver the waste to the central collection point, but at worst he or she would dump items at a roadside. The council would then incur the expense of collecting it, lose the small waste revenue collection opportunity, and experience the dissatisfaction of local residents.

The council recognized that to transform citizen service, it needed to re-engineer its business processes. It adopted a multi-channel solution running on Siebel Call Centre. It developed a single source of citizen and council service information, transforming how the council interacts with its citizens. Whatever enquiry the citizen has – whether it has to do with recreation facility opening times, a council tax payment, building control, or a local environmental issue – the citizen calls the council using a single, central number. Automatic call distribution immediately routes the call to one of the council agents. E-mails are also routed to a central distribution point. Agents use an integrated, complete view of the citizen and council services to respond to enquiries over both channels.

Using this approach, the council now resolves 80 per cent of the 650 average daily enquiries at the initial point of contact. It has also cut dropped calls from 20 per cent to 4 per cent. Now, in one call, citizens can report local environmental issues, schedule an appointment with a planning inspector, arrange transport for the elderly or disabled, enquire about general services, and even pay parking fines. The system is also used to improve efficiency and service quality among the council contractors and a wide network of service delivery partners. When citizens contact the council to request special waste collection or pest control services, the details – location, type of problem and schedule – are routed to the contractor via e-mail or telephone. The contractor notifies the call centre when the action will be undertaken. The agent can confirm this with the citizen and use the complete view of the situation to resolve any subsequent issues.

One reason for problems occurring in customer care is that managers who make policy are remote from customers and from those who serve them, and do not share the insights that arise from serving them. These managers may be unaware of failings in customer care. Performance problems may be attributed to other policies. Another reason is that mentioned in the Introduction, that managers' performance measurements cause them to act against consumer's interests. A third reason is that the complexity of the consumer's decision making may not be recognized.

Focus on the consumer decision-making unit

While database marketers tend to focus on the individual consumer (and might be obliged to, for privacy reasons), in customer care – as in classic marketing – we recognize the role played by, for example, friends, family and neighbours. The roles played include:

- user – the person actually using the product;
- influencer – who influences the buying decision, often someone who works closely with other members of the buying centre, or whose objectives require the use of the product or service to be successful;
- decision maker – who makes the decision, often a budget holder or person in a position of authority;
- gatekeeper – who brings/allows information about the product into the buying centre, including information about the level of customer care experienced by other customers;
- buyer – who implements the buying decision using formal procedures;
- financer – who pays for the product.

These roles may be played formally or informally. Each individual might play a number of roles. Different roles imply different objectives, requirements, levels of influence, and the need for different types of customer care. For example, a parent buying a complex, expensive electronic toy for a child's birthday, the day before the birthday, might require, as financer, buyer and influencer:

- a variety of goods on display, so that the child can choose knowing what each product is really like;
- helpful guidance about the product range;
- payment options or credit facilities;
- immediate replacement if the product proves defective;
- a competitive price;
- availability of the product in stock;
- gift-wrapping;
- robust packaging, which allows the product to be replaced in it many times when not in use.

The child, as gatekeeper, decision maker and user, might require:

- availability of the product in stock;
- robust performance, to specification;
- packaging that can be easily removed.

Of course, the father might be a second, possibly secret user, and have some of these requirements too! Often, the family becomes a 'mobile buying centre'. Shopping is for many families one of the only things they do together as a group. Suppliers have the opportunity of satisfying their requirements as a group, but also the risk of failing to do so. Retailers should cater for the different members of this group simultaneously, for instance by provision of toys for children to play with, chairs for the elderly to sit on, papers for dads to read.

The scope of customer care

Customer care does not just cover sales situations. It covers transactions connected with sales such as reading an electricity meter and receipt of an invoice. It covers service situations that are not directly related to the sale but are in some sense commercial, because the consumer might have to pay as a result. Examples of this include emergency call-out of service staff to check a central heating boiler emitting fumes (a repair would need to be paid for) or flight cancellation (the consumer has paid for a ticket). It also covers definitely uncommercial activities such as treatment of voters or taxpayers, behaviour of security guards, or even arrest by police. Whether all of these activities should be termed customer care issues is a debatable point.

The perceived transaction period

Customer care does not just relate to face-to-face transactions. It includes:

- over the telephone;
- in self-service stores when the customer is confronted by shelves of merchandise;
- in self-service petrol stations;
- at cash machines;
- when customers receive letters;
- when customers see advertisements;
- when customers face computer screens, whether viewing the organization's Web site or to e-mail it.

In fact, opportunities for customer care exist whenever customers perceive that they are engaged in a transaction with the organization. This view of customer care brings many opportunities and problems. For example, consumers who buy new cars may pay two or three visits to the dealer before buying. They may view the manufacturer's and dealer's Web sites, perhaps even 'building their own car'. They may have several telephone conversations with the dealer before and after the sale. They may exchange one or two letters during the transaction. They may visit the dealer after the sale to have a minor problem rectified. Throughout this period, consumers may consider themselves engaged in a transaction with the dealer and possibly with the manufacturer. If a company manages this period of transaction well, consumers are likely to return to the dealer for service and for a replacement car when the time comes. They might also buy a more expensive model, or buy insurance, extended warranty or finance through the dealer. However, the potential for problems is also greater. If this period of transaction is spoilt by failures in customer care, then consumers might not buy additional items. At the worst, they might cancel the deal. So, using the 'perceived transaction period' in defining customer care opens up opportunities for better customer care, but also exposes risks of failure.

The service encounter

A perceived transaction period might consist of several service encounters. In each service encounter and over the transaction period as a whole, the consumer might go through several mental states, such as:

- experiencing the need;
- panic about how to fulfil the need, or whether it will be fulfilled at all;
- sensitivity – about whether the right choice has been made, or whether to accept the way in which the service is being provided;
- dependence – a feeling of being as a child to the 'adult' provider of service;
- happiness or unhappiness – according to the degree of success of the encounter or transaction;
- satisfaction or resentment – after the encounter or transaction is over, according to its result.

Perceptions of care

Perceptions define the period of the transaction. They also define the standard of care received. Suppliers aiming to improve customer care may need to monitor delivery of customer care through internal measures, such as time to answer a query, or frequency of a fault recurring. However, the measure that counts to consumers is the perception of what they are receiving, and how satisfied they are with it. Measuring service just through internal measures is like behaving as an adult to a child. The organization is effectively saying: 'I am an adult and I set the standards. The consumer (the child) will see the wisdom of this in the long run.'

As we identified in the Introduction, another problem with measuring service at this transactional level is that organizations tend to target their staff on the results of these measures, and staff will then head in the direction of these targets. If, as is generally the case, these measures are transactional (that is, relating to how well particular transactions were handled), the organization will become oriented more towards the success of individual service transactions, and less towards fulfilling consumers' main requirement (the 'halo'). This is dangerous when the measures focus on areas that are not productive as far as consumers are concerned. However, organizations often measure attributes because they are easy to measure, rather than because they shape and improve an organization, in particular, its ability to give customers what they really want. Hence the example of health services measuring waiting lists (queues) rather than maintenance of health and well-being.

Customer service and customer care

'Customer service' is an accepted term. Many companies now have 'customer service' functions that are far more than complaints departments. For example, many equipment manufacturers successively named their after-sales activities maintenance, then service, then customer service. In most cases, this renaming was not superficial. It indicated a real transition, through stages that had the following focus:

- maintenance – ensuring failures were dealt with and restoring equipment to its required standard;
- service – ensuring that the equipment performed to the appropriate standard through the intervention, often on a scheduled basis, of the engineer;
- customer service – an advanced version of the previous attitude, with more focus on the interaction between the customer and the supplying company at the time of delivery of the service action.

In line with this move, staff servicing the equipment went through the following (or similar) name cycle:

- maintenance engineers or field engineers;
- (field) service engineers or field service representatives;
- customer service representatives or officers.

The customer service orientation was an advance on the engineering orientation. It did not deny it. After all, equipment must continue to receive good engineering service or be designed to avoid the need for it. The customer service orientation moved the focus to the customer. However, the focus was (and in many cases still is) on the supplier's perception. High priority is given to tasks, costs, procedures, management processes and hierarchies, and internal targets, rather than to consumer insights: in particular the halo, not the head. Thus consumers might say that for urgent calls, they require service staff to come within two hours, and the problem to be resolved within one hour of arrival. This assumes that consumers know how long servicing takes, and that every two hours has the same value. For example, is two hours over a lunch hour or at the end of a working day worth the same as two hours of prime work time? Still, some suppliers insist on asking the question in terms of absolute number of hours because it is only by hours that they can target their engineers. For the consumer, the main desire might be to complete the weekly wash that day. This shows the importance of true consumer insight, and of having the right information to support customer care decisions.

Consider automotive service. The main thing a customer of a repair facility wants is a vehicle that is mended and stays mended. There is no point in fixing it quickly if it breaks down again a day or so later. Service is part of what the consumer buys, but the result, a properly repaired vehicle, is why the consumer bought the service, not a number of hours of repair time. Good insight is required by organizations if they are to understand what consumers really want from them and to market to that need, to measure their performance against it and to motivate their staff to provide it. If an organization is failing to perform long term but its customer service scores look good, it is likely that it is measuring and targeting on the wrong things.

Focusing on customers

The customer care approach focuses on the customer. It considers the customer's perceptions and requirements in the customer's own language and within the customer's own frame of reference. Customer care also focuses on service encounters within the perceived transaction period. Within these service encounters are usually one or more moments of truth – moments when the customer becomes convinced either that excellent service is being delivered, or that the service is poor. Customer care focuses on procedures that allow responsiveness, supportive management and targets that are customer-oriented. In theory, the same is true of database marketing, although the same divergences between the consumer's interest and the organization's direction can exist.

HOW DATABASE MARKETERS USE CONSUMER INSIGHT – STARTING WITH THE OFFER

In this section, we consider the main activities of database marketers and show how consumer insight should support them. In database marketing, the product or service is promoted through 'an offer', which is defined as 'the total proposition made to the customer'. The offer is usually used to close a sale, once awareness has been created or increased by other means such as advertising. The components of the offer are listed below.

Core proposition

This is the key business or product message, usually determined by the organization's marketing strategy.

Formal proposition

These support the core proposition and differentiate the product from others. They include the elements listed in Table 3.1.

Symbolic proposition

This includes:

- **brand:** this shapes the appearance and tone of voice of the organization's communications;
- **trademarks:** these can be used to add further confidence and status to the company brand;
- **logo:** this helps punctuate and support the offer, adds instant recognition and promotes confidence in the communication and offer.

As the best offer the organization can make to consumers is the one that satisfies their needs, the importance of consumer insight should be obvious. Without good insight into consumers' needs, marketing might deliver poor returns. While different offers may be tested and shown to produce different results, it is combining response and purchase data with market research that shows why one offer works and another does not. As we shall see, this also applies to the choice of media used to communicate with consumers.

Table 3.1 *Elements of the formal proposition*

Element	Example
Product features	Number of channels, breadth of programming, flights per day, worldwide destinations for example
Packaging	Visual – corporate identity Content – packaging of offering: value pack, premium movie or sports packs, economy or premium tickets, discounts, last-minute deals
Peripherals	Interactive content, menus on board, lounge access, facilities for business travellers
Service	On-line flight information, one-stop booking line
Customer care	24-hour customer care, freephone calls, technical help desk
Price	Lowest price, entry-level packages, discount or special offer
Terms	Terms of the offer, eligibility, close date, restrictions, conditions
Availability	As part of offer, 'while stocks last', offer period, and so on
Marketing communications	Look and feel, tone of voice, call centre script, Web site layout and design, paper stock, font and so on all contribute to the overall positioning of the offer

HOW CHOICE OF MEDIA REQUIRES CONSUMER INSIGHT

In this section, we briefly investigate the media used in database marketing and CRM, and identify their consumer insight requirements. Before we begin, let us examine a case study which shows how a company uses several different channels or media to manage customers.

AMP

AMP Ltd is one of Australia's leading financial services companies. AMP Financial Services (FS), a business unit, provides a range of products and services in insurance, banking, asset management, retirement savings and income, and financial planning. The increasingly competitive nature of the financial services sector and ever-changing needs of its customers, together with the enhanced market visibility brought about by the demutualization, meant that AMP FS had to compete hard to maintain customer loyalty. AMP FS set itself the goal of building its business on a renewed focus on CRM. To achieve this, AMP FS expanded the number of channels used to communicate with customers. In the past, the company had relied on a network of company-branded and independent financial planners to sell products and services through face-to-face meetings, with information held in filing cabinets. The company recognized the need to market to, sell to, and provide service to customers across its four primary channels: phone, Internet, mail and its financial planner community. It needed to combine face-to-face meetings with other contact points, such as call centres and the Internet. Given its broad range of financial products and services, the company wanted to improve its ability to up-sell and cross-sell to its customer base.

AMP FS needed an integrated CRM solution. It deployed Siebel Finance and Insurance to its call centre representatives and Siebel Partner Relationship Management (PRM) to its financial planner network. With financial planners responsible for approximately 75 per cent of AMP FS business, the implementation focused on providing these critical stakeholders with functionality that would help them increase revenue and customer satisfaction.

AMP FS replaced many of its existing systems and processes, and now has an enterprise-wide system that allows it to collaborate with partners over the Web through a planner portal. The system provides lead generation, routing, and monitoring capabilities as well as access to a unified repository of customer information. Call centre representatives can now deliver personalized service with consolidated information on the customer from back-office systems such as policy and billing systems, and from previous contact across all channels.

The system quickly improved the effectiveness of AMP FS's opportunity-development process. Where a lead was once routed to a planner in hard copy via a spreadsheet or fax, it is now sent electronically via the Internet, along with an automatic e-mail alerting the planner. This has transformed a time-consuming manual task into a fully automated process. Managers distribute the leads to the financial planners by region and monitor the leads throughout the sales cycle. Planners have 48 hours to accept or reject a lead before it is passed to another planner – a process that managers can now track.

The system is also used to measure the effectiveness of marketing campaigns as well as other initiatives such as lead management. Its marketing module enables financial planners to execute targeted marketing campaigns to their customer base and generate more revenue from up-selling and cross-selling. In addition, the solution helps financial planners hit quarterly targets and directly enhance the company's bottom-line results. Marketing campaigns are now generated by marketing analysts and fed to financial planners through the planner portal.

Financial planners then select a channel to execute the campaign for their customer base. The progress of marketing campaigns is monitored in real time, allowing financial planners the flexibility to make adjustments if required, or even opt out should a planner decide a campaign is not suitable for his or her customer base. A given campaign might target up to 300,000 people, but when planners log in to the planner portal and look at the campaign, they see only the prospects targeted in their own areas.

Direct mail

Direct mail has three main uses:

- as a prime medium – a self-contained vehicle for selling a product or service, promoting an event, etc;
- with other media, to support or follow up other activities;
- as support to a channel – before the sale (eg to provide leads) or after (eg to follow up a sales call).

As with all direct-marketing media, targeting is critical in direct mail. In a mail campaign, unlike with telephone marketing and some other media, the response cannot instantly be adjusted at the moment of interaction with the consumer. It is no use finding out after the event whether the consumer is the right one and whether the form of communication is right for that consumer. Although the cost of each communication seems low, the costs of a large campaign are not. Hence the importance of testing.

In a direct-mail campaign, you must be very clear what consumers are expected to do when they receive the letter. You will not be there when the letter is opened to tell them what to do! Customers' motivation in taking the required step must also be understood. For consumers, response equals effort – the effort of cutting out, completing and posting, or picking up the telephone and dialling, or logging on to the Internet, or visiting a branch of the organization. Mail-pack design must take these issues into account. The message and any call to action needs to be as simple and clear as possible. Direct-mail planning requires a good understanding of how consumers receive and deal with direct mail – hence the importance of consumer insight.

The advantages of direct mail are as follows:

- It is possible to target highly specifically.
- It is personal and confidential.

- It is more competitively secret.
- The message can be highly specific, enabling you to dovetail it very closely with messages put out through less targeted media, such as television or the national press.
- Even in the lowest-cost postage bracket, a lot of space is available in which to communicate.
- A variety of formats and materials can be used.
- There are many opportunities to introduce novelty (eg by different formats and types of enclosure).
- Mailings can be scheduled to arrive within a fairly well-defined period.
- Testing is relatively easy.
- The response vehicle can be defined so as to ensure that customers know exactly what to do when they receive the mailing.
- Properly planned, it can be much more cost effective per reply than most other media.

Direct mail has some specific weaknesses:

- It is not appropriate to all markets or consumers.
- It does not suit all objectives. For some products, consumers may not trust direct mail, preferring to visit a retail outlet to gather information. In this case, it might be better to use direct mail to stimulate consumers to visit retail outlets.
- It cannot be used in isolation to build a brand.
- Some customers are very sceptical of direct mail.

Here's how to make it fail:

- **Emphasize short-term response, rather than relationship building.** Now that so many companies are committed to CRM, this approach is less common. Many companies still decide to 'do a mailing' to 'bring in leads'. They rent a list, design and dispatch the mailing, and never work out whether targeting was accurate. The opportunity to learn and improve is lost, as is the opportunity to build a database.
- **Use it tactically.** Even if the organization has a good database, you may be tempted to use direct mail entirely tactically, just to generate leads. You might miss opportunities for building loyalty, developing a catalogue operation, selling additional products and services, cross-selling and researching the consumers.
- **Do not integrate your contacts with the rest of the company's contact efforts.** For example, letters might be going out at the same time that sales or service people are due to call.

- **Choose your own messages,** and do not worry about the other messages the company is sending out, or what branding it is trying to achieve. This is a great way to confuse consumers.

Direct-mail users often incorporate personal details about consumers in the letter copy. So, a letter might say, 'When you bought your washing machine from us five years ago you returned us a questionnaire that indicated that you would be likely to replace your machine after five years. Five years have now passed, so we would like to offer you a very special trade-in price for your old machine…' This might lead the consumer to wonder how the organization has managed to remember what the response was five years ago. The consumer might also worry that information that he or she thought was used for market research has now been used to encourage replacement.

A more subtle approach would be to use the data to target the consumer in question, and make a trade-in offer, without actually reminding the customer about the data. The rule is that in the body of the letter, customer data should only be used where the recipient would expect the organization to have and use it. This applies even if the consumer provided the information directly in the first place. The content of the message must also be based on deep insight. For example, a washing machine company might identify that the 'halo' that consumers want relates to a 'cleaner world and a cleaner home'. It might write to its consumers to say that in the last five years it has worked hard to design a machine that produces better results with less water and energy, and that can be disposed of when obsolete in an environmentally friendly way.

This case study shows how improved consumer insight can increase the efficiency of direct mail.

CENTRE PARCS EUROPE

Centre Parcs is a European leader in short-break holidays. The company operates 15 vacation parks in the Netherlands, Belgium, Germany and France. Centre Parcs focuses on putting the customer first. In recent years, Centre Parcs has invested in improving its proposition and in tuning it to target groups. Every park offers a unique selection of facilities and activities adjusted to visitors' preferences. This focus is also expressed in a multi-channel approach to customers and prospects. Customers can book or request information anywhere and anytime through, for instance, the Internet, a call centre, or travel agencies.

The most important challenge for Centre Parcs is to achieve maximum occupancy for the vacation parks. The average occupancy of the approximately 9,000 bungalows in Europe is about 90 per cent, which is unequalled in the leisure industry. Centre Parcs' objective is to increase further the occupancy rates of its parks and cross-sell more sports and leisure facilities to guests. To achieve this, Centre Parcs has implemented SPSS PredictiveMarketing to revolutionize its marketing strategy.

Before, this activity involved sending two bulk mailings per year. The software enables Centre Parcs' marketers to efficiently create, optimize and execute their marketing campaigns. This has reduced direct marketing costs by 46 per cent, while streamlining direct marketing campaign optimization and execution processes. Centre Parcs now accurately predicts individual customer needs, contacting only those customers who are likely to respond to a campaign. Its main marketing campaigns are now followed by several small, but highly targeted, campaigns that are used to sell remaining accommodations or to cross-sell additional facilities. Each campaign can be built in just a few hours. This is useful for short-term promotions of vacant accommodation. Centre Parcs' objective is to use these online channels to cross-sell additional packages, such as leisure facilities and dinners, to customers at the moment they book their accommodation. The software's ability to determine the most profitable cross-sell offer at the moment of interaction is crucial to successfully achieving this.

Telemarketing

Telemarketing means using the telephone as a properly managed part of the marketing, sales and service mix. It differs from telephone selling, which aims to get sales over the telephone. Teleselling is usually a standalone strategy rather than an integrated element of the marketing mix. In consumer marketing, teleselling is now less common, and many companies now use telemarketing as one of their main ways of managing consumers. Many consumers find teleselling a nuisance. Consumers have ready excuses to deal with poorly targeted calls. 'I've got one already' or 'We had it done last year' are the commonest.

In telemarketing, highly trained staff use telecommunications equipment and networks to achieve marketing objectives by carrying out a controlled dialogue with consumers. These staff are supported by systems that allow companies to manage the workflow, measure it and follow through the outcome of the dialogue. Consumers calling are identified by their telephone number, and this plus other data are used to route the call to the right telemarketing agent, who proposes the right offer. In its most advanced form, the dialogue between customer and company can be switched between telephone and the World Wide Web or Interactive television, or combine them simultaneously.

Telemarketing requires systematic management, measurement and control of every aspect of its operation. Without this, it is not possible to know the relationship between the inputs and outputs of the telemarketing operation. This information is essential to achieve effectiveness. Nonetheless, the costs of running big telemarketing operations are coming under scrutiny. Many companies are moving their contact centres to developing countries, or persuading their customers to use even lower cost channels, such as the World Wide Web. Consumers too are increasingly showing their preference for the Web as a way to learn about and even buy products and services.

Consumers may find the telephone a good way to manage their relationship with the organization because:

- **It saves their time.** They do not have to handle the formality of a sales visit, or travel to see the product.
- **It allows them to feel they control the relationship.** They can indicate when it is convenient for someone to call, and can call the organization when it is convenient to them. They can terminate the call when they want.
- **It gives them information when they need it.** They might find it frustrating to wait for information to come in the post. They can call the organization, and it can respond immediately or quite soon after.
- **It gives them a direct dialogue with your company.** This gives them confidence in the relationship.

Telemarketing is best used as part of CRM. A central principle of CRM is to be in dialogue with consumers. This ensures that their needs are more likely to be met and that the database is kept fresh. In a dialogue, information flows both ways. This dialogue lasts as long as the consumer remains a customer.

Telemarketing requires detailed planning. Whether or not a precise script is used, each call must be under control and planned. Telemarketing differs from telephone selling in that every call is measured and the results analysed. This enables the different elements of telemarketing to be measured and tested in the same was as with direct mail – the list, the script, the offer, the timing and so on. Telemarketing also needs to be tested in competition with other media, and with different combinations of media in the contact strategy. The management of a telemarketing campaign must be very precise, including careful control of costs (such as operator time and list selection), through budgeting and planning of campaigns. Quality must be monitored very carefully. It is easy to target a telemarketing campaign to produce a specific number of requests for further information or for a quote, only to discover that few consumers follow through. So telemarketing must be measured as part of the overall contact strategy, which is designed to yield more sales and profit, not just appointments. The database must therefore allow tracking of the effectiveness of every contact medium from beginning to end of the sales cycle.

Telemarketing helps achieve many objectives. They include:

- **Call handling:** answering consumer calls on any matter, including enquiries about products, requests for service, dealing with complaints or problems.
- **Moving towards a sale:** lead generation, appointment creation, order taking, seeking or closing, selling up or cross-selling, converting non-sales-related inbound or outbound calls into sales opportunities.
- **Cold calling:** normally as part of a campaign or following up a mailshot, subject to telephone preference legislation.
- **Building loyalty:** by meeting needs and by just listening and remaining in contact; by following up a mailshot; by asking what consumers thought of a product, brochure etc.
- **Enquiry screening:** obtaining information to confirm whether the prospect is serious.
- **Consumer and market research:** gathering information to use in making business decisions. This includes screening of lists of customers or prospects to be used in particular marketing campaigns.
- **Delivering customized advice** – by anticipating what consumers need to know, and briefing telemarketers so that they can help.
- **Account management:** improving the quality of account management, so certain groups of consumers benefit from a better relationship with the organization. This may include finding new purchasers within existing accounts, preventing competitive inroads into customers, and reactivating lapsed customers.
- **New business:** identifying and developing new prospects and new markets, extending coverage of existing markets, or launching a new product or service.
- **Quality:** improving the effectiveness of distribution channels.
- **Customer care:** improving customer service and satisfaction. Many customer care departments use the telephone as the main channel for complaints management.

Contact centers are usually highly automated, with on-screen scripting, online access to operational systems to check inventory availability or service delivery, and the ability to key in orders or book service calls. Such centers can be particularly effective for handling telephone responses to mass mailings or broadcast and published media campaigns, or for handling customers who call in often for service reasons (such as bank balance checking or booking service calls). Many companies that manage their consumers on the Web can now browse collaboratively with those customers and push different screens at them to help them.

The progress of telemarketing has been facilitated by the development of telecommunications and computing technology. The telephony requirements are usually provided via an automatic call distributor (ACD) or through computer-integrated telephony that can fully emulate all the features of ACD. An ACD is an independent unit that allows calls to be distributed between call receivers on a variety of programmed bases. It also allows the telemarketing manager to monitor each telemarketer's inbound and outbound telephone usage (since it provides call-handling statistics). ACD statistics help in monitoring telemarketers against their targets. ACD systems enable telemarketing managers to listen to and record conversations. Telemarketers can also record their own conversations. They can then use these recordings to improve their technique.

The ACD directs calls automatically, for example:

- to distribute workloads evenly;
- to give valued customers preferential treatment;
- to ensure that the right person handles each caller (based upon skills, product knowledge etc);
- directing particular calls to telemarketers with special expertise;
- promoting personal relationships with customers.

Telemarketing works best when based on a comprehensive customer database. Some telemarketing is supported by a central database, holding all customer information. The database feeds information to telemarketing systems, which in turn feed new information back to the central database. Various standard and 'tailorable' systems are available. These allow:

- Online scripts or call guides so that telemarketers cover all the required points in a structured way.
- Storing information about customers and dialogues with them. This takes place as telemarketers talk with customers, and is especially effective if call guides are being used. The information can then be used either within the conversation, to trigger decisions about next

steps in the sales cycle, or in a future conversation, to enable telemarketers to 'remember' customer details.
- Diary entry of customer call-backs within a sales cycle.
- Prompting fulfilment, either by providing a feed to an automatic literature fulfilment process, or even directly to a product distribution system, which in turn can be attached to a stock control system.

Packages are sold under the generic title of telemarketing, call center or contact center systems, and run on anything from a PC to a mainframe. Some only perform telemarketing functions. Others offer extra functions such as territory planning, direct mail and sales accounting. Almost all have a database management facility linking different functions. These packages are often sold as part of an integrated CRM package.

In telemarketing, the old management sayings 'You get what you inspect, not what you expect' and 'If you can't measure it, you can't manage it' apply with a vengeance. Telemarketing works with various targets and ratios. Decision maker contacts (DMCs) are defined as making contact with the person who can make the decision to buy (not his or her partner or another colleague). A target is required for DMCs per period, and for the ratio between dials and DMCs. Achieving the target ratio of DMCs per day (or week) is important for two main reasons. First, it ensures that resources are geared correctly and effectively towards the level of customer coverage that is demanded by the telemarketers' role, and second, measuring the number of decision makers contacted ensures that the telemarketers are getting through to the right person in the family or customer organization.

Many ratios also apply to inbound telemarketing, except that DMCs as a target in their own right do not apply (the caller is presumed to be interested). Therefore all other ratios are per caller rather than per decision maker contact. Other ratios include:

- time to answer;
- number of calls answered;
- time taken to deal with each call satisfactorily.

In the case study, we show how consumer insight is used to improve the efficiency of a call center.

SPAARBELEG

Spaarbeleg is one of the Netherlands' larger financial services institutions. Its retail banking products include savings accounts, pension programmes, stock lease products, share funds and tax-saving products.

These are all designed to keep restrictions to a minimum. Freedom and convenience are major differentiators for the firm. Spaarbeleg takes a multi-channel approach to interacting with its customers, using a combination of mass media, direct mail, franchises, independent brokers, the Internet, interactive voice response (IVR) units, and call centres.

Spaarbeleg decided to use real-time analytics to generate recommendations for its call center agents. Originally, the company considered generating recommendations in batch for its entire customer base, but this would have provided call center agents with recommendations that were outdated and did not take advantage of new information gathered during the call. In addition, the batch scoring would not have been a scalable solution, as the number of scoring models and channels was expected to grow significantly.

Spaarbeleg selected SPSS PredictiveCallCenter, and integrated it with its existing home-grown call center system. The application provides Spaarbeleg's call center agents with a highly accurate, personalized product offering recommendations for use during service calls. Using business logic, the application generates real-time predictions regarding each individual customer's needs, recommending the product most likely to be of interest to the customer. In 18 per cent of inbound calls, the software detected a potential cross-selling opportunity, and an offer recommendation was communicated through a pop-up window on the agent's desktop. For one-third of these recommendation opportunities, the agent made a decision to make the offer to the customer. Offers were not made where call center load was too high, so the agent chose to focus on providing service rather than cross-selling, or where the agent decided that the customer was not open to a cross-sell suggestion at that time. Where an offer was made, 50 per cent of the customers responded positively, and were sent additional information. Of this group of customers, 75 per cent converted. The increased profit allowed Spaarbeleg to transform its service call centre into a profit center.

Two factors were crucial to this success. First, the quality of the recommendations needed to be high for them to be used effectively by the agents. Spaarbeleg believed that if the system made too many incorrect predictions, call center agents would stop making offers to consumers after several unsuccessful attempts. Real-time predictions, which take into account the most recent information on the consumer, were needed in order to achieve sufficiently high-quality predictions.

Second, call center agents played a pivotal role. Spaarbeleg allowed agents autonomy in deciding whether to make the recommended offer to the customer. The software not only provided the recommendation offer directly to the agents' desktops, but also displayed information, such as the quality of the prospect (hot, medium, or cold), a reason to make the offer, and sales arguments for this particular customer, to assist agents in closing the sale. Spaarbeleg also implemented an incentive plan to encourage its agents to make the offers and generate new sales.

Other ways to contact customers

The range of media that can be used to contact customers is constantly evolving. Many campaigns combine different media to deliver the elements of the message most suited for each medium, and for which each medium is the most cost effective. The media used in direct marketing are:

- broadcast media - television (including teletext), in all its distribution modes - terrestrial, satellite and cable, interactive television, radio, fax, cinema;
- publications - newspapers, magazines, journals, owned media such as newsletters, customer newsletters the organization issues itself, or those that are issued by other companies but open to its use, such as newsletters for credit card holders or airline customers;
- distributed media - door-to-door leaflets, catalogues, free newspapers, within-customer communications, invoices, bills to the organization's customer database and to third-parties' customers;
- display media - exhibitions, posters, outdoor billboard advertising, point of sale advertising;
- personal media - sales offices and sales forces;
- new media - Internet, kiosks, e-mail marketing, SMS and MMS text messaging, interactive television.

We do not have the space to consider all media in detail, so here we just consider some of the most important points related to consumer insight.[2] Whatever media are chosen, targeting is key. The closer the fit of the target market to the organization's consumers, the higher the likely response to campaigns. By profiling existing consumers to understand their characteristics, and by finding the best consumers, it is possible to find more prospects of the same type, with the same attributes. Once you have this information you can make an informed choice about two things.

The first is who the prospects are. This refers to whether they are male, female, old or young, their social or geodemographic class, their life stage, leisure activities, interests, hobbies, values, priorities and so on. Much of this information can be collected from simply asking customers, but if it is not possible to contact them directly or a questionnaire is not appropriate, suppliers of customer data and modelling tools can help.

The second is where the prospects are. Once the organization has built up a pen portrait of its consumers - and this is very useful to do - the same techniques can be used to map out other areas - postcodes or even regions - with the same characteristics. Analysing the consumers might also reveal certain common aspects, such as that 70 per cent are readers of a mid-market daily newspaper, 60 per cent listen to early morning radio while in the car, or 80 per cent have children aged under 10. These attributes will determine the targeting strategy. They tell organizations how to reach their target customers, through which media, at what time of day. It may even help them to determine the message, as they will better understand the consumers and what makes them tick.

Some media can be personally addressed or distributed so that they are restricted to particular types of consumers. A catalogue can be sent to named consumers, or distributed house to house to areas of known average characteristics, as well as being given to anyone who wishes to take one. A magazine might have a subscription list of people with known characteristics (because of the details included on the subscription application), but it might also be available through retailers. Broadcast media are also more targeted than ever. It is possible to reach private subscription groups (closed user groups), and different types of people by advertising at different times of the day and alongside different programming. Exhibition attendees can be invited individually, and their attendance logged on a database, so it can be seen how effective the exhibition has been in generating sales. Organizations should not lose any opportunity to target individuals and record results on their database, and use this information to determine the next target strategy.

Most media suppliers - often working in conjunction with independent agencies - have developed audience or readership membership systems, enabling marketers to get a precise measurement of the audience reached. The need for this has been reinforced by the rising cost of media advertising, and the need for more controlled, measurable and accountable budget spend. Many companies regularly compare the pulling power of all media. This does not mean different media are always in competition. The best campaigns usually combine different media. Each medium is asked to do a specific job. In some cases, the campaign is sequenced by medium - with the first contact being by, say, published media, which is followed up by direct mail or telemarketing. In other cases, different media are used to generate the first response. This is because different kinds of consumer respond better to different kinds of media. Some are more mail-responsive, others telephone-responsive, and others television-responsive. One an organization has identified the halo it is working towards, then the media chosen must reflect it. There would be dissonance if a company proclaimed its environmental credentials then used door drops consuming huge amounts of paper. Irrespective of addressability and audience measurement, many companies add a response element to broadcast advertising. Executed properly, a direct response element can dramatically increase the effectiveness of this advertising, and also help companies at the early stage of database building.

Mobile marketing

Some newer media open up new opportunities for personal dialogue. For example, short messaging service (SMS) is the text service sent from mobile to mobile. SMS messages can also be sent from PC to mobile, and from digital television set-top box to mobile. This is often called 'message to mobile'. As this channel is fairly new, it has increased impact on consumers, who may be receiving marketing through SMS for the first time. With SMS comes the promise of personal and local marketing that is both interactive and immediate. However, care should be taken to ensure the message is targeted to the right person, at the right time with the right offer, or else the message can be lost and damage be done. Results have shown that the more interaction there is with the receiver, and the more value the organization adds, the better the response.

SMS marketing uses include revenue-generating services such as casting votes, especially during television shows, and information updates – sports, horoscopes, weather and traffic reports, flight delays and local cinema guides. With handsets with additional functionality, such as camera phones, mobile phone companies are launching new multimedia services enabling users to download games, images and ring-tones. Although these present new opportunities to marketers, success depends largely on the uptake of more advanced mobile phones. It also depends on whether users continue to upgrade their phone as technology moves on.

By its very nature SMS mobile marketing is:

- Immediate. It gains a rapid response, which allows brand managers and direct marketers to know very quickly how successful their campaign has been. It also lends urgency to the message.
- Personal. This message gets right through to the target customer's handset. This means it is important to get buy-in from the consumer. However, once consumers have agreed to receive text promotions, they are likely to react quickly. The medium also lends itself to viral

campaigns. Messages are often received when the consumer is in a group and may talk about the message instantly. Messages are easy to forward.
- Cost effective to deliver – the technology used to deliver these messages is straightforward and the situations surrounding a campaign are generally controllable. It is rarely necessary to reschedule a text campaign in the same way a television campaign might need to be rescheduled (perhaps because of a change in programming). Only simple graphics are needed.

With well-designed campaigns SMS marketing can be highly engaging and effective, but for this it must be:

- fun and familiar (billions of text messages are sent daily);
- interactive (the opportunity for two-way dialogue is there);
- viral (people forward messages);
- environmentally friendly: no trees are felled to produce a SMS!

The main measures in SMS marketing are:

- messages sent;
- messages delivered;
- response rates (who responded to the prompt?);
- conversion rates (who went on to purchase?);
- recall (do people remember receipt?);
- appeal (propensity to recommend or forward the service to others);
- brand impact (impact on opinion of the brand).

How new media have changed marketing

When companies began to include interactive media in their marketing mix, they started by creating product Web sites, which they tended to use in the same way as offline press advertising, for publishing information. However, this relied upon users knowing the address, or URL, of the Web site in order to find the information they were looking for. So marketers started putting advertising for their site at the top of other popular Web sites. These included search engines like Yahoo.com, where users could click straight through to the site in question. This banner advertising is one of the most widely used types of Internet advertising. A big advantage of banner advertising (and other online ad formats) is that the marketer can track exactly how many users have clicked through from the banner ad to the Web site. 'Click-through rates' can be tracked for placing the same advertising on different sites, so you can monitor banner performance when targeting different audiences with tailored messages, according to the site where you placed the advertisement. The following case study would now be regarded as typical of Web-based retailers.

US WEB RETAILER

This was one of the first companies to use the Internet. Now it is transforming itself from being based on operational excellence to being based on intimate knowledge of its customers, using SAS Customer Relationship Management Solutions. Its early success was based on convenience, reliability and 24-hour-a-day accessibility. Now every Web retailer offers this. So now consumer data supports the entire decision-support process for managing relationships. Collecting data at all customer contact points, the company turns that data into knowledge for understanding and anticipating consumer behaviour, meeting consumer needs, building more profitable customer relationships and gaining a clear view of a customer's lifetime value.

While cross-selling and campaign management are important features of its marketing, the ultimate goal is to make sure that when a consumer wants to buy, he or she continues to buy from this retailer and cannot be captured by a competitor's marketing. There is a strong belief that loyalty is earned through the quality of relationship offered, with an understanding that not every customer wants the same relationship. Experience in this case shows that some want the supplier to be more involved with them than others; customers grant different levels of permission on how to contact them. Campaigns are planned based on frequency and type of buying pattern, with some consumers happy to be called or e-mailed once a month with reminders and offers.

Broadcast media

Broadcast media such as radio and television are traditionally used to raise awareness of new products and services with consumers. However, this is changing. The growth of cable and satellite television means that subscribers have a wide choice of channels. They can choose channels for specific interests, such as sport, cookery, science and history. For the marketer, tailoring audiences is easier. Niche audiences can be targeted by advertising on specialist channels. Furthermore, if Web site addresses are included in the advertisement, consumers can be directed to additional information on the products or brands featured. They can register for newsletters or for coupons, or can purchase the product straight after they see the advertisement. Interactive television enables digital television viewers to become involved in their viewing. It's more than just television. Involvement takes many forms, but the main features include:

- accessing the Internet;
- use of real-time shopping services;
- interactive guides to television programmes;
- online betting;
- game playing;
- choice of camera angles to view programmes (especially sports);
- additional information on products/services;
- online voting for views on different issues.

Interactive television gives consumers additional choice. It gives them options to personalize what they watch and the opportunity to give feedback, and so puts them in control. It also enables them to react immediately to something they have seen. So, if consumers see a product they like, they can undertake further research and buy the product without leaving their chair. Unlike using a PC to access the Internet, consumers are used to watching television and using remote controls, so the inconvenience is minimized and fear of technology is reduced. Major brands have already been experimenting with interactive television, particularly in the consumer products and services sector, where impulse purchases or additional information are key to the success of the product. Shopping channels on digital television use interactive television as an extension to their product sales process. The viewer presses the interactive button for more information on the product being sold.

The following key performance indicators and measurement tools are used to assess the success of an interactive television campaign:

- Online respondents – who are they? Details can be captured from the set-top box and profiled to obtain geodemographic information.
- Names and addresses of those who opt in.
- Data files (XML or Excel) passed to a fulfilment house.

Reporting (which can be daily, hourly, or even every 10 minutes) includes:

- access point – channel or banner;
- time of interaction;
- time spent interacting.

E-mail

E-mail marketing is a cost-effective way of reaching consumers with targeted messages. It can be used to build awareness of new products and services, inform consumers via newsletters, and cross and up-sell by providing special offers and promotions. Indeed, after consumers have bought a product from a Web site, they expect to receive information confirming their purchase and shipping via e-mail, and increasingly use e-mail for customer service queries. Permission-based e-mail can be very effective, and marketers can either build their own lists as consumers opt to receive information, or buy in lists from third parties. E-mail campaigns and response rates can also be measured and tracked effectively. However, unsolicited e-mails do tend to be perceived negatively by consumers, so care should be taken to ensure relevancy to avoid this.

Some Internet service providers now provide bulk e-mail functionality, to prevent companies bombarding consumers with this type of e-mail, or spam, as it is also known. Bulk e-mails are sent to a separate file in the user's in-box from e-mails sent by individuals, and as such are often left unopened, or can be blocked from a user's in-box completely. It is therefore important for consumers to be able to recognize the e-mail sender's identity in the header, and be reassured that the e-mail is from a company with which they have a relationship, so they are happy to open the e-mail and read its contents.

Even with permission-based e-mail, consumers can react negatively if they receive e-mails too frequently. Marketers should therefore gauge consumer feedback on the frequency with which they should send e-mails. As with traditional mail-based direct marketing, e-mail marketing depends on the accuracy of the contact details in the list, and when consumers change job or Internet service provider, their e-mail addresses invariably change as a result. It is therefore important that consumers are actively encouraged (through online forms, for example) to keep companies updated when they change their contact details.

Companies' failure to respond to e-mails can have a very negative effect on customer attitudes to the company and their propensity to buy. To give an example of how things can go wrong, in a typical e-mail campaign, up to 2 per cent of people will hit the reply button and respond directly to the e-mail (rather than doing what they are intended to do and clicking on the links or response mechanisms they are directed to in the e-mail). This means that in a mailing to 100,000 there may be 2,000 ad-hoc replies to handle over a very short period. People expect e-mail to be an immediate channel, so a delayed response, or no response at all, is unacceptable and will do serious damage to the brand. An automated response as a holding device is fine, as long as consumers understand when someone will reply to them with a proper response, and as long as the company delivers on the promise. Ideally, consumers get a personalized response that takes account of any previous dealings with the company (for existing customers) and provides a relevant answer to any queries. All of this is entirely possible, but it takes a sophisticated e-mail data management system with infrastructures optimized to handle high volumes. Many companies are just not geared up for this at the moment.

A key question is whether to put consumers in control of their own preference management: that is, to provide an online facility where they can review and edit their personal details and contact preferences. As maintaining preferences online means that consumers will be able to view some or all of their data, they will be more aware of the quality of data held about them. With the flexibility of the medium, it is worthwhile considering making preference choices more granular, not just asking consumers to opt in or opt out, but consulting them about what kinds of products, services or content they are interested in receiving information on, how often they would like to be contacted and so on.

This approach is not without its pitfalls, however. If individuals transact through different sites or divisions belonging to the same company, they will see if data about them is not coordinated across different access routes and channels, so a single view of consumer preferences across brands and channels becomes even more important. Consumers may keep their preferences under review, switching them on and off for different purposes, so there is increased complexity in terms of managing the opt-in/opt-out data. The reason it is worth taking on these challenges, however, is that online preference management has the potential to improve targeting and minimize blanket opt-outs. As consumers can choose the kinds of products or content areas they are interested in and even how often they want to be contacted, they feel in control and consequently more receptive to receiving further e-mail communications.

Personalization is essential for minimizing opt-outs. Specialist providers can help organizations to get this right from the outset. The organization sets up the business rules and the software personalizes the e-mail message content for each consumer, based on his or her preferences, interests, and segment or profile. Message content – including images, paragraphs, words and links – can be assembled based on stored data, such as age group, past purchase history, and even data returned at run time from external applications such as credit referencing. All this is not difficult to achieve – the technology certainly exists, but it may be hard for marketing departments to coordinate agency, data bureaux and internal systems providers to bring together the various sources of data.

With the uptake of broadband services, richer media will become the norm. This adds further complexity, but is an excellent opportunity to maintain high response levels and opt-in rates, particularly for technology-literate or younger consumers. To deliver and track audio and video elements in e-mails, a powerful infrastructure is needed. It might not be cost-effective for a company to make the investment required itself unless it is core to its business. With access to the right technology, however, high levels of rich media personalization can be achieved even when the system is accessed by large numbers at peak click-through times, and consumers' interaction with rich media components can be tracked, whether they are sent as attachments in the e-mail or as links.

Most customers respond positively to receiving e-mails if they are asked permission, and feel favourable towards the brand. In fact, consumers are usually enthusiastic about the medium as a convenient way to exchange information with companies they deal with. If they are used only with permission, and if the technology and data are managed effectively to create timely, relevant communications, most consumers will welcome e-mail, and response rates will remain high.

CONCLUSION

In this chapter, we have considered briefly the many ways in which contacts with customers can be managed. Running through the chapter is the constant question, 'What do we know about our consumers?' Organizations need to know about their consumers to target them for action, to choose the right channels to contact them by, or to encourage them to make contact, and to manage their relationship with them - the subject of the next chapter.

NOTES

1 See, for example, Stone, M and Young, L (1992) *Competitive Customer Care*, Croner, San Diego.
2 For more on them and on the previous two media, see Stone, M, Bond, A and Blake, E (2003) *The Definitive Guide to Direct and Interactive Marketing*, FT Pitman, London, chapters 12–16.

4 Customer relationship management (CRM)

Merlin Stone, Alison Bond, Bryan Foss, Neil Woodcock and Jennifer Kirkby

A VARIETY OF DEFINITIONS

As with many management fashions, relationship marketing, customer relationship marketing and customer relationship management are terms that many use, but define in different ways. The set of ideas that we use to improve management of consumers has passed through different phases, including:

- customer relationship marketing, which included a very strong focus on the customer;
- customer relationship management (CRM), which was supposed to remedy the alleged neglect of other functions' contribution to the management of customer relationships;
- enterprise relationship management, which adds the supply chain dimension;
- E-CRM, electronic customer relationship management, which adds the focus of e-business.

However, despite these changes, the main focus of the activities described by these changing definitions has remained the same, namely:

> The use of a wide range of marketing, sales, communication, service and customer care approaches to:
>
> - identify a company's named individual consumers,
> - create a relationship between the company and its consumers that stretches over many transactions;
> - manage that relationship to the benefit of the consumers and the company.

However, this is a little lacking in feeling. In marketing, a good way to define a concept or technique is in terms of what the organization wants its consumers to think or feel as a result of its using it, something it could even explain to consumers. So a company could describe CRM to its consumers like this:

> CRM is how we:
>
> - find you,
> - get to know you,
> - keep in touch with you,
> - try to ensure that you get what you want from us in every aspect of our dealings with you;
> - check that you are getting what we promised you
>
> – subject of course to it being worthwhile to us as well.

From this definition, it should be obvious that unless it is supported by deep insight into how consumers feel about an organization and how it serves them, CRM may be worthless. It must also be supported by a strong vision of why the organization exists and why the relationship it wants to build with customers is required. In the late 1990s, CRM became a heady fashion among managers of marketing, service and information technology, and even general managers. This was despite strong evidence that many consumers did not want to be managed in relationships, and that in industrial markets, many big buyers used their relationships with suppliers to extract maximum value while returning minimum value. We are therefore cautious about over-using the word relationship – we only use it where we feel that it is justified. Consumers can be managed in many ways. CRM is just one of many ways of doing it. In many situations, we prefer to use the term customer management (CM), because it does not imply a particular model of customer management. As we shall see, there are many models of customer management.

MANAGING THE RELATIONSHIP IN STAGES

In markets in which buyers and sellers do experience benefits from developing relationships, these are rarely simple relationships in which a consumer is 100 per cent loyal to one company or to another. Most relationships develop in stages, with consumers sampling different products and often remaining 'switchers' or 'multi-sourcers' – buying from several companies. To help companies manage this situation, we use a simple model of relationship development. We summarize the relationship as a series of stages, and then identify how many consumers are at each stage and what takes them to the next stage. Table 4.1(on pages 92–95) shows the main stages along with some problems companies have in managing them. The implications of this approach are that:

- consumers do not simply move from being 'prospects', to 100 per cent 'loyal consumers' and then to 'lost consumers';
- stages of the relationship can be identified and managed;
- insight can be used to manage this activity.

WHY CRM IS IMPORTANT OR AT LEAST USEFUL

The benefits of CRM are usually in one or more of two areas. The first is improved consumer retention and loyalty – consumers stay longer and buy more, more often, producing increased long-term value, because they want to do so, since the organization is giving them what they need. The second is higher consumer profitability, not just because each consumer buys more, but because of lower costs of recruiting consumers, and no need to recruit so many to maintain a steady volume of business, and reduced cost of sales, as existing customers are usually more responsive.

However, acquiring the wrong consumers and keeping them is often very damaging. Focusing on consumer retention as a top business priority can be damaging if most consumers are not profitable. In many industries, such as banking, general insurance and utilities, a high proportion of consumers are unprofitable, because the cost to serve them is much higher than the value derived from them. In such situations, management techniques can be used to reduce costs to serve, perhaps by developing a 'low-cost' proposition. It is possibly a better option to get rid of unprofitable consumers, and concentrate on profitable consumers.

CRM can act as a mask for problems. Many businesses feel that as long as they retain enough customers, they must be doing something right. However, a retention statistic might conceal consumers who are gradually finding the company's proposition less appropriate, because it is moving away from their 'halo'. It takes a brave and persistent employee to raise issues when a business appears successful. Not all companies encourage staff to speak up. This can lead to the situation where a competitor identifies the weakness, produces a proposition that is in the halo of most of the first company's customers, and wins most of them away.

Consumers usually want these things from an organization:

- When they enquire about the product, it should give advice to them promptly and courteously, and do the things it says it will do, when it says it will do them.
- It should be timely and relevant in its contacts with them.
- It should make it easy for them to contact it, and give them a person to talk to who is able to do something about whatever they have contacted it about.
- It should make it easy for them to buy the product they want at a competitive price. They want it to be complete and working, and if the product is being delivered, for it to be delivered to specification, on time and in full.
- It should make sure that the product or service it provides is what it promised and meets their 'halo'.
- It should use the data they give it properly and ethically and in ways that benefit them, and make sure they can access that data when they are in contact with the organization.
- After the sale, it should not pester them, but keep in touch if there is something to say.
- If they have a problem or ask for support, it should give it promptly and courteously. It should trust them and live up to its promises.

If the organization's proposition matches consumers' needs and its staff are friendly and professional in the way they deal with consumers at all stages, the benefits can be massive. If customer management is aligned with consumer needs, the organization will:

- hold on to consumers longer;
- maintain or even improve profits from existing consumers;
- improve its share of its consumers' purchases;
- get more referred business: this is the most effective way to acquire new consumers too!

Table 4.1 *Stages of relationship*

Stage	Definition	Typical problems and opportunities
Targeting	When the consumer is targeted as being an appropriate consumer for the company, and induced to 'join'	Targeting is not precise enough. So if the company tries to cross-sell to all its existing consumers, irrespective of their suitability, cross-selling can be a loss-making activity. Very large numbers of consumers are targeted, using a variety of approaches – direct mail, off the page, television. This leads to overlapping coverage and wasted promotional budgets. At worst, if the activities of different product managers are not coordinated, the same person might be targeted for several different products at the same time, with the same names being rented more than once. This not only costs money but demonstrates to the customer that the relationship is a sales one and not one of understanding.
Enquiry management	The consumer is in the process of joining	Usually a very short stage, but of critical importance. In many cases, failure to manage enquiries properly leads to many consumers being lost before they join. In fact this stage is the main prospect gathering stage. By capturing prospects in a database and maybe issuing information organizations can convert this interest to sales by targeting these hot leads. Care should be taken to set consumers' expectations for future treatment. They can often be disappointed and the relationship damaged before it starts.
Welcoming	After the consumer has joined, depending on the	This is also often a very short stage, yet it is clear from what happens when consumers have problems or make claims that they often do not know who to call or what to do.

	complexity of the product or service, it is important to ensure that the consumer is 'securely on board': for instance he or she knows who to contact if there are problems, knows how to use the product or service	For decisions involving significant outlays, consumers may need to be reassured that they have made the correct decision, and given the opportunity to say whether they feel they could have been handled better during the buying cycle. In some cases and with some products and services this stage is overstated and over-engineered. Often all that is required is speed and accuracy. Doing too much at this stage can divert attention from the primary thing the customer has bought from the organization.
Getting to know	This is a crucial period, when both sides exchange information with each other. Additional consumer needs may become apparent, and the consumer's profile of use of the product or service becomes known. More is also learnt about the	Many companies assume that this stage does not exist, and that their consumers go straight into a mature state of account management. Yet if we take the example of financial services, the early cancellation that applies to many types of insurance policy and loans might indicate that this is not so. It could also indicate poor targeting of the product in the first place or inaccurate processing in the welcoming stage. Companies cannot expect that no consumers will cancel early, but they can expect to be able, through data analysis, to identify consumers most likely to do so, and implement preventive action. Experience in insurance and banking shows that if efforts are made, there will be some success. Much of this early cancellation can be explained by how companies develop and target their products. The financial services industry in particular is now

(continued)

Table 4.1 *Continued*

Stage	Definition	Typical problems and opportunities
	consumer's honesty, ability to pay, etc.	feeling a strong regulatory hand to prevent this recurring to the same extent. Analysis from other industries with long-term relationships with consumers indicates that communications behaviour, brand attitudes and satisfaction with the category are good predictors of loyalty. Strong preferences can be formed quite early on in the relationship: for instance, if consumers respond to communications, rate the brand highly and are satisfied with how the organization has arranged their portfolio of products or services, they will be more likely to stay with it.
Customer development	The relationship is now being managed securely, with additional needs being identified in time and met where feasible	This is the ideal state, though quite a few consumers never reach it, and often dip into the next stage or remain in the previous stage for a long time. This can be detected by short questionnaires – which can be administered by mail, telephone or by sales staff. However, if the product or service is essentially an ambient one, such as a pension, it might be worth considering a relationship that purely talks about the end result of the pension, rather than extending any expectations beyond.
Managing problems	The consumer has such severe problems that special attention is needed to ensure	This stage is defined in terms of what the supplier should do, but of course the need for it is often missed and the consumer goes straight into pre-divorce, for example after a mishandled service event or a change in need that remains undetected. If a company

	that he or she returns safely to account management. If this attention is not given, the consumer is so dissatisfied that divorce is imminent. If the consumer does leave, he or she will usually, after a cooling-off period, be ready for 'winback'.	does not handle the initial problem well, and the consumer considers leaving, companies often fail to recognize that this is happening. Surprisingly, many companies give up here, and even pride themselves that they make it easy for consumers to cancel. If the reason for cancellation or termination of the relationship was a change in circumstances or a move by the consumer out of the category, then brand loyalty may be intact, and in some cases enhanced if the supplier makes termination easy. Insights from consumers at this stage may relate to how the product was sold and to whom. If the targeting was right, early termination should be less of a problem. If the product or service was mis-sold, this is far more likely to be a reason to use this stage as an information gathering area for future development and insight.
Winback	Sometimes the relationship ends because of high price or the wrong product, so winback can be initiated when these issues are resolved. Winback is hardest if the consumer left due to poor service, unless the competitors' service is even worse!	The targeting of winback campaigns is made difficult because many companies are poor at defining and identifying lost consumers, and because they have no reliable consumer database. Also if they are failing to gain insight at each stage detailed above, there is no reason for them to should win customers back. If they learn something every time a customer leaves, then the organization will be richer in insight, and ultimately less likely to lose the customers it has, as well as more likely to gain new ones.

A MODEL OF CRM

QCi, a specialist CRM consulting company, has developed a straightforward way of representing what doing CRM involves. Rather than describe CRM as a high-level concept, it describes it simply as a list of management activities, which when put together result in consumers being managed better. We describe it below.

Analysis and planning

Customer management starts with understanding the value, behaviour and attitudes of different consumers and consumer groups. Once these are understood, the company can plan cost-effective acquisition, retention and development of consumers.

The proposition

The understanding of consumers derived from analysis and research will help the company to identify groups or segments of consumers who should be managed. The next step is to define the proposition to each of the segments and plan the appropriate value-based offers. This is done through focused 'needs' research, mapped against the values and behaviours discovered during analysis. The proposition is normally defined in terms of Brand, Price, Service, Transactional interactions, Relationship, Logistics and Product. For each element of the proposition a service standard is defined in terms that can be measured. It must involve all functions within the operation that affect the proposition and customer experience – it cannot successfully be developed by marketing and imposed on the organization. The proposition must then be communicated effectively to both consumers and the people responsible for delivering it.

Customer management activity

This is the delivery of customer management. Plans and objectives, based on the retention, acquisition, penetration and efficiency findings of the analysis, and the needs of consumers, lead to activity throughout the consumer lifecycle from prospect, through new consumers and on into mature consumers. This involves day-to-day working practices of marketing, sales and service support functions in:

- targeting, acquisition and retention activity;
- handling enquiries;

- support for new and upgrading consumers;
- getting to know consumers and how they want to be managed;
- account management (service, billing, technical support, field, third-party telephone);
- identifying and managing dissatisfaction;
- winning back lost consumers.

People and organization

People deliver activity. Companies should identify and develop required competencies. Leaders must create and support customer management objectives, in an organizational structure that facilitates good customer management. Clear, understandable customer management objectives should be linked to business goals and employee satisfaction. Suppliers should support the organization with skills not available internally.

Measuring the effect

Companies should measure how people, processes, profitability, proposition delivery, channel performance and consumer activity (such as campaigns) support achievement of the vision and objectives. Identifying performance relative to plan allows a company to refine and redefine plans and activity.

Understanding consumers experience

CRM is about managing consumers. So companies need to ask consumers:

- How well are we doing?
- What can we improve?
- What do competitors do better than us?

They should do this for each experience customers have with them, especially the ones that they consider most important.

Information and technology

Information and technology underpin the whole model. Information needs to be collected, stored and used in a way that supports the strategy, the way people work and the way consumers want to access the organization. Technology needs to be used to enhance the way consumers are managed (from analysis to data at point of contact) and enabled.

HOW CRM IS EVOLVING TODAY

Two new developments are attracting attention at the time of writing. The first is **customer experience management** - managing consumer expectations and their experience of dealing with a company. It focuses as much on the emotional experience as on rational customer satisfaction, and encourages feedback of information to the relationship processes and systems. The second comprises **customer managed relationships, buyer centricity and mutual marketing** - these are new theories based on working more collaboratively with consumers. Communication is equal, two-way and always on. This more advanced form of CRM incorporates the idea of permission marketing, opening up opportunities for consumer self-service, sharing of knowledge with consumers - often in real time, with greater transparency and allowing consumers to form communities and interact with each other - supporting more word-of-mouth communication.

One reason for this evolution has been the failure of CRM to live up to expectations. CRM was a heady fashion in the late 1990s. Companies thought that they could avoid the perils of consumer expectations, competition and commodity pricing by using information technology to help them understand and manage consumers better. However, the technology sometimes failed to deliver promised results. It never could do so without changes to how an organization worked and to its skills. Some CRM activity actually damaged relationships.

The three main reasons that CRM initiatives have failed to deliver their promise are:

- a lack of authoritative leadership;
- a lack of education and understanding about how CRM can deliver value;
- too much focus on technology, too little on understanding consumers.

PERFORMANCE IS DISAPPOINTING

The observations on CRM success and failure cited in this chapter come from the use of QCi's Customer Management Assessment Tool (CMAT), but are borne out by many other studies. A CMAT assessment seeks *'hard evidence'* for the answers to 260 CRM best-practice questions, based on the customer management activities described earlier, and known to be correlated to good business performance. Evidence is important, because time and again there is a difference between what top management honestly believes happens within its organization and the reality. A score of 100 means best practice in a particular activity. In most cases, progress is patchy, uncertain and unconvincing, and therefore unlikely to have a solid and permanent effect on business performance. Companies appear to be experiencing real problems in implementing CRM.[1] Let us see why.

Senior executive ownership and leadership is required

Only one in five companies has executives on the board with responsibility for CRM (in the sense that it constitutes more than 50 per cent of their role). As yet, these executives are not increasing their companies' CRM effectiveness. Why?

- Managers have a short-term focus – financial objectives are often set quarterly or at best annually. CRM approaches often take longer to pay back, unless activities are carefully planned. Managers are often in a CRM role as a 'career development' move, and their performance is only judged over a short period.
- Managers do not see change through. Investment in CRM systems is clearly taking place, but not enough is invested in changing the behaviour and attitudes of employees, so little benefit arises.
- Senior managers ignore the basics of good CRM and business performance. They become obsessed with 'dramatic change' and new concepts. Plans that take a company's current business model, tighten it up in places and adapt it slightly in others, do not seem to appeal as much. Significant benefits can be achieved more quickly and easily, and certainly more cheaply, through incremental change within an overall framework, often fixing areas that senior management do not know are broken!
- Senior managers do not see their companies' CRM strengths and weaknesses. Views on strengths and weaknesses usually differ before and after a CMAT. So project priorities and implementation programmes developed without thorough review of the current position may be founded on myths.
- Senior managers rarely have real authority or appetite to challenge the status quo.

Poor implementation – too much postulating, too little doing

CMAT assessments regularly reveal unrealistic road maps, untested or unpiloted assumptions, irrelevant business cases, poor (often absent) programme management, many failed projects, weak focus on skills and motivation, and too little learning from experience. Also some companies over-complicate CRM. Typically CRM programme design is removed from consumer reality. Processes become over-engineered to cope with the most complex situations, and become difficult to use. Larger companies find it harder to manage consumers than do smaller companies, because of their complexity.

Functional and departmental silos

CRM is often implemented by individual functions and departments. This is dysfunctional from the consumers' perspective – they expect to be managed consistently across departments. Some consultancies offer CRM services despite having no knowledge of CRM. They were attracted to it by the money they could make rather than the skills they could add.

CRM is 'champion' not culturally based

CRM behaviours (such as consumer profitability analysis and managing consumers based on their value) are often not embedded in an organization's culture, through objectives, incentives, structure, skills and knowledge sharing. People change roles. Their thinking is often lost or moves with them.

More skills and education are required

Knowledge of good customer management techniques and practices is not widespread. Education in customer management is lacking, despite the efforts of many institutes, associations and forums. Key concepts (simpler ones such as decile analysis, or more complex ones such as customer value forecasting or measuring the success of retention management against control groups) are still not widely used. Customer service competencies are under-valued. Enquiry follow-up is weak. Good training exists in some companies. Database marketing principles (particularly in relation to analysis, campaign management, lead management, customer retention and measurement) underpin good CRM, but in many companies database marketing has a poor image. This can lead to rejection of its experiences and contributions.

A belief that IT is a panacea

IT is not a panacea. IT enables CRM, but a company must define its CRM strategy first. This then defines IT's enabling role. The rest of the organization must be aligned and usually must change, at least a little but often very much. Data is the building block of many companies' CRM management efforts. Data management remains one of the stumbling blocks to creating value.

WHERE NEXT FOR CRM?

Despite all the above, there are many examples of very effective practices in companies, and after all, if CRM were easy, it would not give the competitive differentiation benefits claimed for it. Analysis of CMAT scores shows which characteristics and activities are most closely associated with higher scores, and thence overall business performance. These are shown in Table 4.2.

CUSTOMER EXPERIENCE MANAGEMENT

Customer experience management (CEM) is part of the discipline of CRM. It is a combination of product, service and the 'feelgood factor' generated by a range of stimuli (visual, tone of voice, smell, atmosphere, care and attention to detail) at consumer touch points (which include salespeople, call center agents, advertising, events, debt collectors, receptions, product brochures and Web sites). It is based on consumers' expectations, determined by:

- brand promotion;
- word-of-mouth communication and reputation;
- previous experience of the company;
- previous experience of other companies (not necessarily competitors).

The customer experience is a step beyond customized service in the 'progression of economic value' (see Table 4.3), and like product and service, needs to be designed and managed. The buying of art for reception and staff areas, the staging of themes at exhibitions, the attention to the details of navigation on a Web site, a supportive attitude in response to complaints and ensuring easy visitor car parking are all part of the same phenomenon, creating a positive customer experience around the value proposition.

Designing the customer experience

In designing and managing the customer experience, it is important to aim to just exceed expectations in the areas that really matter to a consumer,

Table 4.2 *Characteristics of high performers in CRM*

Analysis and planning

Determine the competitive arena and the competitive challenge facing the company.

Determine which companies are trying to win the best present and future consumers, or increase their share of business from these consumers.

Ensure that the organization's strategic objectives are communicated to all staff in a way that links them to retention, efficiency, acquisition and penetration in CRM.

Be clear about profit and where it comes from: in particular, from which consumers.

Determine how much the organization can afford to spend on acquisition, development and retention of different consumer groups, and align resources to value (and maybe needs) segments.

Be greedy for knowledge from consumers, staff and partners.

Proposition

Develop clear and differentiated propositions aimed at those consumers the organization wants to manage.

Determine how loyalty can be built among key value groups.

Cascade the proposition from high-level brand values to influence the organization's behaviours.

Communicate the consumer propositions well to employees, partners and consumers, and measure the resulting behaviour and attitude change.

Customer management activity

Overall	Develop practical, efficient acquisition, development, retention and efficiency plans. Only sell what can be delivered. Ensure the organization is on track to deliver and does not oversell.
Acquisition Targeting Enquiry Management Winback	Develop and measure effective enquiry management processes that identify future consumers and business that will be good for the company (convertible, profitable, retainable, etc). Develop winback programmes for selected former consumers.
Early retention	Provide thanks – as a courtesy and reinforcement of purchasing decision.
Welcoming Getting to know	Get it right first time. If anyone makes a mistake, correct it and apologize quickly. Ensure early relationship service management works.

Table 4.2 *Continued*

	Monitor early transactions for indications of usage, higher future potential or risk of early attrition. Understand consumers – how they want to be managed and what their potential is.
Repeat purchase Ongoing management Managing dissatisfaction	Let consumers service (manage) themselves and their data. Try to predict defections through consumer feedback and contact analysis. Proactively contact high-value groups regularly. Manage key accounts in ways that are mutually beneficial. Identify dissatisfaction and manage it timely and well. Encourage a no-blame and learning culture. Do not underestimate the value of good customer service. In these days of choice and when consumers have the confidence to change, service experience is key.

People and organization

Provide customer management leadership with cross-functional/departmental authority.

Ensure the organization is flexible enough to support consumer-oriented decision making.

Align objectives throughout the organization to focus on profitable customer management.

Recruit and develop people with the right skills and orientation.

Ensure that incentives and rewards encourage desired CRM behaviours.

Understand employee satisfaction and commitment and its relationship with customer management.

Actively manage those partnerships and alliances that affect consumers.

Measurement

Measure consumer behaviours, attitudes and activities and their impact on return on investment.

Measure farther out than just where is it easy to measure. This means that if the product is offering a better life, measure if that is what it is delivering, not whether staff are picking the phone up quickly, as this does not give someone a better life, just less time waiting to be answered.

Measure how different media (touch points and types) affect CRM results.

Measure and learn from campaigns.

Measure the effectiveness and efficiency of individuals.

(Continued)

Table 4.2 *Continued*

Customer experience
Understand how consumer commitment (buying, responding) and customer satisfaction are related.
Understand performance in individual and combined (relationship) moments of truth at all consumer contact points, absolutely and relative to the competition.
Benchmark against others, in the company's competitive arena and outside it.
Information and technology
Understand priorities and how success in CRM depends on success in IT and vice versa.
Understand consumer data application, acquisition and maintenance.
Increase visibility of appropriate consumer data to employees and partners.
Increase visibility of consumer data to consumers.
Understand and implement support for the business integration requirements driven by CM.
Process
Define and integrate processes based around the proposition.
Replicate or grow successful processes for improved RoI.

and just meet expectations for the rest. Research techniques can establish what parts of the consumer value proposition and experience, at which points of the life cycle, via which channels, consumers value most, which are merely necessities that all suppliers are expected to provide, and which are potential torch points (as opposed to touch points). Exceeding expectations can be time-consuming and costly, so must be done where it will have the most effect and where it takes the organization further into the consumer's halo, not away from it or into a whole new one, unless that is a specific choice.

The major steps in designing the experience are:

- Confirm by research that the company's brand values and image are valued by consumers and are seen as different from those of competitors. Also confirm what staff and managers think, what they believe the organization to be and how this matches up to what the customers are saying.
- Carry out strategic relationship management research to establish relationship determinants: how consumers currently feel about the experience, what they expect and value.

Table 4.3 *An example of the evolution of customer experience*

Product	Model
Birthday cake cooked by parent from basic ingredients	Ingredients sold as a product
Premixed birthday cake	A service added to the basic product
Ready made and iced cake	Greater value service added to the basic product
Parents buy a complete party experience including cake	An experience is built around service and product

- Using a combination of touch point analysis, consumer life cycle interaction processes mapping and known relationship determinants, map out the moments of truth (MOTs) in consumer interactions (that is, where the experience makes the most positive and negative impact on consumers).
- Establish the gap between desired and actual customer experience at the MOTs.
- Establish the employee experience at each MOT, and compare it with the customer experience.
- Design and pilot new consumer and employee experiences.
- Recruit, train, coach and provide incentives to staff to support the customer experience.
- In CRM strategy, build the required experience for each segment into the consumer value proposition.
- Develop a measurement tool which makes it possible to measure far enough out to see if the organization is moving towards or away from the consumer halo. If it wants families to love birthdays and have more parties to celebrate, measure there, not just how they liked the cake.

The benefits of managing the customer experience

The three benefits of CEM on word-of-mouth communications are:

- improvements in customer loyalty;
- differentiation from competitors;
- improvements in retained business and consumers and the 'stories' being told in the market.

Table 4.4 *From presence to halo*

Presence	I tried it before and I am familiar with it
Relevance	It's for people like me
Performance	It does a good job
Advantage	It does a better job
Bonding	It's my brand, I'm committed to it
Halo	It really does everything I want in this category, long and short term

Customer loyalty

The customer experience is important in building up longer-term emotional 'loyalty' or commitment to an organization (see Table 4.4 for our view of the hierarchy). Experience is the ultimate conveyor of value to consumers, and is a primary influence of their future behaviour. A poor customer experience is a step on the path to defection and poor word of mouth, while a good one is likely to lead to retained business, recommendations and greater loyalty. Consumers have the biggest propensity to recommend just after a major interaction. The more loyal consumers are, the easier it is at these times to encourage them to make recommendations. Companies that build emotional loyalty, therefore create a big advantage over those who still only look at rational customer satisfaction.

Competitive differentiation

Brands are becoming less distinct in consumers' minds. How can favourable word of mouth be generated? Brands should be distinguishable from the competition. They need a 'personality' that can be promoted and brought to life at touch points, then they are easier to talk about. Brand promotion gives the promise; CEM is the physical delivery of that promise. This can be achieved by:

- basing brand values on what consumers want;
- involving employees in developing the values;
- linking the values to the main brand promise;
- encouraging staff to align their behaviour with the values;
- rewarding employees for delivering the brand values.

Consumer stories

The management of CEM comes in two parts, strategic design and continuous improvement. Continuous improvement is enabled via consumer feedback - or experience stories. Feedback allows the company to resolve complaints and to improve the day-to-day customer experience. It can have an immediate effect on business by reducing the level of defection and business at risk, while increasing the likelihood of favourable word of mouth. Feedback can cut consumer defection alone by 2 to 3 per cent per year. There are several ways to collect feedback - surveys, projective research techniques, complaints management, feedback calls, consumer surgeries, analysing telephone and Web interactions, user groups. However, the data so collected must be converted into knowledge and then into improvements. There are two main uses: to make immediate improvements to the experience, through procedures, process and behaviour, and as input to the consumer strategy to ensure that consumer investment and objectives are on track.

MAKING THE STRATEGIC SHIFT TO CRM/CEM

CRM is a necessity of modern business. CEM is a necessity for CRM and to gain the benefits of word of mouth. To make CEM powerful a halo needs to be in place, and that halo must work at all levels: staff, managers, stakeholders and consumers. To improve in these areas, companies need more unifying, cross-functional capabilities. In particular they need:

- a marketing/CRM strategy - how consumer value is to be created;
- human architecture - the way people collaborate, use knowledge, plan and provide consumer solutions;
- IT architecture - based on process and data integration, with open standards for external interoperability.

Each area should include the following actions.

Marketing/CRM strategy

- Audit the consumer base to find the asset value - the segments, the potential value, and the fragility or strength of relationships.
- Design the customer experience.
- Outline a consumer strategy that ties corporate financial goals to consumer objectives: acquisition, retention, development and cost to serve.
- Establish the tactics and capabilities needed to achieve the objectives.
- Pilot business initiatives, especially those that encourage consumers to

talk to each other, such as consumer value group communities and consumer forums.

- Evolve the strategy through feedback and metrics.
- Improve consumer interaction processes, using consumer feedback. Process redesign is often a catalyst for organizational changes to the human architecture.
- Build an information and data strategy to support the business initiatives – what information, built from what data, from where, how sourced, how often.
- Develop interlinking metrics to include the value obtained from customer management and to the consumer. For CEM important metrics are brand experience dimensions (BEDs) – the elements of the company's image and service that consumers really care about. BEDs can be monitored daily.

Human architecture

- Benchmark current culture with staff via 'story' techniques about consumers, their work and CRM. Establish the problem areas and use the information for internal brand alignment through change programmes.
- Spread consumer insight among staff and ensure they can use it in their work. Link knowledge management processes to consumer interaction processes for greater collaboration and learning. The big mistake of previous process re-engineering phases was in not doing this. Good customer experience depends on the learning and support that staff give each other as a natural part of everyday life.
- Establish the new skills required and 'cast' staff in the new roles. Develop skills through continuous coaching in delivering the brand values.
- Redesign organizational structures to support new ways of working. Put flexible delivery teams together, pulled from 'communities of practice' (similar skill pools) as and when required. CRM and CEM challenge old structures because of the need for a segmented approach to consumers, non-siloed thinking and working, and new and scarce skills.
- Link key performance indicators through performance management to staff incentives – banish incentives that misdirect activity. The right incentives are vital. Do not just focus on 'what' is being delivered in terms of financial targets. Focus also the 'how' of good performance delivery.

IT architecture

Technology is a curse and an enabler for CRM/CEM. Ill-conceived Web sites that damage brand values and the appalling experience of many call centres have created a need for more technology to monitor and improve the customer experience. Much of the software that enables better CRM delivery is not pure CRM software. Software applications needed for CRM/CEM include:

- knowledge management;
- content and collaboration, such as instant messaging; community support on Web sites;
- business information and analysis;
- experience feedback;
- enterprise process management;
- portals and self-service;
- applications that turn call centres into interactive contact centres.

The ways of providing the technology are also growing, with hosted, outsourced and Web-service solutions increasingly available from service suppliers. Organizations should make the most of these.

Broader systems and management issues

Many companies assumed that having a single system to manage consumers was all that was needed. In fact, managing consumers is a new discipline, often conflicting with existing disciplines. It requires different data, decision processes, skills and incentives. Also, the discipline is changing rapidly with the introduction of e-business techniques, and it will continue to change. So many companies have recognized that transforming customer management is a long and never-ending journey. Multi-year planning horizons are common, with different systems gradually introduced to support the steadily improving customer management process, and clever systems integration work ensuring that the different systems talk to each other in real time.

Where customer management via the Web is concerned, skills are even scarcer, as this involves blending CRM and Web skills. Companies are mostly weak in analysis and planning of customer management. Companies use their consumer data poorly to determine which consumers to obtain more value out of, keep or discourage. When the e-approach is introduced, life is even more difficult, so a stronger foundation is needed. This is because as the e-approach generally passes more control to outside the organization, consumer (and supplier) behaviour may start to change in unanticipated ways - and faster. This implies the need for smarter systems and processes to manage consumers - or allow them to manage themselves. Without these, consumers, suppliers and companies will probably not get the benefits of e-commerce. This applies particularly when it is running alongside established ways of doing business (channels of distribution).

The informed consumer

In many areas of customer management, the exchange of information has traditionally been a key to managing consumers. As we have seen in many examples above, consumers' involvement in becoming informed is made dramatically easier by the Web. This is the more so in areas where consumers have traditionally been deprived of relevant information by experts, such as health services.

The entitled consumer

Governments have similar problems in managing large numbers of taxpayers. Here, the consumer entitlement is the right to transact efficiently with government, not stand in queues, wait for telephone replies, complete forms and deal with the whole panoply of bureaucracy which governments are so expert at generating. This will have particular consequences for less developed countries, where state bureaucracies have always been a prime way of maintaining employment.

CONCLUSIONS

The way in which CRM has developed is the main reason for this book being written! It has focused managers' minds on their consumers, what they do to consumers, and what their consumers want them to do. It has not always worked for organizations or their consumers, for the reasons we outlined in this chapter. One reason for this is their failure to develop and use consumer insight. In the next chapter, we explore how market research can help.

NOTES

1 See Woodcock, N, Stone, M and Starkey, M (2002) *The Customer Management Scorecard*, Kogan Page, London, for detailed evidence on different aspects of customer management and for trends over time.

5 Consumer insight and market research

Merlin Stone, Alison Bond, Clive Nancarrow and Sharon Rees

INTRODUCTION

In most consumer markets, customers are too numerous to research or understand as individuals. They tend to be researched on a sample basis. The aim of this research is normally to identify what types of consumer exist, and group them coherently, according to some common factors. This allows sensible statements to be made about the group. The statements may be demographic - the types of people they are (age, occupation, location, type of housing), or behavioural or psychographic - how they think, feel act, respond and so on.

In this chapter, we describe the research CRM practitioners use to understand consumers. This includes:

- Qualitative research - depths and groups to explore and get beneath the surface and identify what could be important.
- Buying behaviour or audit research - investigating what consumers buy, when and how. This is often provided by a few large companies who pay retailers for their data from their tills, repackage it and sell it to the manufacturers. These services are called retail audit. Consumer panels are one way of doing this.
- Usage and attitude surveys (U&A) - investigating consumers' perceptions and attitudes and relating them to their buying decisions. In the

last decade U&As have given way to satisfaction surveys that measure levels of satisfaction.

- Tracking studies – studying trends in the above over time.
- Mystery shopping – trained observers posing as customers.

This research-based approach to understanding consumers is becoming more rare among users of database marketing or CRM, because of the amount of response, sales and other data that they collect about individual consumers. However, this can lead to a failure to understand consumers' wants, attitudes and perceptions. Eventually, CRM marketing can get out of touch with consumers. So wise users of CRM continue to research their consumers about things that are not revealed by patterns of response and purchase.

As we discussed in previous chapters, the need for the understanding of an organization's halo is vital if the information it has is to be kept in context. The wins an organization can make using CRM can be greatly enhanced if it understands its halo and works towards it. The opposite is also true: if it practises the science of CRM, but does not understand its halo, the long-term prospects for customer loyalty will be poor.

SEGMENTATION

Grouping makes it easier for marketing policy to be formulated and implemented, almost in a modular fashion. This applies whether or not a company uses CRM. However, given the richness of data available to CRM users, it is all the more important to use the best available techniques to make sense of the very high volumes of data that are available. For example, a mobile telephone company with 5 million users, each making 10 calls or sending 10 text messages a day or some combination of the two, will have at least 50 million 'transactions' a day. However, each transaction has a number of characteristics – timing, who sent, who received, from where to where, whether the voice call was broken or stored as a message, and so on. Typically each call contains 20 data items that are useful for marketing, service or billing purposes. So that makes a billion new items a day, and this assumes the consumer is not using the phone to browse the Web or send picture messages. Clearly, the data needs to be reduced so that it can be understood.

In CRM, one of the first steps is to try to group consumers into segments. To segment consumers is merely to group them by shared characteristics. The aim is to find segments whose members are as similar as possible to each other in some respect (such as attitudes, perceptions, buying behaviour, location or responsibility) and as different as possible from members of other segments. This is done because if such segments are identified, it is possible to predict their behaviour more accurately, design offers for them more easily, and target them more precisely. Getting segmentation right often requires significant research and testing. Some segments will change over time, and consumers will move between segments.

Commonly used CRM approaches to consumer segmentation include:

- demographic – age, social class, marital status, number of children;
- socio-economic – occupation, income, assets (eg house) – usually of great interest to marketers because it indicates buying power and aspirations;
- geographical – location (physical and relative to people with specific socio-economic/demographic characteristics);
- general behaviour and attitudes (shopping, leisure, etc) such as who enjoys shopping, who does not (this gets into the mind of consumers);
- behaviour/attitudes in relation to product/category (whether or not user, frequency of use, loyalty, etc);
- psychographic (eg extrovert/introvert, optimist/pessimist, planner/improviser, consumer/saver);
- in some cases benefits sought, based on database questionnaires.

Demographic segmentation

Many more sophisticated approaches to segmentation are now used. Several specialist data suppliers have produced advanced socio-demographic classifications, combining census, electoral roll, credit and other data. The classifications give up to 50 or more types, and data are available at to the lowest postcode level (group of houses – the average number is 15 per postcode). The main segmentation products are classifications of neighbourhoods rather than individuals. This is because the original source of the data is by area, not individuals, through census enumeration districts. However, companies are increasingly able to supply data on individuals, provided that it has been gathered according to the terms of data protection or privacy laws.

Neighbourhood classification data falls into three main categories:

- demographic – such as how many people live in a household, their ages, and family structure;
- socio-economic – such as value of house, income of household, occupations of household members;

- physical – such as type of dwelling (house or flat), size (number of rooms).

This approach allows companies to enhance their customer files (which usually cover names, addresses, telephone numbers, response to promotions, and purchases) with other data relatively cheaply and quickly. However, while segmentation based on neighbourhood classification systems works on mass-market products, using it on niche products and services can be misleading and wasteful.

Psychographic segmentation

Another development is advanced psychographic analysis, using data on consumers' attitudes, interests and opinions. This started with basic psychological categories, but has developed much further. It provides useful categories to use when analysing purchasing behaviour in relation to new products or new channels of distribution. It is also possible to develop categories that are specific to particular products and services. Psychographic segmentation can be produced by combining response and sales data with research data. If it is not possible to identify beforehand consumers who belong to segments defined using this data, then it will not be possible to use it for CRM targeting.

One source for this approach to segmentation is 'lifestyle' questionnaires, which are sent out to millions of consumers, to gather data on media and buying habits. In exchange for this data, consumers are sometimes sent coupons giving reductions on the kind of products they say they like, or are given the chance to take part in a prize draw. The data is then sold to CRM users, which use it as a promotional list or to enhance their files. The sheer volume and depth of data produced in this way can provide source material for segmentation. It also makes it easier for companies getting started in consumer CRM to obtain data on their target markets. However, many consumers are becoming wise to these questionnaires and return them only to obtain the coupons or enter the prize draw, so the information contained in them can be unreliable. Use this kind of data with great care and test the value of the information by running campaigns using this information alongside campaigns using data from other sources.

Combining sources

Many data agencies now supply combinations of the main marketing data sets. They started by combining census, postcode and credit data. Now they combine their original data with lifestyle surveys, media surveys (such as readership surveys) and shopping data from retail audits, to give much greater depth of information on consumers of particular types. This combined data shows companies how to reach consumers of particular kinds through published and broadcast media (for instance for 'hand raising' campaigns to get prospects to identify themselves, or for branding campaigns to provide a positive context for CRM campaigns), and what coupons to distribute in which areas to encourage the purchase of their products through retailers.

Other sources of segmentation data

Some agencies provide forecasts of social, economic and market change. Consumer goods and services companies use forecasts of the impact of changing demographic and social patterns as input for their strategic plans. Important factors include ageing, home-centredness, changing shopping habits, and the growing computer and mobile telecommunications culture. This is useful if organizations want to look beyond the horizon imposed by current buying data, to the state of their consumers and database in a few years.

Response-based segmentation

CRM routinely generates the data needed for market segmentation. Response data include:

- information consumers give during their response: for instance simple facts about who they are and (if their address was not known beforehand) where they live;
- the fact that they have responded to a particular approach;
- where appropriate, the fact that they have bought, and if they have been asked, whether they are satisfied with the company's service or offering.

This data can tell you:

- what products and services consumers have bought and when – and what they have not bought, so by implication what they are most likely to buy in the future, and when they are likely to buy it;
- what kinds of promotion they have responded to, and by implication are likely to respond to in future;
- how they paid (or not) – type and timing, and by implication whether a consumer constitutes a credit risk.

Although it might seem tempting to customize an entire communication to individual consumers – a market segment of one – in practice this is rarely possible (except for *personalization* – addressing the consumer by name). Products and offers must normally be designed to meet the needs of groups of consumers. It is expensive to customize both communications and products and services to individuals. Letters must be mailed and advertisements shown such that they reach cost-effectively the groups of consumers most likely to respond and/or buy. So the aim is to find the best groups – the ones most likely to respond, buy and pay. Years of experience have shown that consumers' needs are not that varied, so organizations can confidently expect to group their consumers according to their needs.

Sometimes the data source used to segment consumers is very rich, and this enables the owners of this data to make some highly tailored offers. This applies to retailers with loyalty cards. The data collected enable retailers to tailor offers to individuals. They send out voucher and offer packs customized to the shopper's known purchasing habits, perhaps several thousand different combinations of offers each time they mail. They also use this understanding when consumers shop online. When customers log on for the first time to use the home delivery service, they are asked for demographic data. This is used to bring up a likely list for the shopper to choose from, cutting the time the shopper has to stay on line selecting items.[1]

HOW TO DEFINE SEGMENTS

Segmentation analysis aims to find the characteristics of consumer groups or segments who will respond differently to marketing programmes, for example finding that people who live in one area have a greater chance of liking a particular product than people who live in another area, or finding that people who buy product X are more likely to respond to a mailing on product Y than people who buy product Z. To target as precisely as possible, organizations may want to find associations between several variables. They might, through analysing their databases, find that people who bought product X last year and product Y this year, who live in upper income areas, are very likely to respond to a promotion on product Z.

Purchasing variables

In CRM, the main segmentation variables are purchasing variables – particularly frequency, recency, amount and category. These were mentioned in the case study in Chapter 1. Now let us examine them in more detail.

Frequency

Frequency is defined as how often the consumer buys, typically the figure over the last period (say a month or year). Just as important is the trend in frequency: is it rising or falling? Suppose there are two consumers with the same very recent purchasing behaviour, but one's purchasing frequency is rising and the other's is falling. The former is likely to be of more interest than the latter, other things being equal. Any analysis of frequency must take into account promotions history. Where consumers receive varying numbers of promotion, a better statistic to use might be average frequency of response per promotion, measured for each time period: last half year, the half year before that and so on.

Recency

This measures when the consumer last bought. Again this depends on promotional factors, or when the last few promotions took place. Other things being equal, more recent purchasers have greater value. Small changes in recency might be a harbinger of doom - or great success. If recency is found to be increasing - consumers are on average waiting longer before rebuying - it is important to find out quickly which consumers are concerned and why. Are promotions failing in their objective because of problems with the offer, or is there a problem with the product or service?

Amount

This measures how much the consumer bought - usually in value terms. It might be defined for individual products, or for the whole product range. The latter definition usually only makes sense if the consumer knows that the products come from the same supplier. The points made about frequency also apply here. For example, a consumer could be buying with the same frequency, but the average value of purchase might be falling. It is important to find out whether this is due to factors that cannot be controlled (perhaps the consumer's income is falling), or whether it is due to marketing or product failures.

It could also be that the halo is no longer working because consumer opinion or needs have shifted away from it. Thus, fast food chains whose emphasis was on convenience and price have had to respond to calls for healthier options. Their initial failure to do so contributed to a fall in profits. On the other side companies like Pret A Manger have thrived as they are seen as offering a range of healthy alternatives to fast food. As food starts to be perceived as more than just something you refuel with, companies need to adjust their halos to offer something that draws consumers to them, in order to stay competitive. Understanding the direction of a halo that will promote profitability and possibly growth requires insight, and deriving that insight from existing data is one of the best ways possible to ensure that marketing is going in the right direction.

Category

Category defines the type of product bought. The point made above about amount bought per consumer applies here. Cross-selling as a concept only makes sense, from a measurement point of view, if the consumer knows that the product is coming from the same source, unless it is just being used as a measure of success in employing targeting data. In financial services, as companies from different sectors move into each other's territory, and the market becomes more competitive, the cost of acquiring new customers rises. So the key to success is how many categories the consumer buys from one supplier.

Speed of order following promotion

This can be an important variable. Fast orderers may be very interested in new offers and keen to try them. So it pays to find out the characteristics of fast orderers, profile them using whatever consumer data is at hand, and apply this profile to other data sets to try to find more fast orderers. If fast orderers can only be identified through psychological variables, then it may be necessary to use lifestyle questionnaires to identify them.

Mode of payment

Unless all payment is by the same method, the mode of payment can be a very important discriminator. Credit card payers might be regarded as safer, because there is no risk of default.

USING MARKET RESEARCH IN CRM

Compared with traditional methods of marketing consumer goods and services, CRM has not used market research enough. The question for database marketers is whether market research can add to their understanding of consumers, given the rich data provided by their customer databases. Research should be used to find the link between information on a database and the knowledge, attitudes, motivations and emotions behind consumer behaviour. Qualitative groups, possibly using a viewing facility, so all personnel using the database can attend, bring to life the reports and statistics produced by the database. They may also produce ideas about campaign design – who to target, with which products and service, and with what offer and creatives.

Groups are also an excellent vehicle if campaigns start to be less successful. They help to show why. Researchers experienced in the use and techniques of CRM will be able to help use the findings constructively around the business.

Where consumer insight can be used

There are a number of areas where market research can add value to CRM:

- Product/concept testing – to get an idea of the viability and acceptability of a new product or concept, before investing money on producing it and test marketing it.
- Product features – to find out which product features are important to consumers, and what advantages and, importantly, benefits they provide.
- Creative guidance – to direct the creative effort. Research enables organizations to understand whether a message is being understood, whether wording is appropriate, whether consumers have hidden objections, or whether opportunities are being missed.
- Missing features – to uncover hidden emotions and feelings behind consumer response.
- Purchasing channel – to understand which channel consumers would rather use to buy goods and the level of service consumers expect when purchasing. For example, will they tolerate a voice-activated system if using the phone? Are they prepared to go so far with an online purchase then expect human contact?

Therefore research, by creating a true understanding of the awareness, attitude and interests of consumers, can help to focus testing programmes and avoid some test failures. It can also be used to evaluate and diagnose campaigns after the event, and so help refine CRM marketing programmes.

UNDERSTANDING CONSUMERS

The results of campaigns provide CRM marketers with lots of information about who responds and to what degree they respond. However, why consumers respond in a certain way can only be inferred. Why consumers do not respond is hard to infer, as they have given no additional data except the fact that they did not respond. Reasons for lack of response may include:

- Poor targeting.
- Poor product.
- Poor offer design – consumers might have wanted the general concept but not the way it was embodied in the offer.
- Competitors providing better offers.
- Poor company image – consumers liked the offer but did not trust the source, because the supplier's image was poor or nonexistent. This is inextricably linked to a company's halo. If the things that the company stands for and represents turn off consumers, it will affect response rates enormously. It could be that the halo has stayed the same for many years but it is not far-reaching enough to be ageless. As we showed in our fast-food example, consumers' perceptions moved on, but the halo of some of the chains did not.

A market research programme can answer these questions.

MAIN RESEARCH TECHNIQUES USED IN GAINING CONSUMER INSIGHT

Group discussions

Group discussions are often used before a campaign or approach to managing consumers is finalized. They should be externally moderated by a research professional. The results of this research are presented, then usually argued over to establish the implications for campaign design and relationship management. Group discussions are used for many more purposes, including:

- basic need studies for new product idea generation;
- new product idea or concept exploration;
- product positioning studies;
- advertising and communication studies;
- background studies on consumers' frames of reference;
- establishing the vocabulary consumers use, as a preliminary stage in questionnaire development;
- determination of attitudes and behaviour.

Depth interviews

Depth interviews are usually used to find out why individuals buy various products and what buying, owning and using means to them.

Interviews last anything from a few minutes to two hours or more. This method can uncover basic predispositions, such as why a consumer does not order through the post. People's attitudes can be probed and their cause, intensity and implications uncovered. If the subject is sensitive, personal or complex, depth interviews can be better than group discussions. This applies particularly in business marketing, where topics being researched may include complex buying procedures. The other reason it works better than groups is that recruiting specific individuals for groups can be very difficult, and the offer of an in-depth interview at an individual's office is generally far easier to organize. Also at a senior level people tend to be more used to 'holding the floor', and this is tough to manage in a group discussion but excellent for a depth interview.

Mail questionnaires

Mail questionnaires are sent to consumers to complete by themselves. It is wise to include a stamped addressed envelope and an incentive such a free draw. This helps response rates but may slightly bias the results. These are used widely in CRM, usually when a large sample is needed to derive valid results. The more companies collect e-mail addresses or use Web marketing, the more online questionnaires are used. Consumers might be sent questionnaires by e-mail to be returned in the same way (or less often by post), or the e-mail might direct the consumer to a Web site where the questionnaire is online. Mail and online questionnaires are also used to gain further information about consumers already on a database. If qualitative information is required, this can be elicited through more detailed questions about why they respond in particular ways to particular questions. Some responses may be triggers for action for a company, when a consumer indicates an immediate need or raises a customer service problem.

Open-ended questions add greatly to analysis cost, so it is best to carry out a few focus groups and/or depth interviews to identify what consumers' needs and concerns are likely to be, and the language they use to express them. Then the questionnaire can be structured to cope with most of the likely variations in consumers' responses.

Mail and online questionnaires have these advantages:

- Both, but online in particular, are more economical and convenient than personal interviews.
- They can be anonymous.
- They avoid interviewer bias and, if anonymity is assured, can reduce socially desirable responding.
- They give people time to consider their answers.

- Online computerized routing of questionnaires allows for complex patterns of behaviour to be captured.
- Online can provide rapid results.

They have these disadvantages

- The questions need to be very straightforward if the response is to be valid.
- Answers must be taken as final.
- It is impossible to be sure that the right person answers the questionnaire.
- They sometimes throw up more questions than were started with when the data is analysed. If this is the case, consider holding some focus groups to ensure the results are fully understood.
- For mail, respondents see the whole questionnaire before answering it.
- For mail, the research process can be slow.
- For online, some consumers pay for online time and so this potentially forgotten cost must be mentioned.
- For online, the concern about the representativeness of those who can access online is a declining concern. Other methods of data collection are also increasingly meeting access problems, for instance screening out calls by use of telephone answer machines, and caller line display.

One frequent problem with mail and online questionnaires is non-response and the consequent likelihood that non-responders will be different from responders. The higher the response rate, the more valid the result. However, one way to check this is by chasing up a sample of non-responders. Another way is to analyse results by how quickly people respond. The laggards may be closer in characteristics to non-responders than those who reply immediately. Of course, researchers should examine ways of maximizing response by careful research design and motivating or incentivizing respondents.

Telephone questionnaires

Telephone questionnaires are used in similar contexts to mail questionnaires, with the addition of those administered when consumers call in, for example to respond to a promotion or to contact a help line. Telephone surveys are normally more accurate than mail surveys. They combine many of the advantages of mail questionnaires and in-depth interviews. Their strengths are:

- They are one to one.

- The consumer cannot see the whole questionnaire.
- Any problems of understanding can be dealt with.
- Careful scripting helps avoid interview bias.
- Computerized routing of questionnaires allows for complex patterns of behaviour to be captured.
- Response rates are higher – consumers can be called until they reply.
- Costs are lower than for personal interviews.
- Speed – telephones get higher priority than post, and the results are immediately available.

Their disadvantages are that:

- Some consumers object to the approach.
- Increasingly answerphones, voicemail and caller display are used to screen out unwanted calls.
- The call is at the organization's convenience and not the consumer's. This can produce a negative response from the consumer. For this reason, telephone is often not the best medium for customer satisfaction work. However, if there is a long questionnaire to be administered, this problem can be overcome by scheduling the call at a time agreed with the respondent.
- The costs of setting up a telephone questionnaire can be high.
- Calling costs are higher than postal costs.
- It is a voice medium only, so consumers' reactions cannot be seen.

Observation, for example mystery shopping

Participant observation by 'trained evaluators' might seem more objective than asking customers about consumer perceptions. However, there are problems. Observation focuses more on what seems to be 'transmitted', but does not necessarily capture the consumer's experience. The advantages are that:

- It provides a 'reality' check against the perceptions of consumers.
- It can be very thorough, so telling small details that might have significant impact are picked up.
- It provides a useful complement to consumer studies.

Disadvantages include:

- The high cost of in-person visits (telephone contact is of course cheaper).
- Some transactions and relationships in particular cannot be faked.

- The potential artificiality of the engagement.
- There are limits set by various Codes of Conduct when it comes to mystery shopping one's competitors (visit MRS Codes of Conduct at www.mrs.org.uk).

Using market research in post-testing

Post-testing, which uses the same techniques as pre-testing, is used to find out why things went as they did in a promotional campaign. Typical questions include:

- Why do particular kinds of consumers order or not order a catalogue or a product?
- Why are members cancelling?
- Why is the conversion rate low or high?

THE 10 KEY CRM QUESTIONS

The key questions CRM practitioners face are:

1. With which consumers does the organization want to create and manage a relationship?
2. What are these consumers' behaviours, wants and needs, and perceptions?
3. What is their relative importance; do they constitute a hierarchy?
4. How far do the organization's policies meet its needs today?
5. What are relevant competitive offerings against which the organization should position its offering?
6. What are consumers' experiences of the organization's products, services and of the relationship as a whole?
7. What do the organization's staff believe about their role in its relationship with consumers?
8. What do commercial indicators of relationship success (such as brand loyalty, market share) show?
9. Can consumers be grouped into coherent segments, to enable CRM policy to be structured to meet their needs?
10. What are these segments, and are they stable?

THE RESEARCH PROCESS

Clearly, many answers to these questions should be sought from consumers. You cannot build a relationship without talking to the other party! The research process must be integrated with the policy process. Information is not being gathered for the sake of it, but to influence policy. This means that the content, coverage and timing of research should be integrated within the planning process. To ensure this, each piece of research should:

- have specific objectives;
- improve the quality of the next piece of research;
- have clear policy outcomes.

Relationship performance requirements

The most important activity in researching customer relationship needs is to define consumers' general perceptions, wants and expectations in relation to the relationship. To this must be added information on the relationship that is actually achieved (as perceived by consumer and supplier), and on changes that are planned in relationship management. The result of this analysis should be a comparison between current and planned levels of relationship management and consumer needs. This will be fed into the next stage of the process.

The contact audit

CRM practitioners need to understand how the different contacts consumers have with a company affect their attitudes and perceptions concerning the relationship. The contact audit begins identifying all the contact points. The audit shows the type, nature, frequency, and quality of contact with consumers. It should also show how these contacts affect consumers' perceptions and attitudes. You may be surprised, as many managers are, to find how many points of contact exist between some organizations and their consumers.

APPLYING MARKET RESEARCH TO CUSTOMER BASE ANALYSIS

Consumer profitability

Aside from understanding consumers' needs and wants, it may also make marketing and market research sense for organizations in certain sectors to determine the relative profitability (*actual and potential; current and lifetime*) of individual consumers, and analyse other behavioural and attitudinal data, perhaps by decile segments of these measures of profitability. Highly profitable consumers might need to be treated differently to those who are not so profitable. There may even be a case for demarketing to non-profitable individuals or segments. The consumer's propensity to deal with and buy from the company is also relevant, as in the end this leads to the company achieving different 'share of wallet'.

Market researchers, of course, are used to sampling to ensure a good representation of 'heavy users' for analysis, but they should also consider the possibility that users of different categories can be (too) costly to serve. For example, in business-to-business markets, heavy users may also be very demanding users in terms of special terms and conditions, perhaps even special prices. Conversely, in consumer markets, a common problem is light users (and therefore low revenue providers) who are very demanding – high cost to serve can result from users being inexperienced. Measures need to be refined to take account of profitability and to be comparable (where possible). Few (though a growing number) of companies segment by customer profitability, due to problems of measuring or estimating customer profitability. On occasion, this can be derived by weight of purchasing or weight of use, but these are far from perfect measures. There is a need in many organizations for the development of more sophisticated measures.

Loyalty, commitment and retention

Rather than just customer profitability, another basis for CRM marketing strategy is the degree of 'loyalty' or commitment a consumer exhibits. However, this raises another market research issue – how best to measure loyalty, or even whether to do so? Some may even question the use of the term 'loyalty' in relation to brands where there is no interpersonal dimension. While brand 'personality' discourse is useful and illuminating in some respects,[2] the fact that a brand is not a person (and is rarely a cause) means loyalty as a metaphor for commitment or disposition may be misleading.

There are of course both behavioural and attitudinal measures or indices of commitment. Indeed there can be a confusing array, as shown in Table 5.1.

There is still much to do in terms of organizations having clear definitions and appropriate operational measures. Clearly marketers need to focus on what precisely they are trying to achieve in terms of buyer behaviour and attitude (see Table 5.1). Indeed, there is an argument that measuring both attitude and behaviour provides particularly useful insights.

Dick and Basu clearly define loyalty as a two-dimensional construct – behavioural and attitudinal – and on this basis developed a potentially

Table 5.1 *Measures of commitment*

Behavioural	Attitudinal
Recency, frequency, monetary value (RFM)	Brand preference
Share of budget/wallet	Willingness to pay a premium
Recommend brand/product to others	Declared intent to consider/purchase
Loyalty card schemes	Disposition to recommend
Buy across range/trade up	General evaluation

useful matrix for loyalty classification (see Figure 5.1).[3] The Dick and Basu grid helps marketers understand who is to be rewarded (the northwest quadrant), who is vulnerable (the northeast quadrant) and who offers an opportunity (the southwest quadrant).

Possibly the biggest help market researchers could give in this area is to help organizations discern what their halo is, and to show what path they are on with that halo. This can be achieved though qualitative and quantitative research on perceptions of the offering, ideally on a trend basis. Overall satisfaction is by itself a poor indicator of commitment. Consumers who are satisfied can defect to a perceived better offering. As regards what is most important to a consumer and leads to retention, we can ask consumers directly. However, rationalizing and posturing might mean direct questions are misleading, so it might be better to infer statistically the factors that seem to lead to a good retention level. Also, too many satisfaction surveys focus on measuring what is easy to measure rather than things that are of genuine importance to the customer.

		Attitudinal commitment	
		High	**Low**
Behavioural commitment	**High**	**True loyalty**	**Spurious (inertia)**
	Low	**Latent loyalty**	**None**

Source: adapted from Dick and Basu (1994).

Figure 5.1 *Attitudinal and behavioural loyality/commitment*

The customer experience and timing of research

Qualitative research with consumers and discussion with front-line employees and first-line managers can help identify the different ways in which an organization touches its consumers. However, it is not easy to ensure the research is conducted at the 'moment of truth' for everyone, especially in some business-to-business markets where there is a constant stream of such moments for many buyers. Tracking studies in some markets may offer a solution, but in others it just has to be accepted that only some of the experiences can be sampled and related to commitment models.

Getting measurement right is vital. We know that organizations go in the direction of their measures. If the organization's measures are inward-facing, then that is the way it will start to face. Thus, many financial services companies have embraced customer satisfaction measures. They have been measuring things like the speed of answering letters and the usability of documentation. Customers are, however, deeply dissatisfied because investments – their pensions and endowments – are not going to produce the returns they expected. The measurements did not show this was going to be the case, and gave few clues that the industry would be facing a retention crisis, just that it could answer letters quickly. The companies had become inward facing, expert at administration, but were not fulfilling the customers' needs. Market research has let these organizations down. If the measures had focused on the real reason consumers bought their products, then the companies could have responded to their real concerns, rather than the inward-facing ones. And perhaps this same thought should be applied to market researchers themselves. If their halo is to do with thought and understanding , this is what they need to contribute, not just reports and presentations. If market research were managed in this way, then market research clients should be more successful!

Market researchers can provide useful conceptual and operational definitions and measure the total market, not just consumers on the database. Both market researchers and database marketers should strive to use common measures and units of measurement so data can be compared, contrasted and fused where this might be useful. (Note: data fusion involves the merging of two studies A and B so that the relationship between variable X in survey A and variable Y can be inferred based on the relationship they have with a variable or set of common variables in both studies.[4]) Standardization across database and traditional market research should cover demographics, psychographics, category measures, commitment, satisfaction and so on.

One further issue relevant to monitoring customer experience is that some consumers become over-researched and in the end less cooperative.

This has become more acute with the advent of Internet-based research.[5]

Other measures of consumer importance

We noted earlier the potential of segmenting consumers by profitability and commitment. However, there are many other bases for segmentation (products bought, benefits sought and so on). Also we should not forget the influence some consumers have. Opinion leaders exist in both business and consumer markets, and there is a tradition of research in this area. Methods to identify consumer opinion leaders are by self-designation (self-ratings), key informants, observation and socio-metrics (asking who influences whom in a circle of contacts, friends or acquaintances). Recommenders may be important to new initiatives and may warrant special marketing attention, to ensure they become effective advocates of a brand. This also applies to identifying potential innovators and early adopters, who, because of their importance and different characteristics from late adopters, may require a different marketing programme.[6]

The focus of research: consumers and staff

CRM researchers clearly wish to understand their consumers, test activities and evaluate these when rolled out. We have noted some of the preoccupations above. However, employee research or internal market research is also valuable. Research into employee attitude and behaviour (just as with consumers) during the implementation programme, helps to:

- identify strengths and weakness;
- identify and evaluate training and support needs;
- move towards improving results.

We have noted that customer management research suggests a high correlation between having the right people and people programmes in place and achieving results. This may explain why some successful managers extol the mantra 'the customer comes second', meaning that where there is a positive focus on employees, they in turn will be able to understand consumer needs and manage relationships effectively. Furthermore, given that service elements such as the telephone contact experience often play an important role in determining a consumer's overall commitment towards a provider (and clearly consumer-facing employees often have a great influence in this area), companies depend on motivating their employees to deliver the required service levels.

Sears implemented a set of total performance indicators using the 'soft' measures of employee satisfaction and customer loyalty, which enabled them to estimate their effect on financial performance and to set targets for employee and customer satisfaction.[7] 'Every 5 point increase in [employee] satisfaction is related to a 1.7% increase in customer loyalty which in turn is associated with a 3.4% increase in earnings.' So it is evident that researching employees is highly relevant to business success with service-oriented categories. Employees can provide early warning of problems as well as opportunities. This is closely connected with an organization's halo. If enough staff understand their organization to have a halo, which reflects what it does in a very positive way, then this will translate into higher employee satisfaction and in turn customer satisfaction. There is a close fit between what staff say about their employer and what customers say about the business. If the halo works for staff, and increases satisfaction among them, it will also work for customers. This may become even more important as organizations increasingly use call centres based abroad.

Research culture: 'If you can't measure it, you can't manage it'

There is undeniably a strong quantitative research culture in CRM. This may create the impression that the CRM research management platform is, 'If you can't measure it, you can't manage it.' Of course, this is not the case – many good managers work by feel. They might produce better results than their peers who feel exposed without measurement. Indeed, a policy of managers themselves 'staying close to customers' and ensuring that staff do the same can be just as effective as measurement-driven management.

Many of the biggest CRM users spend a fair share of research monies on qualitative research, to get beneath the metrics. What is measurable may provide a distorted picture of the market. This distortion may be due to classic research biases or simple omission of key influences or factors because of problems of measurement. Where the value of qualitative research is not appreciated, organizations may find they are moving towards a quantitative, data-rich culture that is perhaps not 'information rich'. What data is collected often depends on what has always been collected or what is easily collected. Both may lead to a serious distortion in the view the organization has of consumers.

Another tendency in some CRM operations is to base analysis on the measures available rather than trying to collect vital missing data from consumers. We believe some customer metrics being used, such as customer numbers, churn rates and customer satisfaction, are useful, but on many occasions they can be misleading:

- A focus on **customer numbers** normally results in a strategy to 'acquire at any cost' and the acquisition of many unprofitable or even loss-making customers.
- A focus on **customer satisfaction**, as typically measured by large companies, gives misleading results, as consumers who rarely transact with the company, and spend little with them, are asked what they think - and their views dilute the views of heavy users and loyalists. It is the satisfaction of the most valuable and/or most loyal buyers that counts.
- A focus on **customer churn** is misleading because it is rarely defined or measured accurately (see Chapter 7) and 'received wisdom' is the norm. Thus, any figures put forward by companies are likely to be doubtful. Also, the really telling figures may be the churn of heavy users and loyalists.

All of the above problems and issues spell opportunities for market researchers interested in CRM to bring to bear their understanding of consumers across many issues and studies and, of course, their research expertise. However, some users of CRM believe that sales or service personnel make good research interviewers. In our experience this is often not the case, as training rarely takes place, and there is the problem of competing interests (selling versus research).

CONCLUSIONS

There is a risk that client-based market researchers who do not adapt to the new customer information reality will be sidelined. Market researchers should consider their role in the organization and the need for someone to pull all the consumer research together to see the bigger picture, maximize insight and disseminate this throughout the organization. To achieve this, researchers need to understand the mindset and culture of those in CRM. Key bases for CRM strategy include the consumer life cycle, acquisition and retention, and the historical and lifetime value of customers. Many market researchers have the skill sets, aptitude and techniques that can add value. New lines of research on opinion leadership, word of mouth and networks also seem highly relevant, suggesting new bases for targeting influential consumers. Sophisticated models of commitment based on more meaningful, composite measures of commitment that identify what fosters commitment will provide actionable findings. New ways of assessing what is important to consumers can also be very useful.

While CRM practice is far from perfect, the evidence is that where it is appropriate and executed intelligently and sensitively, it makes a real difference to business success. Some barriers to its success include poor research focus and weak problem and concept definition, as well as unsophisticated measures and models. This is territory in which the client-side market researcher should at least be involved, and the agency researcher should be prepared to act as consultant and researcher.

At the heart of the CRM implementation problem is often lack of appreciation by senior management that for CRM to succeed, a company must take a different approach not just to customer service and marketing management but also to people and operations management. For consumer contacts to be managed better, those managing the contacts must be trained, motivated and supported with all relevant information. They also need to be confident that other parts of the organization will provide the necessary support and deliver to expectations. To ensure that this happens, the connections between employee satisfaction or engagement, operations, customer service and customer acquisition, retention and profit need to be understood and monitored so that corrective action (and employee reward) can be planned and implemented.

Market researchers must be prepared to shift from the often ivory tower operation, to think not just strategically but tactically, and perhaps just as importantly to champion the consumer and bring together managers involved in the consumer experience. They will be helped by a much stronger focus in the marketing profession on customer experience management. Researchers should ensure that they are discovering what experience consumers receive and what they would like to receive, and make sure that those whose actions affect the experience of consumers understand what the research says. To ensure acceptance of this kind of research, those whose customer management activities are being researched should be involved in the research from the beginning. This can be achieved by proper consultation with internal stakeholders, at all levels of the organization, at all stages of the research process, in the form of workshops, meetings, one-to-ones and e-mail, newsletters, suggestion 'boxes' and the like as appropriate. This also ensures all business and consumer issues are identified and covered in the research.

The market researcher with good research skills can lead in the research design of internal surveys of employees to determine strengths and weaknesses in the organization's customer management, particularly where these involve connections between different customer-facing functions. Finally, it is worth noting that although questionnaires are still a prime research tool, they may not be enough to ensure understanding how changes to customer management strategies and processes affect consumers and the staff who manage them. Properly conducted mystery shopping and participant observation are increasingly regarded as a very important part of the battery of techniques used to understand the customer experience.

CALL TO ACTION

Here we present a call to action, as a series of questions to be answered by client and agency researchers.

Client researchers where CRM is practised

- Are you involved in all consumer research and knowledge management?
- Should you be the guardian and manager of all such knowledge? Or at least work more closely with those who are?
- Is the optimum set of data collected from consumers in order to manage them effectively and profitably?
- Do you know what your company collects, why it is collected and the impact of using that data?
- Have you been involved in efforts to correlate market research-based measures of the quality of consumer management with the outcomes, such as sales and profit?
- Do you identify best prospects in terms of value, profitability, influence?
- Is the consumer life cycle relevant? If so, how, and what research is needed to understand how it affects what and how consumers buy and respond at different stages of the life cycle?
- What is the relative importance of acquisition and retention for your organization? How is this reflected in market research activity?
- How are retention, loyalty and commitment defined and measured?
- What in an organization drives these?
- What benchmarks are used to evaluate, say, retention activities?
- How do you determine what drives and fosters commitment and what is really important? How does this apply to consumers of different net profitability to your company?

- Do you distinguish between claimed importance versus statistically inferred importance?
- Are you involved in relevant CRM employee research?
- How would you evaluate the organization's CRM activity?

Agency researchers

- Do you know the answers to the above for your clients?
- What value could you add against the above?
- Does your organization successfully implement CRM?
- Do you check this?
- How?

NOTES

1 For more on this, see Humby, C, Hunt, T and Phillips, T (2003) *Scoring Points*, Kogan Page, London.

2 Fournier, S (1998) Consumers and their brands: developing relationship theory in consumer research, *Journal of Consumer Research*, **24**, pp 343–73.

3 Dick, A and Basu, K (1994) Customer loyalty: toward an integrated framework, *Journal of the Academy of Marketing Science*, **22** (2), pp 99–113.

4 Baker, K (1998) Multivariate analysis of survey data, in *ESOMAR Handbook of Market and Opinion Research*, ed C Mcdonald and P Vangelder.

5 Nancarrow, C. Pallister, J and Brace, I (2001) A new research medium, new research populations and seven deadly sins for internet researchers, *Qualitative Market Research*, **4** (3), pp 136–49.

6 Oxley, M and Nancarrow, C (2002) Managing the diffusion of innovation: a new research concept and new marketing tools, paper from ESOMAR Congress Barcelona; and Oxley, M and Nancarrow, C (2003) Spreading the word: fast-tracking new products to market, *Admap*, February.

7 Norquist, M *et al* (1987) A great place to shop, work and invest: measuring and managing the service profit chain at Sears Canada, *Journal of Interactive Marketing*, **3** (3), pp 255–61.

6 Analysing computer data to get insight

Merlin Stone, Bryan Foss, David Selby and Julie Abbott

PRODUCTS, PROPOSITIONS AND CUSTOMERS

Before the age of database marketing, much marketing data was about products – how much they sold, where, at what price. Still today, many companies do not know the identity of their consumers, so while applying consumer management disciplines to their immediate direct consumers (such as retailers), they must use product management to get the best results. We call these the 'product or proposition optimizers'. Their own and market data on price, promotion, inventory levels and movements, and shipments are used to determine marketing and distribution policy. Their data are organized by product, and the main analysis task is to make sense of the possibly daily millions (for example, for a grocery brand leader) of transactions in which their products are involved.

By contrast, companies that can manage their consumers as individuals need to become expert in analysing consumer data, to answer questions such as:

- Which consumers do I want to market to, and which not?
- How do I want to manage my consumers?
- Which products and services would I like to sell to particular kinds of consumer?

- At what price, through which channels of distribution, and when?

These questions apply whether the contact is managed directly or through an agent. The key point is that individual consumers are known to suppliers. Data requiring analysis is in-depth consumer data, combined with transaction and promotional response data. These organizations are 'consumer optimizers'. Consumer-optimizers express marketing strategy in terms of acquiring, retaining and developing customers. Here is an example of how a company approached this through direct marketing channels.

CORONA DIRECT

Corona Direct is Belgium's second largest direct property and casualty insurance company. It markets via four channels: direct marketing, call centre, Web site and affinity schemes. Corona Direct has been growing rapidly. Direct marketing campaigns play a key role in this growth, enabling Corona Direct to acquire new customers by offering attractively priced insurance products. To sustain its current level of growth, Corona Direct's customer acquisition campaigns must be profitable – that is, first-year revenues generated from new insurance policies should pay for the cost of acquisition. However, in the past, the cost of acquiring new customers exceeded first-year revenues by almost 50 per cent, putting Corona Direct's growth strategy at risk.

To turn its unprofitable acquisition strategy into a profitable one, Corona Direct implemented SPSS PredictiveMarketing. The software identifies groups for Corona Direct that are likely to respond to a campaign, and then performs a profit – cost analysis, balancing growth targets against profit margins. With this focus on likelihood of response and expected profitability, Corona Direct is able to optimize its potential for growth. After modelling with the software and then fine-tuning its prospect mailings, it has cut its direct marketing costs by 30 per cent while maintaining new customer conversion rates. The company's acquisition campaigns are now profitable. First-year revenues cover campaign costs, enabling Corona Direct to sustain its growth strategy. Also, long-term customer profitability has increased by 20 per cent and product sales have risen significantly. Payback for the software implementation was achieved within six months.

The next example is of how a company approached this through its branches.

NATEXIS ASSURANCES

Natexis Assurances is a leading French insurance and investment company. Its marketing includes direct-mail campaigns followed up by local branches. The central marketing department defines campaigns, contacts individual local branches to see if they are interested in participating in them, then executes the campaigns. As branch participation is discretionary, the marketing department must demonstrate that its campaigns generate high-quality responses.

To increase the quality of its direct marketing campaigns, Natexis uses SPSS PredictiveMarketing to support the creation, optimization and execution of targeted marketing campaigns. Using this application, it can better understand customer needs, optimizing campaign response rates by selecting those customers that will generate the highest value for the company. Now Natexis can target its best customers for each campaign, and provide highly qualified leads to the branch offices for follow-up. As a result, direct-mail volumes have been reduced by 50 per cent, while revenues have doubled. For example, the company implemented a life insurance campaign, which included a direct mailing followed up with phone calls by the local branches. Compared with similar campaigns that were run earlier that year, the size of the campaign was reduced by 46 per cent, while the number of policies sold was increased by 55 per cent. In addition, since the software selected only those customers who were most likely to make higher investments, actual returns generated by the campaign increased by 109 per cent. A life insurance campaign also demonstrated the software's ability to predict precisely the response rate and results of the campaign. The number of policies sold within the group of customers selected was three times higher than within other groups, while the average revenue per customer investment was 92 per cent higher.

Some companies are hybrid product and consumer optimizers. Many service retailers (for instance, in retail finance) can identify final consumers individually, but must work hard to optimize product marketing so as to make the best use of their sales capacity. Some retailers focus only on product-optimizing merchandising, but others find that individual consumer management is now possible through store cards (credit, debit and loyalty cards). In practice most companies are hybrids to some degree, requiring both product and consumer optimization. Note that in some cases, what appears to be a problem in one area (such as product) might turn out to be a consumer acquisition and/or retention problem.

Segmentation

An important requirement in consumer optimization is for consumers to be classified into different groups to be managed differently, either tactically or strategically. Here is a useful hierarchy of segmentation, as follows:

- contact management;
- analytical segmentation;
- response segmentation;
- strategic segmentation;

Contact management

This is using data at the point of contact with the consumer to improve management of individual consumers. It may use the output of the segmentation categories described below to change the action or response of the company: for instance, alter the telemarketing script, accept or refuse a consumer. For example, contact management might at first be based on simple analytical segmentation techniques, but over time usually matures to be directed by response segmentation (or predictive scoring), supplemented by analytical segmentation for improved understanding of relevant wants and needs.

Analytical segmentation

This is the use of consumer and market information to identify that there are indeed different groups of consumers with different profiles, needs and so on. This approach often starts with very broad questions such as 'What kinds of consumer do we have? What is their behaviour? Which products or channels are the most successful?' The segments identified in this way might never be subjected to different promotions, policies or strategies. For example, they might be aggregated into a target market for a promotion. The main criterion for successful use of analytical segmentation is that any resulting strategies work overall, because they are based on in-depth understanding of consumer needs. Analytical segmentation often provides the foundation for the other three types of segmentation.

Response segmentation

This is the identification of different groups of consumers for targeting particular promotions. A given consumer might belong to a whole series of different segments, according to the objectives of individual promotions. The key criterion for the success of response segmentation is the success of individual promotions (that is, whether response rates met expectations; whether final purchases hit target). As the case study below shows, apparently small differences in response rates can make a very big difference to profits, so a segmentation approach that delivers such an increase can be a key source of competitive advantage. Put simply, a 0.1 per cent increase in the response rate means a 5 per cent increase in sales if the response rate was 2.0 per cent before. As costs will not usually rise 5 per cent, it means a much larger increase in profit.

US RETAILER

This company does much of its advertising via direct mail. Using data collected from its own credit cards, the retailer already has extensive background information on its customers, including their purchases. Based on intelligence gleaned by accessing its two-terabyte data warehouse, the retailer can reduce the number of customers mailed to 1 in 300 who buy a particular type of product. The retailer also builds models to determine which customers are brand-loyal and profitable in order to cut the lowest 10 per cent of responders from its mailing lists. This retailer has moved away from the traditional recency, frequency, monetary (RFM) mode and into behaviour and life cycle modelling.

Response segmentation has become more important. Direct marketing relies on tight targeting of consumers and well-built consumer databases to ensure high-quality data. Direct marketing practice has been weakened by many companies crossing industry frontiers and targeting each other's consumers. Banks offer insurance, insurers offer banking. Utilities are offering telecommunications. Retailers offer everything. Everybody offers credit cards. They all see direct marketing as the answer to their prayer. This is in part because they see it as a cheaper option than above the line, and in part because of its perceived measurability. In these circumstances, unless there is amazing increase in the propensity to respond, or to buy direct, response rates are more likely to fall than rise. Improved targeting will be the only way to make direct marketing pay - hence the need for better targeting. Simple predictive modelling is giving way to more complex modelling based on classification techniques, achieved through data mining, covered later in this chapter.

Strategic segmentation

This is the identification of groups of consumers who need in some sense to be handled differently. This should be driven by a study of key performance indicators to provide the maximum benefit. For example, in mass-market financial services, it is particularly important for suppliers to identify:

- loan consumers who are likely to be higher credit risks (in which case they are usually only accepted as borrowers at an interest rate which covers the risk premium);
- mortgage consumers who are likely to be rapid switchers (eg of mortgages), in which case they may only be accepted for loans with higher penalties for earlier cancellation;
- low-risk or infrequently switching consumers, who will be targeted and marketed to intensively, and particular attention paid to the quality of consumer care they receive.

The idea of strategic segmentation is to ensure that each consumer is allocated at a minimum to at least one strategic category, membership of which carries certain implications for the marketing policy likely to be directed towards him or her. Also, one should avoid creating too many categories, with attendant risks of overlap (a given consumer being subjected to too many marketing initiatives or restrictions, which have to be resolved by prioritization rules) or over-complexity (because of the number of segments to be addressed with different marketing policies).

While this approach sounds exciting in theory, it is not easy in practice. A particular issue is the movement of consumers between categories. The best example of this is the life cycle category. For example, a mother with very young children will be in the market for disposable nappies (diapers) for two years after the birth of each child. During pregnancy, the mother can be considered as about to enter a strategic segment (current buyer). So the supplier's main strategic segments are women in the late stages of pregnancy and mothers of children under, say, two years old. However, when the child is trained, the mother moves into another segment – a candidate for other products and services, as well as a potential recommender to others. This shows that where life cycle segments are important, it is necessary to be able to identify not only which consumers are already in the high-usage segment, but which consumers are likely to move into or leave it.

The same competitive pressures that apply to direct marketing apply to strategic segmentation. Companies are trying to target their products and services accurately. The ultimate aspiration is often expressed as 'the market segment of one', implying that the whole marketing mix can be attuned to individuals. Most large companies find the idea of 'mass customization' more helpful. This involves creating a modular marketing mix, with the ability to 'package' the offer individually, for instance by changing the information that forms part of it. The simplest example of this is the personalization of communication. Mass customization is attractive because products and services can rarely be changed quickly to meet the needs of different segments. Product and service features are usually determined as part of a strategic process (although of course modularization allows flexibility). Tightly defined strategic segmentation - in which the characteristics of consumers who make up particular target segments are defined in some detail - is becoming more common, as products and services are targeted at smaller segments. Older methods of segmentation, based upon quite large groupings defined using broad socio-demographic or economic characteristics, are giving way to more tightly defined segments, often defined through data mining. For both response and strategic segmentation, senior management is starting to ask that investigative work, questioning the definition and value of segments, becomes part of the routine of the marketing department rather than a once-and-for-all exercise which determines marketing policy for years to come.

CONCLUSIONS ON THE DEPLOYMENT OF ANALYSIS

Here are the most important points that arise from the above and from our research in this area.

1. The analysis required by product optimizers and consumer optimizers is different, but many suppliers now realize that they have to do both.
2. Companies should recognize that they will normally need to consolidate and synthesize data from different sources (internal, commissioned market research, generally available market data and so on) and functions (marketing, sales, finance, consumer service, manufacturing, etc).
3. A successful approach to analysis requires the company to define the key analysis dimensions in some detail, and then to ensure focus on a few areas which can be backed by management action.
4. The needs of different users vary, and different users will require different tools to support their different management actions, but this must not lead to data being dispersed to different users so that the capability for coordinated analysis is lost. Hence the need for central consolidation of data to facilitate reporting to all parts of the organization.
5. This approach will be much facilitated if data and analysis requirements are defined as part of the wider business systems requirement, and if the consortium of suppliers is built around this concept.

6. If the underlying data is not in order, many conclusions will be invalid.
7. When deploying data-mining tools, start with a clear business understanding and identified business problem. Do not expect data mining alone to be a 'silver bullet'.
8. Successful joined-up business processes require joined-up IT systems and underlying data structures.

ADVANCED DATA ANALYSIS

Improving marketing results while minimizing marketing expenditure, thus increasing the return on investment in marketing, can be achieved by combining CRM systems with a new approach to consumer insight. This can increase consumer satisfaction, stimulate purchases, increase loyalty and retain valued consumers, while controlling costs. It requires the combination of analytical techniques and computing technologies that enable businesses to communicate with individual consumers, regardless of contact channel, by offering service and purchase suggestions that reflect precise buying habits, needs and desires, preferably in real time. Consumer insight is key, but the ability to use it profitably via closed-loop CRM systems is rare. As Hirschowitz points out, 'no matter how sophisticated a company's ability to generate consumer insight, it delivers little value without the processes in place to exploit the understanding to build stronger consumer relationships.[1]

Treating the consumer as an investment

In many companies, consumers are not viewed as longer-term valuable assets but just as prospects for the next contact list from which to make the next sale. When a company starts to think of consumers as valuable assets, it can justify investing in individual consumers so as to get the best from them and to ensure that the consumer gets the best of the supplier. English noted that 'Businesses fail when management focuses too much attention on today's immediate needs, such as quarterly profits, at the expense of solving tomorrow's problem, such as discovering and satisfying consumers' emerging requirements.'[2] This is the problem we discussed in the previous chapters, which is resolved by taking a halo approach to business.

Many marketing systems use a point-in-time (that is, a campaign by campaign) logic to make marketing investment decisions. However, consumer-focused analytic software now allows companies to take into account the effect of one campaign on another before an offer is presented, provided of course that they have managed their consumer insight data properly. The idea is to develop a marketing plan for each individual consumer. This plan is continually re-evaluated and designed to feed campaign management with a set of offers that maximizes the return on investment for each consumer. This allows organizations to plan and manage consumers to a budget. Where most event-based marketing triggers an action whenever an event is seen, this approach first evaluates if this is the best use of the marketing budget for this individual.

Single view

Consumers should believe they are dealing with one integrated firm, rather than a disjointed set of business units which only take ownership of a consumer for those interactions relating to their particular part of the business. The integration facility of many CRM systems enables this via a real-time data management system. This uses a data store incorporating analysis models to generate propensity scores, and a consumer behaviour profile which can be used at all consumer touch points. When consumers interact with a company, their behaviour profile develops, giving each touch point hard accounting data (for example, what was spent or invested) and soft facts (such as attitude to risk and price sensitivity) that are used in conjunction with powerful technology to generate personalized messages for each individual consumer. 'You really understand me' is the impression the company wants to create. Such a system enables consumers to acknowledge that the firm understands them and meets their needs, ensuring that they continue to do business with that supplier. What is important here for business is to take the interaction to the level beyond spin, where the organization does not just show that it understands its consumers, but really does understand them; this understanding is insight. For consumer insight to be deployed like this, it must be supported by the right systems. Here it is important to determine how the insight will be deployed in practice. The following case study gives an example.

AN AUSTRALIAN BANK

This bank's retail business incorporates checking and savings accounts, credit cards and loans. It has a customer base of several million. A team of analysts built customer models to analyse and predict customer behaviour. This initiative, part of a commitment to CRM, was the largest customer-focused project ever undertaken by the bank's analysts.

Phase One involved the identification and preparation of thousands of possible characteristics and the development of tens of behavioural models. Around 70 per cent of the time spent on Phase One was dedicated to defining and preparing the characteristics. The behavioural models produced were each able to predict the likelihood of a given behaviour in areas such as marketing, retention and credit decision initiatives. Project stages included initially carrying out basic analysis in order to understand what drives behaviour. Once this was done the models were built. Prediction of customers' behaviour is possible from previous experiences. However, the models also identify unusual or unexpected behaviours which can then be used as a marketing opportunity. The bank runs its standard set of models regularly and automatically. The information the models provide is used by the bank's decision makers for marketing purposes such as direct mail, as well as for collection strategies and cost/risk estimations.

For Phase Two, the team was able to develop a streamlined approach that made it possible to refine and automate the data preparation process, exploit the data sources and drastically reduce the number of variables to hundreds from thousands – once it was understood which were most predictive and valuable.

The bank also creates one-off models for specific campaigns, giving even better results and potentially doubling the effectiveness of the campaign. For example an early model-based credit card campaign resulted in a 67 per cent increase over earlier campaigns. Now that the bank can develop its models in-house, the cost of the exercise is minimal, and the return on investment runs to thousands of per cent.

Developing or enhancing the technical infrastructure

Real-time decision making requires new capabilities. After collecting data and transforming it into insight, it is necessary to focus on its storage and retrieval to ensure it becomes a useful corporate asset. In many companies some form of data warehouse already exists. Certain data types require focus to ensure sound corporate decision making. Examples include campaign information, campaign responses both positive and negative, consumer characteristics, channels preferred and used, and cross-product behaviour, as well as more obvious consumer details such as name and address. Where Web marketing is used, more dimensions are necessary such as traffic sources, online behaviour segments, and content or image categories.

This record of historical behaviour provides a vital piece of information for generating analytical models to predict consumers' propensity to respond to a marketing event. It allows organizations to create a view of the consumer before a significant event, such as a Web page or kiosk screen presentation, or a direct-mail offering. These events stimulate consumer behaviour, and provide important ingredients for predicting behaviour of consumers before an event and analysing consumers after the event. With this evidence – a prior view and a response to a stimulus – sophisticated data-mining algorithms can be used to generate models that predict the consumer's next behaviour. This prediction can then be applied to other consumers within the population.

DATA MINING

A simple definition of data mining in marketing is:

> Extraction of previously unknown, comprehensible and actionable information from large repositories of data, and using it to make crucial business decisions and support their implementation, including formulating tactical and strategic marketing initiatives and measuring their success.

The aim of data mining is to obtain a sufficient understanding of a pattern of market behaviour to allow *quantifiable* benefits to be derived from changes in behaviour suggested by the analysis. This involves learning previously unknown facts about market behaviour, and answering specific questions, including forecasting questions.

Of course, it is not always possible to finalize expectations before data mining starts, as the results usually determine what can be done. However, you must not overestimate the company's capacity to change. Marketing budgets may be set for a year ahead, and with them plans. New promotional initiatives may have to replace existing ones, unless the organization has adopted processes and systems that allow it to change its marketing approach immediately or quickly, based upon mining results. The latest marketing software is designed to allow companies to do this.

Data mining starts with the idea that companies hold a lot of data about their businesses, but do not have full understanding of what is happening in detail. By 'digging' in the data it is possible to 'mine' the nuggets of buried information. This approach is mainly relevant for companies that have lots of readily available information, but have not analysed it much. In these cases almost anything discovered will be interesting but more importantly of use to the organization. Remember, apparently small gains achieved through analysis can give big long-term gains, particularly when repeated over a long period. For example, in one company, increasing cross-sell rates by 2 per cent yielded 22 per cent more profit, and 8 per cent better retention.

However, data mining is more than simple data analysis. It is machine-aided consultancy that requires:

- understanding of the industry conditions;
- appreciation of specific factors that apply to the company;
- familiarity with a wide range of analytical tools;
- the ability to present extracted information in informative ways.

Data mining consultancy can provide advice on what can be determined and how to interpret it, for instance:

- what can be learnt from particular types of data;
- the answers to certain questions about the data;
- the way to collect new data to answer other questions;
- the limits of what can be learnt.

What data mining offers to marketing

The exploration characteristic of data mining software is made possible by advances in computing, in particular comparison of very large numbers of attributes of cases, to see which cases are similar. In particular, it helps marketing managers understand and predict consumer behaviour. Take for example the phenomenon of the frequent flyer. Here there are many variables requiring analysis, such as where and how far in advance the ticket was purchased, how often the flyer has not shown up despite buying a ticket, what class he or she is flying, and how complex the total itinerary is.[3]

Managers are also enabled to discover consumer groupings that would be hard to discover using theory-based hypotheses. For example, a life insurance company discovered a low-risk group of smokers within the high-risk group of all smokers. These were consumers who were prudent in every other way – except that they smoked. These consumers could be profitably retained by offering them a slightly lower premium.

The questions companies want answered

The last few years have seen many companies applying data mining to their marketing data. These applications are designed to answer a variety of questions. Here are some examples:

Consumer-based

- What kind of consumers does the company have?
- How do they respond to the marketing proposition?
- Which consumers are more desirable and which less?

Product or price

- Which products are bought together?
- When is the best time to sell a product?
- Which combination of tariffs yields the maximum revenue?

Distribution and communication routes to market

- Which campaign design works best?
- Which distribution channel is most effective?

Combinations of the above

- Which consumers are most responsive to which communications for which products?
- Which consumers with low lifetime values can be deterred by higher prices?
- Is it possible to identify groups of consumers, within groups considered homogeneous, that can be managed more profitably and/or less riskily?

Some examples of data mining activity in marketing

Here are some popular types of data mining activity that are encountered in practice, with a short description of the type of business problem associated with them.

Consumer gain and loss analysis (churn)

Why have some consumers been gained for certain products, and others lost? Variation in behaviour may be random, or may correlate with business trends, economic or social factors, or competitors' activity. The case study below gives an example of churn analysis.

MOBILE TELEPHONES

The telecommunications industry in Europe is becoming very competitive, and preventing customer attrition is a key focus for suppliers. As part of an effort to enhance its customer-relationship marketing, this

European cellular phone operator sought a churn model that would indicate clearly which customers were most likely to leave. This would enable the company to take action before 'good' customers discontinued service. The company also sought to discover cross-selling and up-selling opportunities.

The company asked IBM to research and implement a data mining-based churn model, with clustering, classification and predictive algorithms. With IBM's scalable data mining algorithms, the company develops models using all its customer data: that is, without sampling the data. The output of these models provides a list that assigns a probable attrition value to each customer. This business intelligence approach brings together both transactional and customer-base data, and helps the company understand the various segments of its customer groups. It provides the company with crucial insight into the characteristics of different customer groups and their churn probability. The probability scores it generates can give the company an understanding of the customer base, which allows it to devise different marketing strategies for different groups.

Consumer migration

What factors cause consumers to move to different products? Their buying pattern may show that they buy one particular product followed by another (for instance, after buying a dress the consumer buys a matching hat in the spring in 70 per cent of cases). The link between product types, and the susceptibility of a consumer to follow a sequence, could determine how items should be placed in a store and merchandised at certain times in the year, or which consumers to target in a marketing campaign.

Consumer solicitation

How effective are marketing campaigns in reaching the right consumers? Increasing campaign yield (a higher proportion of positive responses), or decreasing the cost of finding new consumers can yield big savings. The propensity of consumers to buy certain products can be used to predict future behaviour for new products.

Consumer response analysis

What causes consumers to respond – or not – to a campaign? Which respond most often, to which offers?

Promotion analysis

What are the results of a marketing promotion? Which consumers bought particular products, and why? The key task is to explain observed behaviour in terms of a mix of consumer and product types. This can be achieved by comparing the segmentation of consumers before and after the promotion in question.

Purchase analysis

What types of products and services are specific consumers buying – or not?

Seasonality analysis

How does the buying profile change during the year? Seasonal patterns in products (soda and popcorn in the summer, hamburgers in the winter) and in strengths of links between products can be studied.

Priority analysis

What order do consumers prefer to buy products in? How does this vary by consumer type?

Consumer loyalty

Which factors cause a consumer to remain loyal to a company or product? Consumer loyalty and lapsing are two sides of the same coin.

Cross-selling

What additional products could be offered to existing consumers? The propensity of consumers to buy a product can be used to infer how they will respond to new cross-selling opportunities.

Niche market determination and target marketing

What segments exist or have specific buying patterns that have not been identified before? The existence of many, often small, previously unidentified and possibly high-value (or low-value!) segments may suggest new products. For example, finding a small group of older drivers with fast cars that were costly to repair but had very few accidents led to a special insurance offering for vintage sports car enthusiasts.

Channel of communication and media analysis

Which channels do particular types of consumer prefer to use? Do their preferences vary for inbound and outbound communications?

Channel of distribution analysis

Which channels are different types of consumers using, when and for what products? Which would be most suitable, given consumers' geographic location? What is the optimum number of branches to cover the market?

Basket analysis

What associations are there between products – within the shopping basket, between products bought in the same week, month or year? This is the classic application of product link analysis to determine dependencies between otherwise unrelated activities.

The following case study shows how several different objectives are met.

BANKING

A North American bank aimed to be the only bank its customers needed. But to get to know customers on an individual basis and treat them personally, it needed a systematic approach to anticipating and meeting client needs. To improve productivity and build market share, it needed to:

- establish a central repository for customer information;
- unite customer information that had become fragmented within product-centric legacy systems;
- rely on a comprehensive, long-range predictive customer-segmentation model rather than using ad hoc methods that required expert statisticians to spend lots of time sourcing and extracting relevant data.

It realized that its segmentation was too product-centric, and focused on finding the right customer for the product rather than vice versa. So it sought a solution to help it segment customers and create a framework for a systematic approach to CRM. In turn, the bank would know its customers better and would be able to assure consistent treatment across channels.

The bank now scores all its nearly 10 million customers monthly through IBM data-mining tools. Scored profiles are made available to branches, contact centres and support employees. Advanced campaign management software uses these new profiles to select customers for targeting. The bank has developed and deployed various models. Now, in each segment, the group has a model-based approach to determining how to engage with each customer. With relevant information tailored to each customer's financial needs, the bank's employees can treat customers consistently whichever channel they use to interface with the bank. The bank now sends each customer three tailored offers monthly. Through relevant bundling of products and services based on individual needs, the financial group is better positioned to retain customer loyalty and expand its market reach. Using additional credit analytics and event triggers prompted by various segmentation-driven initiatives, it handles overdrafts more efficiently. Now the group automatically extends overdraft protection to help retain customer loyalty and reduce handling costs. Delivery speed for products and services has also increased through event triggers for next-business-day leads. The bank's decision implementation time has improved as well, because:

- householding (identifying which individuals constitute a household and the portfolio of products held by the household) and customer matching are performed monthly rather than quarterly;
- more than 40 models are run against the full customer base in a two-day period, improving efficiency and significantly reducing the cost of segmentation analytics;
- the new campaign management system allows better marketing techniques to be used more quickly.

Is data mining essential?

You do not have to use data mining to answer the kinds of questions listed in this chapter, but the more complex the question, and the larger and more complex the data set, the more likely it is that data mining will shed additional light. Data mining not only helps you find better answers – it also makes it easier for you to find these answers.

The methodology of data mining

The basic steps of a data mining analysis are data collection and cleaning, data analysis and presentation of the results. The first answer to the question 'Which data should I mine?' is simply 'Whatever you have that is likely to be relevant to the business problem and may give business insights if analysed effectively.' Most of this is transaction data, that is, data collected at the time of sale of the product. Often only a part of the available data is captured and retained at that time. This data is primarily product, not consumer data. Response data may also be available. Negative responses are often not collected, yet these are equally important. The full data set includes campaign responses, survey or research data, and complaint data. Data on consumers – how to access them, their characteristics and so on – might be collected during transactions and responses, or by a special collection effort. It might also be sourced externally.

Volumes of consumer interactions and resulting response and transaction data vary dramatically by type of business (for example, between retail, where card holders may transact daily, and insurance, where there may be one transaction a year). In some cases, data will also be held on the relationship: for example, on renewals of contracts. This data can be supplemented with external sources (demographic, geographic, lifestyle and so on). Combining one or more product sources may provide more insights into consumer behaviour and the relationship between consumer and company, and also on past consumers and relationships.

The steps typically involved in data mining are:

1. Understanding the business issue and the factors which affect it.
2. Data collection and warehousing (extraction, transport and loading).
3. Data cleaning, merging and purging, and grouping (including householding).
4. Variable redefinition, and transformation using mathematical techniques.
5. New data collection – typically items revealed as missing.
6. Data mining – often in several steps as 'internal clients' learn about type of results that can be achieved.
7. Data visualization.
8. New requests for analysis, additional information to be collected and analysed.
9. Assimilation.
10. Planning – including action and monitoring, and deciding whether to do it online rather than offline.

Traditional market segmentation approaches tend to be weak when it comes to understanding how consumer behaviour varies over time and space. This is partly because adding these dimensions makes data analysis much more complex. The increased availability of geographical data (where a consumer lives, where he or she has bought) and the ability to map it and show changing patterns mean that marketing managers are becoming more demanding when it comes to understanding spatial dimensions. Where time is concerned, time series analyses often led to simplification of the specification of the problem because of the difficulty of handling complex sequences of behaviour. The difficulty in both these areas was not that the statistical techniques could not handle them in theory, but that their introduction multiplied the complexity of the problem and made it hard to implement hypothesis-led approaches.

Too often, companies lose historical data. For example, a consumer's new address overwrites the old one. As prediction usually involves analysing current *and* past relationships, companies should consider keeping past versions of the database 'frozen' for analysis. The simplest example of problems caused by failure to keep frozen slices would be if a retailer tried to understand why a consumer bought at a number of different branches without knowing that the consumer had lived at three different addresses!

Basic techniques of data mining

Data-mining techniques are often classified as being either discovery-led or as hypothesis-led.

Discovery-led

This is the usual situation for new data-mining users, as the first question is usually: how can the data I have help me solve my business problem(s)? The aim is to use self-organizing methods to determine the nature of variation (correlations) within the data, without preconceived ideas about how the data might be organized. Thus, a company might believe it has three consumer types: average consumers – 'run of the mill' takers of the service or product – very good high-value consumers, and bad consumers – debtors or defaulters. A marketing campaign might aim to reduce defaulters while increasing cross-selling to high flyers. A discovery-led analysis of the data might show that there are several types of high flyers with different needs, or that defaulting is related to particular factors, to which some parts of the general group are also susceptible.

Hypothesis-led (also known as verification-led)

This is the conventional approach of standard querying, reporting and statistical techniques. A hypothesis is formed as to which types of consumer have certain characteristics (such as those making them good prospects, or those making them vulnerable to competition), and a test performed to see if this view has significant support from the data. While this approach is still valid, it has the drawback that the hypothesis must be invented before it can tested. A hypothesis-led approach may lead to critical issues being missed. The hypothesis might be confirmed, but it might not be in the best form or as complete in coverage as it could be. However, later on, hypotheses come into their own as discovery techniques start to suggest new areas for hypothesis formation. It may be better to use discovery-led procedures to identify possible hypotheses, and then focus on particular factors for testing. For example, a general segmentation of consumers into retail buying groups could suggest that there exists a large group of elderly couples on low incomes. The hypothesis that this group also correlates with those who take up low-premium insurance policies could then be tested.

Data mining operations – for hypothesis or discovery-led work

Data mining operations can be classified into the generic activities of correlation, segmentation (often referred to as clustering) and propensity. These are defined below. The division between these three is not fixed – there is overlap between them. Some authors give a different division, although there is a good general agreement that this is an informative way to consider the various types. Within each type there are many individual methods, and each method may be applied to a number of different business problems. Note too that each method can be used as part of a discovery approach or a hypothesis approach. For example, we could ask 'Which factors are related to each other, and how well, and which are more related to each other than other factors?' (discovery led), or 'Is factor X related to factor Y, and if so, to what extent and how significantly?' (hypothesis led). It is the sheer volume of the data that pushes companies towards discovery-led approaches, because of the difficulty of determining which factors to hypothesize about!

Correlation (or association, or sequencing – if over time)

How does one factor relate to another? More generally, how does a group of factors relate to some other group of factors? Simple correlations between two factors (whether linear or some other form such as algebraic or rank), usually with an associated confidence factor, are the easiest to understand. Income may correlate with the propensity to buy retailer own brands. But whether higher income causes this behaviour is a different question, not answered by that analysis, but suggested by it. The hypothesis that higher income causes more buying of own brands might depend on a psychological argument about a diminishing need for the reassurance provided by a manufacturer's brand.

In retailing, correlation analysis is known as 'basket analysis', for obvious reasons. For example, correlation analysis might show that there is a group of consumers who buy bacon with eggs and ketchup. The store might want to place bacon, eggs and ketchup close together for consumer convenience, or far apart to ensure that the consumers see other products that they might be tempted to buy. Consumers found to buy gin and tonic might be offered coupons for a different gin type when they buy tonic. Sequencing is association over time, and is a key area for applying data mining, as if buying or response behaviour is very frequent (as in grocer retailing or frequent flying), data mining is needed to explore possible sequencing patterns.

Segmentation (or clustering or classification)

This involves defining classes and assigning individuals to a particular class based on one or more criteria. For example a set of consumers can be classified according to age, or according to home location. It typically tells us little about the members of the resulting groups, as there is still high variability in each group. Multi-dependency classifications can be created by techniques such as neural networks, which learn to discriminate between individuals based on a composite view of their behaviour. For example a neural network trained on product-buying activity could learn the past behaviour of consumers, and be used to predict if new ones would or would not buy the product.

Cluster analysis, or clustering, is a term for grouping similar items together using some numeric criterion of proximity or similarity, and seeing what groups emerge. The groups are chosen such that they maximize the differences between the groups, while minimizing the differences within each group. There is no prior decision on which groups might exist, or which factors may be important. Relational analysis is used to associate similar consumers and put them in the same group. A method of ranking preferences was first proposed by the Marquis de Condorcet at the time of the French Revolution for electing the least unacceptable politician, and has been adapted to the task of choosing the least controversial clustering of consumer groups. The characteristics of each group can then be examined. For example a segmentation of bank consumers might show that older, retired couples in the UK have smaller mortgages than middle-aged couples with children. Very often the segments found do not correspond to exact definitions. They do, however, show tendencies that all the members in a group follow to some degree.

Segmentation is a much-abused term, and carries with it the dangerous implication that once grouped, all consumers within the group behave in the same way. In some companies or industries, the use of the term implies the use of certain determining variables (geodemographic or industry sector, for example), even though these may not be the most important dimensions by which consumer behaviour differs. Segmentation is the process of separating out groups of consumers who are similar (but not the same). Some segmentation methods presuppose that the number of groups is known, and try to find them. Other methods assume that only large groups are important, and try to find all such groups. Some methods require an estimate of the typical members of the group, and attempt to find all the other less typical members; other methods try to find the typical members at the cost of including some who are not typical.

Note that there is no mathematical proof for segmentation. Many outcomes are possible. A good answer is one that is actionable by the business, and the best answer is the one that produces the best commercial results. Note too that data-based segmentation is normally validated by market research techniques. This can create confidence about the validity of the approach, or conversely cast doubt on the model produced.

Text and web mining

Text mining is the mining of words, showing how they are associated. For example, complaints e-mails can be mined to find out what kinds of complaints people have. Many companies mine data about how consumers interact with their Web sites (in particular Web logs), to find out which types of consumers are interested in particular products, offers and communications. The most advanced form of text mining is IBM's WebFountain project. This uses a massive storage facility to keep an up-to-date copy of the World Wide Web. This copy is used for data mining purposes, via various text-mining applications. Here are two examples of its application to consumer insight.

Reputation tracking: in every enterprise, a healthy reputation is the foundation of the business. This application develops an early warning system that can monitor and identify issues as they emerge online. It can identify and track global issues that could affect a company's reputation, spot new and emerging issues, and provide a 360 degree view of how the client is perceived by consumers and others. This is useful in industries where public perceptions heavily influence a company's operations, such as those concerning sustainable development, the environment, or health risks, for example petroleum/energy, consumer packaged goods, retail, automotive, financial/investing, health/pharmaceuticals.

Buzz tracking: this enables monitoring of 'buzz' or 'consumer chatter' about a company or its products. This is used to develop or adjust marketing strategies. Even simple buzz measures can provide useful insights. For example, 'active buzz' is a leading indicator for pop chart movement.

The following case study shows the use of text mining.

TEXT MINING FOR TOURISM

The Agencia Regionale per la Promozione Turistica del Piemonte wanted to learn why visitors were attracted to the Piedmont region of Italy (*Piemonte*). It had found that while Piedmont rated comparatively low against other Italian regions for, say, the number of overnight hotel stays, it rated very highly in the area of gastronomy. Because most of the tourists to Piedmont came to sample the excellent wines and local cuisines, gastronomy was the focus of the first study. To market

Piedmont based on this clear strength, the organization designed a research study to focus on the restaurants of the area. The idea was to analyse the number of typical high-quality restaurants and their densities and distribution, and to compare them with other regions of the country. The results of the study would be the basis for new, better-targeted promotional materials. The project goals were to obtain objective perspectives on restaurants from external sources, to build a database of restaurants, to compare the region with the other regions of the country in terms of number of high-quality restaurants, to study customers' preferences and to get an estimate of restaurant patronage during different periods of the year.

The Agencia extracted the information on restaurants from published tourist and restaurant guidebooks, including both hard copy and online sources. Researchers chose a wide selection of guidebooks in order to get a well-balanced overall view. The project approach was to extract and analyse the relevant information, and to conduct surveys and interviews of restaurant owners and their customers. Restaurant guides contain both quantitative information (including prices and number of tables) and qualitative information (such as cuisine descriptions). They were analysed using SAS text-mining. Taking into account both quantitative and qualitative characteristics, restaurants were divided into a manageable number of different clusters. This made it possible to choose small, but still highly representative, samples of restaurants for ad hoc interviews. For example, in one analysis using clustering procedures, restaurants were divided into six clusters for analysis: spacious traditional restaurants, novelty restaurants, traditional rural restaurants, creative cooking, very good traditional restaurants and prestigious restaurants. Each cluster is homogeneous in the sense that it contains all of the restaurants that have similar characteristics, and therefore it is much easier to analyse all of the restaurants that belong to a group. Further, clusters can be compared based on the percentage of low/high word frequencies in each cluster. Fortunately many guidebooks are now becoming available as online guides and through Web pages, enabling easier access and supporting the transformation of unstructured text to structured data, to combine qualitative and quantitative inputs. One guidebook alone might list thousands of restaurant entries, and if you multiply these numbers by several guidebooks, there is obviously an enormous amount of text.

Results of this analysis provide an understanding of the number and type of restaurants in Piedmont, average meal prices, seating capacities, cooking styles and specialities. This information is matched to the needs of customers from various countries and in different segments for successful promotion. Other departments use this information for operational marketing results. Future text-mining projects include the automated analysis of customer e-mails for further insights into their needs.

Propensity (including prediction and scoring)

Given certain types of things, what can be expected for the remainder? This type of analysis is an extension of correlation or segmentation, but is often used differently. For example, the likelihood of policyholders to lapse, or buyers of toothpaste to buy razors, can both be phrased as propensities: what is the propensity of x to be associated with y? Special techniques exist to do this type of study, and there are applications in diverse areas such as basket analysis and consumer loyalty. Learning what are the important factors that predispose to a particular type of action, such that a numerical score can be assigned to some event, is typically done by fitting an optimization function on multi-dimensional data, and measuring the difference between a given individual or group from the general behaviour of all the groups. For example, a predictive model fitted to the lapsing behaviour of an insurance company's consumers can assign a probability to the likelihood that some groups of consumers might lapse. The size of the group can be used to calculate the risk to the company, and the features of the group can be used to plan a marketing plan aimed at retaining those consumers.

Prediction (or propensity modelling) of likely consumer actions and characteristics, such as to lapse, to remain loyal, to be stable, to buy more, to be profitable, is the key to financial services scoring and direct marketing, but the same mindset is being transferred to many other areas of marketing. In many cases companies want to apply these ideas at the point of contact with the consumer, so that appropriate offerings can be made at this point. The ability to do this has been enhanced by the use of telephone channels and laptop computing (for instance for financial services sales staff). They both allow additional data to be collected from the consumer and input into a scoring module. Of course, there needs to be appropriate and efficient scripting to support the staff member handling the consumer. Identifying 'key questions' and logic structures for scripting is critical to effective use of consumers' telephone time, and to and maximizing sales and profitability. Scripting can now be more dynamic and dependent on consumer responses. It can use the latest version of algorithms that can be easily modified on a regular (learning) basis. In financial services, this may be needed to conform to regulatory requirements, for example for fact finds, where one must demonstrate that the quality of data collection is high, and that needs analysis and financial advice are appropriate.

Following prediction should come testing. This is usually a sample-based marketing activity to validate the prediction – or discover where it does not work. Data mining techniques can easily be adapted to this process. From the discovery of several segments of high-value consumers, a model can be built to predict high-value consumers, and then to test whether the prediction proved accurate when applied to new consumer data sets.

WHERE DATA MINING IS TODAY

Industries that use data mining in marketing include those that have recently started to develop very large additional data sets, for instance because they are starting to use direct techniques in integrated operations companies (as for utilities and retail card providers); and those that have been gathering these data sets for some time, and are now in a situation where better analysis is more important (because of recent competitive pressure) or where they have realized that data holds clues to competitive advantage (for example frequent flyer programmes and retail product data).

Major user industries therefore include financial services; retail and distribution, especially those using direct mail; telecommunications and utilities; and travel and transportation. Many such companies now treat data mining as a normal part of their activities. In fact, the software they use to analyse data, in particular for clustering, may incorporate data-mining approaches of which users are unaware, so routine has data mining become. This strong analytical foundation is the key to advanced understanding of customer attrition and retention, as the next chapter shows.

NOTES

1 Hirschowitz, A (2001) Closing the CRM loop: the 21st century marketer's challenge: transforming consumer insight into consumer value, *Journal of Targeting, Measurement and Analysis for Marketing*, **10** (2), pp 168–78.

2 English, L P (1999) *Improving Data Warehouse and Business Information Quality: Methods for reducing costs and increasing profits*, Wiley, New York, p 339.

3 Selby, D (2003) Materialisation forecasting: a data mining perspective, chapter 20 in T Cirani, G Fasano, S Gliozzi and R Tadei (eds), *Operations Research in Space and Air*, Kluwer, Dordrect, Netherlands.

7 Using consumer insight in developing and retaining consumers

Merlin Stone, Clive Nancarrow, Bryan Foss, Alison Bond and Nick Orsman

THE PROBLEM

Many companies market various products or services to consumers. Consumers buy them with different frequencies. So retaining and developing consumers is rarely just a question of whether the organization sells one or other product or service occasionally to a given consumer, but rather of how often it does it (compared with your competitors) and how long it can keep it going. This chapter investigates how consumer insight is used to help organizations sell more to given consumers, more often, and for longer. For many companies, the prime focus is selling more (cross-selling) and keeping consumers longer (customer retention), but for some it is also selling more of the same (increased frequency) or selling more expensive variants (up-selling). The latter two are quite well understood by marketers, but cross-selling and retention are a minefield. Before examining why, let us look at a case study which shows the kind of insight techniques used in this situation.

TELECOMMUNICATION UP-SELLING

This case study shows how consumer insight was used to support the launch of a new product – 'unlimited UK', from the BT Together range of pricing options, to meet two objectives, high levels of product take-up and increased customer satisfaction. It illustrates the use of intelligent segmentation, targeting and insight to achieve 'personal relevance'. It shows how database marketing can be used as a lead discipline to support the launch of a new product by targeting more valuable customers, before mass communications are launched.

BT is the UK's leading telecommunications services supplier. BT Together with unlimited UK calls was an option added to BT Together pricing options for consumers. It followed the launches of BT Together, the basic option (which includes £2.40 free calls each month) and then of BT Talk Together (renamed as BT Together with unlimited local calls), which also offered free local calls in the evenings and at weekends. The marketing premise of these BT Together options was that customer satisfaction would increase if consumers experienced better value for money, which they would get by choosing the best option for their specific calling behaviour.

There was a market trend towards pricing options, particularly unlimited-type options. Most notable of these was Telewest Unlimited, from a cable provider, offering unlimited local and national calls as well as a basic 14-channel television package for £25 per month. BT Together with unlimited UK calls offered free local and national calls in the evenings and at weekends. It cost £18.50 per month. Also included was line rental and the basic benefits of having a BT Together option – £2.40 free calls per month, reduced international and mobile rates, additional 'Friends and Family' overseas discounts and ability to use the online bill viewing and paying service. The other two options were BT Together with local unlimited calls (includes basic benefits) for 14.50 per month, and BT Together (basic benefits) for £11.50 per month.

The task given to Ogilvy One was to stimulate uptake of the unlimited UK option among BT's consumers, to increase customer satisfaction by making consumers think that they were getting better value and that BT cares about customer needs, and to position the BT Together portfolio of options. The introduction of previous BT Together options had shown that while penetration targets were achieved, awareness and understanding of options tracked by market research was lower than expected. Research showed that many consumers saw telephony pricing 'packages' as 'sneaky'. Consumers suspected there would always be a 'catch'. Fixed-line telephony and pricing options were low interest for most consumers. It was not surprising that many consumers wanted a brand to make sense of the complexity and do the work for them. As many consumers put it, 'Why don't BT look at the calls I make and suggest which package I should be on?'

Unlimited UK was 'new news' (because it covered calls to all UK numbers). However, there was a risk that if it was not explicitly positioned as different from previous options, it could confuse consumers. So the marketing approach selected was to make naming and pricing simple and clear. Naming should be of the 'what it says on the tin' variety: that is, unlimited UK calls. Open and honest pricing meant not using £x.99 but £x.00 or £x.50. Unlimited UK was to be positioned as different from the basic BT Together option and the unlimited UK option, by focusing on the addition of national calls and thus on the emotional and rational benefits of 'Bringing the UK Together'. If consumers could not be bothered to work out which option they should be on, the idea was to take the benefit to them, by introducing unlimited UK relevantly to consumers who would benefit, based on analysis of their calling behaviour. The leading message was the 'new news' of unlimited UK and then the focus was to be on communicating the positioning of the BT Together and its different options.

Role for direct marketing

Direct marketing was used to reach customers with the highest propensity to take up the new product. There were other reasons for the use of direct marketing versus other media during the launch. As the overriding objective was to increase customer satisfaction, it made sense to maximize the moment of generosity – better to bring someone a present (direct marketing) than to ask them to collect it (broadcast). Also, consumers were confused about 'packages'. This suggested using a more explanatory medium to introduce new options. Print allows customers to absorb enough information to make an informed decision. Only if they make a confident, informed decision are they likely to be satisfied. Finally, direct marketing allows different messages to be sent to different customer segments. For example, the message to a customer not on a BT Together option would differ from that to one who was already enjoying the benefits of free local calls.

Targeting and segmentation

Research suggested three dimensions to customer segmentation. The first was financial and based on the saving customers could make with the new option, unlimited UK, typically for customers making many national calls. The targeting algorithm was based on each customer's last three months' calls. The second dimension of segmentation was based on whether the customer already used an unlimited-type option such as unlimited local. This was a proxy for openness to unlimited options. That this might be important came from the insight that not all customers who chose the unlimited local option benefited financially. This was because these customers derived an emotional benefit from 'unlimitedness' – peace of mind that they could call as often or as long as they wanted without a huge bill.

Using these two dimensions, the most likely to benefit (financially and emotionally) were targeted with the unlimited UK proposition, and the less likely to benefit were targeted with a proposition about the BT Together portfolio. The third dimension captured all existing pricing option holdings, of telephony-based options or any Internet option (that is, one of the unmetered Surftime options). This was also a way of reminding consumers of their current option and its benefits. Even if they did not change to another option, customer satisfaction could be created – reaffirming their previous choice of option.

Measurement

This covered the objectives of unlimited UK 'take-up' and its effect on customer satisfaction. The take-up of unlimited UK was measured by response, conversion, sales, and revenue achieved versus targets set. Responders also taking a Surftime option (unmetered Internet usage) with their unlimited UK option were included. Response was recorded through inbound telephone calls through a unique telephone number and through bt.com. The effect on customer satisfaction was measured through telephone research, two weeks after the mail drop. Matched test (with direct marketing (DM)) and control (no DM) cells were set up and sampled from each segment, so the same audience was sampled and any difference between the test and control cells was attributable to the direct marketing communication. Key measures were satisfaction with BT and 'BT cares about customer needs'. Questions on these were asked before diagnostic questions about the communication piece itself. No mention was made to the respondent about direct-marketing activity or the launch campaign as a whole, so there could be no conditioning of the respondent. This meant shifts in any attributes were real perceptions about BT and the result of the direct-marketing activity. 'BT cares about customer needs' was deliberately included as a more specific measure of the 'personal relevance' delivered by the direct-marketing activity.

Conclusions

The activity over-achieved the response target set by 318 per cent. Even without the support of mass communications, which is typically used to initiate the launch of a new mass-market product, the initial direct marketing activity over-achieved response and sales targets. The efficacy of the segmentation is shown by the different response rates achieved: for example in the hottest segment (financially benefit and already on an unlimited option) one in four customers responded to BT. This case also shows that the effective 'take-up' of a new product can be achieved at the same time as improving customer satisfaction. This was achieved by delivering 'personal relevance' (through intelligent segmentation, targeting and insight). After the launch, tracking and analysis focused on the longer-term effects: retention, value over time to BT, share of call volume, and the longer-term effect on customer satisfaction.

The next case study shows the importance of having the correct systems infrastructure for retention.

VODAFONE GREECE

Vodafone Greece is Greece's leading mobile operator. The liberalization of Greek telecommunications created increased competition, from both domestic and foreign telecommunications providers. To succeed in this situation, the company aims to minimize customer churn rates and deliver better service to existing customers, while recruiting new customers. It is reducing customer churn by introducing a streamlined approach to call logging and problem management, while deploying a campaign management system that improves its ability to acquire new customers.

Vodafone Greece introduced Siebel eCommunications, a customer relationship management (CRM) solution tailored to telecommunications. It gives Vodafone a comprehensive view of its customers, helping it to understand its customers' preferences and deliver improved service. By synchronizing and coordinating all customer interactions across different channels, such as telephone, e-mail, face to face, mail and fax, the new system helps improve customer service, increase productivity and maximize revenues. The workflow automation capabilities of the system enable the company to manage every service call efficiently and professionally. Vodafone Greece has integrated the Siebel solution with computer telephony integration (CTI) software to support inbound and outbound call routing. Agents are automatically connected to customers and prospects based on product and service expertise, named account, availability, geography, and other criteria.

CROSS-SELLING

The cross-selling idea sounds simple - sell different products to existing consumers. However, it is more complicated than it sounds, for these reasons.

Supplier–consumer relationships

For many consumers, relationships are much shallower than suppliers believe - even non-existent. In some cases, consumers deliberately choose a portfolio of suppliers for different requirements. They might have their first car serviced by a franchised dealer, but a smaller car serviced by a local garage. They might want current account banking from a major bank, but a credit card from a grocery retailer.

Intermediation

Many markets are intermediated, with intermediaries performing a product election function.

Consumer value – uncertainty and variations

Much of the discussion on cross-selling assumes that a customer base consists of a number of consumers, each of known value, propensity to purchase, media preferences and so on. In fact, this ideal rarely exists. It is only recently that many companies have organized their databases such that their data is high quality and updated properly. Even with this, determining a customer's potential value for other products depends on whether insights from one product are relevant for others. Targeting consumers with high value based on one product for sales of another product assumes that value in the two products is correlated. However, needs patterns might be very different, or the consumer might have very different costs to serve in the two product areas. Thus, in financial services, the consumer might be a high insurance risk but a low credit risk.

Apart from product cost, the cost of managing a consumer, for instance, will vary depending on:

- which channel the consumer uses for regular contact (eg retail, Internet, telephone);
- how often the consumer contacts the supplier with complaints or queries;
- how often the consumer requires non-standard service.

Net profit margin per consumer is often skewed, with a large proportion of lower gross value consumers actually causing a loss. Of course, the Internet can be used to reduce the cost to serve.

Systems to deploy the consumer data

Having good-quality consumer data, which indicates where the opportunity lies, is one thing. Having the business systems and processes to deploy the data so action can be taken at the right time, in the right place, is another matter. In some markets, such as financial services, utilities and telephony, many consumers only buy a single product from each company. Consumers who buy more than one product can be very profitable. They may stay longer, although only a properly constructed time-series analysis can show whether this is true, or whether the relationship is the other way round: that is, consumers who are loyal tend to buy second products. The supposed correlation between holding more than one product and customer profitability has led many companies to justify investment in customer databases primarily on cross-selling potential. The justification is in terms of:

- A lower cost source of leads than, for example, external list rental or media advertising.
- Possibly higher response rates, if consumers are more receptive to offers from a company whose product they already hold. This depends partly on branding and customer service. Many companies have invested much in establishing a wider branding, to encourage consumers to generalize a supposed positive image from their experience of buying only one product.
- Reduction in duplicated mailings: that is, not trying to sell products to consumers who already hold them. This is important if a company has been formed from a series of mergers, or if new products have been added over many years, and each product has its own customer database.

Just focusing on increasing the number of different products bought per consumer can also attract larger numbers of unprofitable consumers. For example, cross-selling household insurance to motor insurance consumers irrespective of their propensity to claim can lead to a higher claims ratio than if prospects were selected primarily on the grounds of low propensity to claim. The same could happen with selling mobile telephony to land-line telephony consumers regardless of their propensity to use either, although here cannibalization might also be an issue. Some marketing managers may have unrealistically high expectations or aspirations about the productivity of cross-selling. 'Cross-buying' might take place anyway – consumers might buy more than one product not because of cross-selling activity targeted at them but because of their exposure to marketing activities for each product, or simply because the two products are brand leaders.

The two case studies below show how two companies approaches cross-selling.

FBTO

FBTO Verzekeringen is a Dutch insurance company selling car, health, home and life insurance policies. Its strategy is to offer attractively priced products and to grow profits by maintaining an above-average level of customer satisfaction. To support this strategy, FBTO depends on fast, reliable operations combined with optimal use of information technology. FBTO uses only direct channels to market its insurance products, interacting with current and prospective customers through direct mail, its call centre and the Internet. Through these channels, the company can reach both customers and prospects with customized, targeted messaging. Call centres are supported by extensive direct-mail campaigns.

FBTO formerly marketed its products through many mass mailings. However, as marketing campaigns were not targeted at those most likely to respond, there was a relatively low conversion rate of mailings to sales. To remedy this situation, FBTO management set three objectives – reduce direct mail costs, increase efficiency of marketing campaigns, and increase cross-selling to existing customers, using inbound channels such as the company's call centre and the Internet. To reduce direct-mail costs, FBTO needed a system that would allow it to model customer behaviour, predict customer needs, anticipate customer reactions to special offers, and then use these insights to make its marketing campaigns more effective. Because FBTO planned to move from few large bulk mailings to many smaller, more highly targeted campaigns, the system needed to allow marketers to create, optimize and execute these campaigns, without having to rely on statisticians.

FBTO now uses SPSS PredictiveMarketing to identify FBTO customers or prospects with a better than average propensity to purchase a product. It enables FBTO to determine individual preferences regarding openness to multiple contacts and preferred distribution channels. FBTO's marketers use the software to create, optimize and execute marketing campaigns. Based on the probability of conversion, customers are selected for personalized product offers and prepared for subsequent interactions. Through this effort, its combined use of different channels is coordinated more effectively, taking into account the latest changes in customer behaviour.

FBTO conducted a one-year test of the system's effectiveness, by rolling out marketing campaigns in an experimental fashion using a control group. Comparing its previous approach of mass mailings with its new, more targeted approach, FBTO found that its conversion rate increased by more than 40 per cent and its direct-mailing costs decreased by 35 per cent. Now FBTO's marketing team can simulate different scenarios and calculate conversion rates and mailing costs in advance. Based on this information, the outbound channel and target groups are selected for each marketing campaign, increasing their effectiveness. FBTO is using SPSS PredictiveCallCentre for real-time cross-sell and retention efforts in its service call centre, as well as PredictiveWeb, to generate highly targeted banner ads and other content on its MyFBTO Web site.

NYKREDIT

Nykredit is one of Denmark's leading financial institutions, offering customers an integrated range of mortgage, banking, insurance and real estate services. It began as a supplier of wholesale mortgage services. When banks launched their own direct mortgage services, this bypassed Nykredit and introduced acute competition into a market that Nykredit had dominated. So in response, Nykredit diversified into banking, insurance, and real estate services and rebranded itself as a full-service financial services company.

Nykredit's decision to diversify beyond wholesale mortgage services presented many new challenges. Established banks were adopting a multi-channel distribution strategy, but they were hampered by years of investment in a retail branch structure. Nykredit did not have this problem, as it had not dealt directly with retail customers, dealing instead through banks and real estate brokers. However, information about customers was contained in separate systems, depending on the products they used. It had many disconnected systems – one mortgage system, and one each for banking and insurance. Using Siebel CRM applications, the company united customer and product information across product divisions and channels of communication, leading to increased cross-selling revenue, improved marketing effectiveness, and a 10 per cent increase in customer loyalty.

Initially, when customers contacted Nykredit it struggled to respond well. Customers were frustrated because it could not maintain a coherent dialogue with them from one call to the next. Customers had to repeat enquiries each time they moved between its representatives. This meant that it took too long to respond. The fragmented customer and product view was undermining customer satisfaction and hindering sales and marketing efforts. The company struggled to cross-sell services, and found it hard to segment customers and develop targeted marketing campaigns. By introducing new systems into all sales offices, its customer contact centre, the sales centre and among insurance agents, Nykredit now has a comprehensive understanding of its customers. The integrated system ensures that each and every customer receives a satisfying experience, increasing the likelihood that he or she will remain a long-term loyal customer. In addition, the system equips Nykredit to cross-sell services to customers more effectively and efficiently.

Now when a customer calls Nykredit, CTI technology generates a 'screen pop' that provides the agent with the customer's complete profile, including the Nykredit services the customer is using, recent mailings, and the status of any outstanding service inquiries. Agents use this information to handle the enquiry. In addition, a customer can be transferred midway through a call to a dedicated specialist if the inquiry cannot be resolved at the first point of contact.

Besides enhancing the quality of customer service, the system makes it easy for agents to target customers with complementary services. For example, if a customer calls Nykredit to raise the amount of an existing loan for the purpose of funding a holiday, the agent may if appropriate recommend a salary account with a credit limit to the customer. If there is no time on the call to discuss this proposal, the agent uses the system to record the customer as a credit-limit opportunity. The agent notes when the customer is due to return from the holiday and uses the system to automatically generate a personalized letter about the loan. This is then scheduled to arrive at the customer's home when the customer returns.

The system also enables Nykredit to route sales opportunities generated in the call centre directly to the customer's local branch. Here, staff have a complete record of the opportunity and all associated activities and can follow it up with a template-based personalized letter or a call. The flexibility of the system enables agents to alternate between accepting inbound sales or service calls, and initiating outbound calls associated with marketing campaigns. Although the telephone and the branch network are the main focal points for the bank's customer activity, the new system also helps Nykredit integrate the Internet as a key sales and service channel. More than half its customers visit the company's Web site every month. Over a quarter check their bank statements and make payments online each month. Many prospects use the company's online Mortgage Calculator service. Together, improved cross-selling and enhanced loyalty have enabled Nykredit to maintain its market share in the face of fierce competition from other Danish financial services providers.

Nykredit uses the system's marketing module to enable the efficient creation and implementation of targeted, multi-channel marketing campaigns. Before, marketing teams had to ask much-pressed IT staff to give them a suitable database of contacts for each marketing campaign, and this took a long time. There were few processes for segmenting customers, managing campaigns and analysing results. Sales and service teams were often unaware that a campaign was taking place, meaning that when a customer follow-up call was received, the teams were ill-equipped to respond. Now marketing teams execute all aspects of the campaigns themselves, including planning, segmentation, campaign set-up, scheduling and workflows. Integration with the sales module ensures that agents are aware of which customers have been targeted for which campaigns.

Data and infrastructure are two of the essentials for achieving higher value per customer, but it is also important for managers to be able to see what is being achieved, so that the company's resources can be utilized.

AXA

Axa Financial in the United States uses Siebel Analytics and Siebel Marketing to determine which products should be offered to a customer based on a sophisticated analysis of that customer's profile. As a result, each customer gets fewer but more clearly targeted offers. Axa built a Campaign Tracking Dashboard, where users select a campaign and track various measures. For example, for a prospect campaign, it can identify how many prospects turned into leads, which leads converted into sales, what kind of sale, and how long it took to determine if the campaign generated additional revenue. It has also developed an Advisor Dashboard, which gives a complete view of each sales associate's business – customers served, number of contracts, number of households, how many contracts per household, share of wallet, cross-sales, household gains and losses over previous year, sales by market segment and product. The data are also aggregated to branch level. Several associates work out of each branch, in some cases hundreds. Everyone accesses the same dashboard, but the dashboard view is personalized by role and level of management, up to regional and national levels. Marketing campaign performance can be viewed in similar detail.

CUSTOMER RETENTION

Retaining good consumers (or those that might become good) is a central topic in CRM, as well as in customer service and branding. The following case studies indicate how a bank, a telephone company and an insurer manage retention using customer data.

THE DREYFUS CORPORATION, UNITED STATES

To manage customer relationships effectively, this bank relies extensively on SAS data warehousing and data-mining techniques. The bank has created a 1.2-terabyte, 4 million household database used for all marketing, sales and strategic planning. Focused on retaining assets, a team of statisticians analyse the data, which includes demographic information, credit and loan applications, spending habits and transactional history, to find out which customers might be thinking about leaving. Warning signs include surges or decreases in the amount of contact from customers and increased numbers of transactions between funds. It can predict that a customer is going to exit three to six months ahead, with accuracy of 80 to 85 per cent.

The bank telephones clients who seem likely to leave, in an effort to convince them to stay. Calls are tailored to each client using offers based on age, wealth, portfolio and recent investment activity. The team applies statistical modelling to the feedback, to find products that might appeal to each individual customer. As a result, the attrition rate for its main product has fallen over the past five years from 22 per cent to around 7 per cent annually – a great achievement given an industry average of around 25 per cent.

The bank also builds models that show how personalized product offerings can reduce attrition rates, enabling it to understand why customers leave and what customers want. Marketers and product managers rely on these models as they build marketing strategies and campaigns. The bank sees payback from these campaigns within four to six months. Data analysis also helps it model a customer's propensity to buy certain products or services, thus enabling it to compute potential lifetime value. Customer attrition has decreased by almost 50 per cent, while the average customer balance has increased substantially, and customer satisfaction has also risen substantially.

US LONG-DISTANCE TELEPHONY RETENTION

Low-cost long-distance tariffs no longer work to keep customers, as many companies offer them. This US telephony market leader has, like many of its peers around the world, switched its emphasis to high-growth areas such as wireless and broadband communications. It relies on data-intensive applications that it builds using SAS Customer Relationship Management Solutions to support customer retention and acquisition efforts.

A recent project integrated customer information across all strategic business units and this company's millions of customers. Analysis of the new integrated customer database allows it to predict and act on likely attrition. Its attrition rate has fallen from 6 per cent to 2 per cent per annum. Existing capabilities such as reporting, segmentation, campaign management, promotion tracking, customer life cycle analysis, and trending and modelling were enhanced to achieve greater return on investment, from both increased sales and decreased churn. The system exploits product bundling capabilities, enabling easier cross-sell to existing customers, potentially doubling revenues. Targeted marketing efforts include focus on customers who are close to existing network facilities, reducing network costs.

US INSURANCE

The Customer Segmentation and Analysis Group of this company focuses on determining more quickly and efficiently which customers hold what products and customer preferences for new offerings. Eighty per cent of the company's cross-sells come from the top 30 per cent of customers, resulting in considerable savings in cost and time, and increased profitability. To identify this required combining policy purchase history, profitability metrics, and demographic and lifestyle data from multiple sources and platforms.

The company's main database, accessed using SAS Customer Relationship Management Solutions, provides data that is supplemented from other sources to create an integrated, customer-focused analytical database. The group develops cross-sell and up-sell models based on 350 variables per customer. This has helped the company reverse a trend. The group used to spend 70 per cent of its time finding and accessing data, and only 30 per cent analysing the resulting information. This has been reversed, allowing more time for both business and IT groups to translate customer data into marketing and sales strategies. The company's greatest gains have come with the company's existing customers, through developing a greater understanding of potential cross-sell opportunities and share-of-wallet estimates. Tracking proves that these developments are successful. The company is also redeveloping relationships with orphan policy-holders who formerly had relationships with financial professionals.

> Modelling has enabled the pairing of prospects with financial professionals. As a result, sales among the orphan group have increased by as much as 276 per cent across product lines.

The kind of good practice illustrated above is being deployed by many companies.

Focus on retention is important where:

- The acquisition costs (including marketing, sales and administration) of new consumers is very high.
- Existing marketing budgets and management are traditionally focused on acquisition, not retention.
- Retention rates vary greatly by product and channel.
- Retention rates are low, so acquisition rates need to be high for the customer base even to stand still.
- A pervasive brand supports high lead generation and acquisition rates, but the same brand is undermined by poor retention, breaking the 'virtuous circle'.
- Not all consumers have the same value. A small percentage of consumers can generate all the profit of a bank or insurer. Retention and development of profitable and marginal consumers becomes critical.

The meaning of customer retention

Success in business is dependent on clear thinking on the fundamental conceptual issues. If customer retention is a major focus, then a key question is what exactly is an organization trying to retain? The list of possibilities is long (see Table 7.1). Behavioural definitions may seem more relevant in some respects, but in other respects may blind marketers to underlying weaknesses in the consumer franchise or disposition. Apathy might lead consumers to demonstrate apparent 'loyalty' or 'commitment' as measured behaviourally. Consumers might resent buying from an organization but be locked into the supplier for various reasons. Here, the reason for staying 'loyal' or 'committed' is that the emotional and financial cost of changing supplier is too great. However, if one or more competitors identify this weakness and make it easy, even rewarding, for a consumer to switch, apparently loyal consumers may do so in droves. Some consumers who do *not* buy feel some 'loyalty'! Barriers (price, access and so on) might prevent a purchase. The customer might not need the category for the time being. However, once barriers are removed, the loyal consumer can demonstrate loyalty or commitment in behavioural terms.

Table 7.1 *The multifaceted nature of retention: some examples*

Behaviour	Hearts and minds (attitudinal variables)
Number of consumers (including dormant)	Salience of brand proposition and its components
Number of active consumers	Brand preference
Frequency of buying decisions	Psychological commitment/loyalty (eg NFO/BJM and Millward Brown models)
Recency of buying decisions	Trust
Size of expenditure	Empathy
Share of expenditure (wallet share)	Propensity to consider buying/use again/contribute resources
Possibly even extent of cross-sales	Propensity to pay more/a premium (eg RI's equity engine model)
Contract	Customer satisfaction/delight
Adjust buying/usage procedures to fit supplier	Likelihood to recommend/advocacy
Routinized re-ordering	Possibly even top-of-the mind awareness
Join club or loyalty scheme	
Proven advocacy	
Enquiries	
Provide information when requested re needs and/or characteristics	
Notify complaints and successes	
Give you more time than competitors/before	
Pay attention to organization's announcements	

Changes in attitudes are more often than not antecedents of changes in behaviour in all but very low involvement product categories. So while behaviour attracts the attention of hard-nosed marketers seeking hard evidence of retention, attitudinal variables (soft evidence) are also valuable. Behaviour is a reflection of the current or more likely historical situation, while attitudes provide clues to future behaviour. In a perfect world, one would examine both behavioural and attitudinal variables and at the same time examine the relationships to determine what drives behavioural disposition. Various research models attempt to do this. For example, RI's Equity Engine and the NFO/BJM Brand Equity Model[1] both link brand attribute ratings to behavioural disposition rather than behaviour itself. The link between the psychological and behavioural is sometimes far from perfect, in terms of consumer satisfaction and behavioural measures of retention or loyalty.[2] Ideally, management should adopt a consumer behaviour model that incorporates all the relevant variables and describes the relationship between them and the organization's halo. This model would be a simple qualitative description of what the organization is there to do. It would create the measures that take it towards this goal. In some organizations it might be possible to develop sophisticated statistical algorithms that permit 'what if' analyses.

As companies have deployed models for retention, they have also gained skills in data mining and data discovery. These make it possible to predict (typically with a reliability of 60–80 per cent) the likelihood of retention, for example predicting the likely lapsers of long-term life insurance products within the first 6, 24 or 60 months, or predicting the time of purchase of a new car. Such exercises (when supported by current knowledge and segment-focused market research) highlight the main predictive indicators and specific data items that help a company develop an agreed definition of customer or product retention. However, from a conceptual or an operational viewpoint, a single variable can rarely represent 'retention'. Any one variable is likely to have shortcomings as a measure of commitment or brand strength.

THE CONCEPT OF LOYALTY

Before moving on to the measurement of retention, we need to address very briefly the concept of loyalty. References to brand 'loyalty' can be found in the early years of marketing.[3] Brand loyalty was a term commonly used in marketing before the wide adoption of the principle of relationship marketing. Brand loyalty is often a consumer device to limit search time and effort. There are so many providers of products and services that it is hard for the consumer to investigate and compare them all. Consumers who are ready to carry out comparisons themselves, rather than choose the most recent offer, will typically only review offerings from a shortlist of between 3 and 10 brands that they already relate to the type of product they need.

'Loyalty' as used by marketers does not have the full significance of loyalty in interpersonal relationships. It is better interpreted as a positive disposition or commitment to a brand that transcends transactions, making repurchase likely in the face of adversity (competitor brand entreaties). The power of such competitive entreaties may prove too much and disloyal behaviour may result. In some markets, such as power supply, telephony or motor insurance, switching benefits vary from year to year and the barriers to switching are low. Nor are unpleasant feelings implied when the consumer is disloyal, as might be the case with an interpersonal relationship. Of course, in some service categories such feelings may exist (when customers abandon local shops, post offices and service providers, hairdresser, restaurant, football club, a friendly financial services adviser and so on).

Although using a single variable as a measure of loyalty (or retention) may not be valid, organizations should try to narrow the variables used to a small range that accounts for all or most aspects of the phenomenon. Use of too narrow a range of variables might explain why the same consumer is defined as 'loyal' in one study and 'not loyal' in another.[4] Stratigos recommends three indices:[5] likelihood to use and renew, to contribute or to recommend. Purchase behaviour and advocacy are both important in some categories.[6] A number of authors clearly define loyalty as a two-dimensional construct - behavioural and attitudinal - and on this basis Liddy developed a two-by-two matrix for loyalty classification, as shown in Figure 7.1.[7] Classifying and counting the consumers in each quadrant might show opportunities and vulnerabilities.

However, this matrix suggests loyalty is binary. In reality there are several different categories of loyalty (exclusively buy from one supplier; preferred brand amongst several; one of many the customer regularly buys; and so on). Some companies also include negative aspects of consumer loyalty, or relationship terrorism rather than advocacy. While a highly satisfied consumer might recommend the supplier to a few others (perhaps encouraged by member-get-member schemes), a terrorist will typically influence many more against such a relationship.

Retention criteria and their measures differ in relevance and importance from product category to category, especially as there is variation in relationship length and in the effect of switching barriers between different products. Finding the best definition and measures is clearly vital to how well an organization can evaluate its performance and link performance to marketing actions. However, even if customer retention is measured, it is not clear how retention levels should be evaluated. It would be useful to know how far senior management monitors customer retention as a key performance indicator, and to determine the extent to which consumer information relevant to retention is collected, and more importantly, used.

THE RESEARCH PROGRAMME

The primary aim of the research for this chapter, which was commissioned by the Royal Mail, was to identify where weaknesses in consumer information, in particular definitions and measures of retention and the use of the information, are most likely to undermine customer retention strategies.

		Behavioural loyalty	
		Low	**High**
Attitudinal loyality	**High**	Latent	High
	Low	Low	Spurious

Figure 7.1 *Framework for loyalty classification*

The main objectives of the research exercise were as follows:

1. To assess the relative emphasis on customer acquisition and customer retention across business sectors, and so focus on organizations that are retention-oriented.
2. To determine whether organizations have agreed clear definitions of what constitutes customer retention.
3. To determine how customer retention is measured.
4. To determine benchmarks used to help interpret customer retention measures.
5. To determine how well organizations use customer retention information.
6. To determine what other consumer information is used.
7. To determine the extent of the belief that cross-selling builds loyalty or helps retain consumers, and the evidence for this.

Method

Using a centralized telephone interviewing facility, 314 telephone interviews were conducted with employees at managerial/director level who were responsible for the marketing from a customer database (or databases) within their organization. The fieldwork was conducted by BJM Research & Consultancy, part of the NFO Worldwide group of companies. Certain business sectors were selected on the basis that they were more likely to be involved in customer management of some description, and that they had databases of at least 400 consumers. In addition, quotas were imposed on larger companies to ensure that a sufficient number of those with 250 or more employees were interviewed. The research included 24 mail-order and 24 dot.com companies for analysis.

The reader should bear in mind the low sample sizes for these companies when examining the findings. Interviews were conducted with managers and directors who might have a relatively 'rosy' picture of how well customer retention is implemented within their own organization. When asking about the customer management process, interviewers were allowed to accept practices even if they only applied to certain (key) consumers. Therefore the survey will probably show an optimum state. This should be borne in mind when looking at the overall results achieved. At the analysis stage, the retention research data were weighted so as to bring the sample into line with the business universe in terms of number of employees and service versus other sectors.

Importance of retention

To establish which organizations were retention-focused, we asked respondents to allocate 10 points between customer acquisition and retention, reflecting the weight they put on each. Over half of the sample (54 per cent) considered customer retention more important than customer acquisition. Only 12 per cent rated customer acquisition above retention. Retention was particularly important to larger companies, those involved in mail order, and those marketing to business customers rather than consumers. A high proportion of dot.coms also focused on retention (the median business life of our sample of dot.coms was one year). Perhaps it is not surprising that retention focuses strongly in the minds of dot.coms given the example set by Amazon and others. It has been observed that 'the success of online marketer Amazon.com can be traced to its emphasis on three all-important business elements'.[8] These are:

- loyalty (the consumer side of retention);
- quality;
- dependability.

Definition of customer retention

We asked respondents if their organization or sphere of operation had an agreed definition of what constitutes customer retention, and if so, what this definition was. Interviewers were instructed to encourage the respondents to state the definition 'as fully as possible'. Only a quarter of the sample claimed that the company had a definition of what constituted customer retention. Those more likely to have said this were larger organizations (39 per cent), those with larger databases (39 per cent), mail-order companies (38 per cent) and dot.coms (40 per cent). At the same time, 20 per cent of those with a claimed definition stated that they did not know what it was. Among those who knew, the majority gave behavioural definitions. The results are summarized in Table 7.2.

Table 7.2 *Definitions*

Keeping customers	23%
Repeat/renew	11%
Response to activity	6%
… rather than attitudinal ones such as:	
Satisfaction	17%

Measurement of customer retention

Although relatively few respondents claimed to have an agreed definition of customer retention, 58 per cent stated that their organization measured customer retention. The larger the organization and the bigger the database, the more likely it was to measure retention. Just over three-quarters of mail-order companies (76 per cent) claimed to measure retention. Dot.coms were the least likely to measure retention.

Interviewers then probed the nature of the measures used, and were instructed to seek precise definitions. Examples were given at the briefing as well as for the analysts coding the answers. Once again, behavioural rather than attitudinal measures were more frequently used. Many of the measures were basic rather than sophisticated. The results are summarized in Table 7.3.

Table 7.3 *Methods of measuring customer retention (base: all claiming to measure – 180)*

	%
Behaviour	**(80)**
Trends in sales, etc	34
Sales (unspecified)	6
Sales at individual level	12
Percentage of customers buying	15
Bought in last period (recency)	5
Frequency	3
Attitude	**(12)**
Measure of declared loyalty/commitment	2
Consumer attitude	8
Product preference	1

Table 7.4 *Benchmarks used to evaluate customer retention*

Base: all measuring customer retention (180)

	%
Comparison with past performance	27
Arbitrary target set by ourselves	14
Level of sales	14
Comparison with key competitors	7
Comparison with best available	4
Against national quality standards	5
Other	14
None	15
Don't know	23

Benchmarking customer retention levels

Among those measuring retention, 38 per cent either did not have a benchmark against which to measure customer retention, or did not know what benchmark (if any) was used. The main criterion against which retention was measured was a comparison with past performance (an introverted perspective). Only a few compared performance with competitors (external perspective). Other external benchmarks used appeared to be more challenging, such as 'comparison with the best' or 'against national quality standards'. Benchmark comparisons in financial services are made more difficult by the large variations in retention by product, within and across companies. The results of this research are summarized in Table 7.4.

How well organizations use customer retention information

Among those claiming to measure customer retention, almost three in five (58 per cent) stated that their senior management regularly monitored retention levels, and a further 23 per cent stated that management monitored them occasionally. Fourteen per cent claimed senior management did not monitor customer retention levels. Those most likely to monitor retention tended to be in larger organizations, in ones with a definition of customer retention, and in particular, in ones with a strong campaign and mailing culture. Sixty-one per cent of those who measure customer retention claimed their organization had a process to ensure retention measures actually had an impact on their business. These tended to be the same company types as those who monitored customer retention levels.

Other consumer information from the database

The survey was also designed to establish the types of information made available on a regular basis from customer databases to help put the internal distribution of retention measures into context. Trend data regularly available from the customer database covered various customer-related issues, but mainly:

- frequency of purchase (61 per cent mentioning);
- number of customers (58 per cent);
- complaints (52 per cent).

Customer defection levels (both actual and predicted) were least likely to be drawn from the database. The results of this are summarized in Table 7.5. Interestingly, between 10 per cent and 15 per cent of those focused on retention thought the individual measures above were 'not relevant' or of 'no value'. One wonders about the logic of this. Perhaps it reflects scepticism about the quality of data collection and research in general!

To determine how sophisticated the analyses of database data on consumers might be, we presented respondents with a prompt list of analyses. The results indicated considerable scope for more sophisticated and

Table 7.5 *Trends regularly available from database*

Total sample	Sub-groups above the norm
Frequency of consumer purchase (61%)	Larger companies (68%), mail order (68%)
Number of consumers (58%)	Larger companies (63%), mail order (68%), those with 10,000+ on database (66%)
Customer complaints (52%)	Manufacturers (64%)
Customer retention (47%)	Mail order (70%), charities (60%)
Length of time have retained customers (47%)	Mail order (51%), charities (66%)
Customer satisfaction levels (42%)	Dot.coms (53%)
Customer loyalty levels (39%)	Mail order (65%), charities (49%)
Customer defection levels (30%)	Mail order (49%)
Predicted customer defection levels (15%)	Mail order (30%)

potentially useful analyses. Overall, in the organizations interviewed, the customer database was broken down principally by the status of consumers (71 per cent mentioning whether customer was new, current or lost) and type of product bought (63 per cent). In detail, the findings here were as follows:

- The most likely company types to organize databases by customer status were mail-order companies (89 per cent), dot.coms (77 per cent), those marketing to individuals (79 per cent), and those with 10,000+ on their database.
- Larger organizations and service-orientated companies were most likely to organize by product/service bought.
- Almost three-quarters (73 per cent) of those with a 10,000+ customer base organized by product/service bought.
- Consumer spend (mentioned by 57 per cent in total) was most likely to be used by mail-order companies (81 per cent), and those with a 10,000+ database (69 per cent).
- Customer profitability, current and forecast, was mentioned by 39 per cent and 32 per cent respectively.
- Current profitability was most likely to be mentioned by large companies (45 per cent), mail order and dot.coms (54 per cent and 60 per cent respectively).
- Breakdown of customer database by forecast customer profitability was most likely to be mentioned by mail order and dot.coms (38 per cent and 44 per cent respectively).

Of course some organizations may market to consumers who all spend a similar amount and are equally demanding in terms of cost to serve. In many markets, such as financial services and telephony, the 80/20 rule often applies, where a small proportion of consumers generate most or even all of the profit due to the wide variation in spend and servicing costs. The implication is that in the absence of good retention and value, resources are unlikely to be distributed efficiently in many organizations.

Respondents were read out a list of information about named consumers that might be collected. They were asked which, if any, was made available to staff who communicate with consumers either on an individual basis (sales rep or service personnel for instance) or en masse (for direct marketing segmentation strategies such as consumer life cycle stages). Nearly three-quarters (74 per cent) claimed to pass on the identity of consumers who had complained – this was higher among small and medium size companies (91 per cent) and dot.coms (88 per cent). The results of this research are summarized in Table 7.6. Note that the figures in Table 7.6 are

Table 7.6 *Information made available to staff in contact with consumers*

Base: all respondents

Identity of consumers …	%
who have complained	74
who are not satisfied	67
who are likely to be lost (based on past experience)	46
who are not spending as much as expected	45
whose purchase pattern has changed	45
And	
important dates for consumers	60
competitor activity	60
none of these	7

higher than in Table 7.5. This is because the question in Table 7.5 referred to trend data being made available regularly, while in Table 7.6 we know from respondent feedback the practice of making information available to staff in contact with consumers included respondents who might do it less than regularly.

The special case of cross-selling

One way to use consumer insight is to look for cross-selling opportunities. Loyal consumers, it is argued, buy a larger cross-section of products or services from an organization.[9] This has double significance as it not only provides additional income but can also be one way of retaining consumers (by increasing dependency between products, and on the knowledge and services of a supplier). We examined the latter argument in an attempt to gauge how credible this retention strategy was, and whether it was ever tested in practice. There was overwhelming agreement with the statement 'encouraging consumers to buy other products helps your business retain customers' – 67 per cent agreed strongly, with a further 17 per cent agreeing slightly. The level of agreement was highest among service organizations and those who marketed to both business and private individuals. The basis behind the strength of agreement tended to be judgement (52 per cent) rather than hard evidence (47 per cent). The company types most frequently claiming to have hard evidence to back up their reaction to cross-selling were mail order and dot.coms, again demonstrating that the marketing culture related to mail and mail-related offerings made the adoption of these processes more likely.

Research carried out relevant to customer loyalty

These findings suggest that much research was carried out that is relevant to customer loyalty. However, this research focuses much more strongly on customer satisfaction (81 per cent) and rates of follow-up after significant contact, rather than on the relationship between customer satisfaction and retention (64 per cent) or on the impact of retention on profits (55 per cent). The reason for customer loss is researched in up to 60 per cent of situations.

Media

Very strong consistency was observed in the current and planned future use of channels and media to separately retain, develop, update and win back consumer relationships. Mail, personal contact and telephone were by far the biggest contributors to each of these objectives, and were anticipated to remain so. The use of e-mail and the Web are growing rapidly, but these are not expected to topple the primary contact methods. Advertising, fax and digital television are perceived to be low contributors to retention practices.

CONCLUSIONS

This chapter shows that despite the enormous attention that has been paid to customer retention in the academic and management press and elsewhere, much is lacking in practice. Many companies that claim to consider customer retention as an important business objective do not define it well or measure it. Companies that are serious about improving customer retention should first define it clearly (and most companies may need several definitions of the term), and put in place operational measures that tell them clearly whether they are achieving improvements in it.

Most companies claim a stronger focus on retention than acquisition, yet only around 25 per cent have a clear definition of retention. This may explain why only half of those rating retention as more important than acquisition go on to measure it, and also why retention measures are often basic, behavioural and short-term focused. Database analyses are limited, with profitability and lifetime value rarely calculated, and neither are behavioural warnings and signs of disaffection. When evaluating retention, benchmarks are often arbitrary or non-existent or historical. Less than one in six used external benchmarks including best practices and competitors. Less than half had activities to understand what drives loyalty or loss, or examined the impact of retention on profit.

Although the optimism of the participants was undermined by the survey findings to a great extent, there seems to be good business potential for many organizations if they:

- Define customer retention fully and in a relevant way for their business and customer base. Good thinking at this point should be the foundation for good practice.
- Operationalize the measures, and also consider attitudinal and behavioural measures.
- Monitor these measures with management attention and meaningful benchmarks.
- Act on the above.

NOTES

1 Morgan, R P (2000) A consumer-orientated framework of brand equity and loyalty, *International Journal of Market Research*, **42** (1), pp 65–78; Wright, L T and Nancarrow, C (1999) Researching international brand equity: a case study, *International Marketing Review*, **16** (4/5), pp 417–31.
2 Kangis, P and Zhang, Yangwei (2000) Service quality and customer retention in financial services, *Journal of Financial Services Marketing*, **4** (4), pp 306–18.
3 Styan, G P H and Smith, H (1964) Markov chains applied to marketing, *Journal of Marketing Research*, Feb, pp 50–54.
4 Backman, S (1988) The utility of selected personal and marketing characteristics in explaining consumer loyalty to selected recreation services', Texas A & M, USA.
5 Stratigos, A (1999) Measuring end-user loyalty matters, *onlinemag*, Nov–Dec, p 74; 7 Kangis, op. cit.
6 Kangis and Zhang (see note 2).
7 Liddy, A (2000) Relationship marketing, loyalty programs and the measurement of loyalty, *Journal of Targeting, Measurement and Analysis*, **8** (4), pp 351–62.
8 Margolis, B (1999) An Amazon.com story: lessons learned? *Direct Marketing*, **62** (3), p 57.
9 Griffin, J (1996) The Internet's expanding role in building customer loyalty, *Direct Marketing*, **59** (7), p 50.

8 Sharing consumer insight – partnerships and loyalty schemes

Merlin Stone, David Bearman, Alan Tapp, Stephan A Butscher, Paul Crick, David Gilbert, Tess Moffett and Nick Orsman

WAYS OF SHARING CONSUMER INSIGHT

In this chapter, we investigate the sharing of consumer data and the value of partnerships, with an extended case study of retail loyalty schemes, one of the dominant forms of data sharing. We start by noting that how companies share insight with business partners is influenced by the type of data, the sharing process (level of detail, timing of transfer and access, and hosting), and data protection legislation and industry conduct guidelines.

Types of data

These are the commonest types of data relating to consumers likely to be of interest to partners:

- demographic and lifestyle data, including interests;
- product preferences;

- media preferences and responsiveness;
- buying behaviour – transactions (what, where, how often, etc);
- complaints, merchandise returns, claims, risk management and exposures;
- mode of payment;
- use of loyalty scheme;
- product data – inventories, orders of partner's consumers;
- product movements within the company;
- promotional outcomes – redemptions, sales;
- promotional plans, targets, performance and histories – what works, how well;
- revenues and profits from customer relationship.

Sharing process

Data can be shared at an aggregated or individual level, and sometimes using a halfway house, with data made available in small consumer segments; or perhaps some at an individual level, but with other data grouped. In general, the more detailed the transfer, the greater the perceived risk. The timing of transfer (or access by one partner to another's data) can vary from online to batch. Hosting may be by swapping: that is, each partner imports the other's data, partially or completely via a third party. The role of a third party (which is discussed further in Chapter 11) is already well established, and includes:

- standard list rental, where the role of brokers as experts in managing data acquisition is well understood (eg selection criteria, data quality, control of contractual terms);
- tagging of client databases by data suppliers – adding data to an existing consumer or prospect file;
- prospect pool supply – finding prospects that match a client's existing good consumers, or in its negative form, identifying prospects to be avoided because they match a client's 'bad consumer' profile;
- one-off data pooling – assembly of a consumer/prospect file from various client and external sources;
- outsourced management of a consumer or prospect file.

Data protection legislation and industry conduct guidelines

Data protection standards have typically varied by country, according to regulation and privacy expectations, and the general culture. In some

Table 8.1 *Arguments for and against sharing insight*

For	Against
■ Improved targeting of marketing strategy ■ Improved targeting of marketing communications ■ Improved/more relevant content of marketing communications ■ Improved product planning ■ Improved pricing ■ Reduced costs of data acquisition ■ Reduced costs of data processing ■ Reduced media advertising ■ Reduced direct-mail expenditure ■ Increased responsiveness to changing market conditions ■ Gaining an advantage over competition at the same level of the value chain ■ Bargaining more effectively with other value chain partners (eg divide and rule) ■ Reducing market risk ■ Learning/skills transfer	■ Accentuate marketing skills difference between partners ■ Increased complexity of the marketing process ■ Increased marketing costs ■ Increased problems with data management ■ Conflict caused by mismatch in objectives/types/pace of marketing/sales process ■ General conflict of interest ■ Conflict of interest over consumer ownership ■ Conflict of interest over data ownership ■ Temporary nature of some business relationships ■ Systems incompatibilities ■ Legal complexities (regulatory, data protection) ■ Data security ■ Political difficulties ■ Skills shortage – data analysis ■ Skills shortage – data management

cases these are supplemented by the business conduct guidelines of an industry or market, for example in insurance and banking. More recently Europe has aligned its data protection legislation. Demand is increasing in some markets (such as the United States) to tighten regulation that can protect individual privacy, as data use and sharing becomes more prevalent. For more on this, see Chapter 9. The arguments for and against sharing consumer insight are given in Table 8.1.

What influences the sharing of consumer insight

The reasons for or against sharing data include the following.

Sector-specific issues

These might be regulatory, but they can also be cultural: for example, a history of conflict; or to do with the channel: for example, the supplier is more remote from consumers than are retailers.

Competitive situation

This includes factors such as how many major companies are competing on each side of the market, their size distribution, their relative competitive strengths (in products, distribution, branding). These factors tend to determine the risks if competitors get hold of information that has been shared. For example, if the customer list of a weak company gets into the hands of a strong company, the latter will be in a good position to mount a competitive attack.

Relative strengths and weaknesses of different partners

This can apply to areas such as consumer insight management or information technology – where sharing with a partner perceived to have a greater or lesser capability can lead to the perceived risk of better/worse exploitation of data, and consequent problems with consumers or competitors. Skills and systems compatibility problems can have their origin here.

The particular marketing/sales approach of the different companies in the supply chain

This includes the extent of use of targeted marketing. In many distribution chains, the level nearest the consumer is involved in direct marketing.

Perceived costs and benefits of sharing

This is usually determined by partners' views about the above factors. There is little doubt about general benefits – the issue is whether it pays particular companies, or whether they can work with each other well.

Availability of trusted independent intermediaries to help with the process of sharing

Third parties are generally trusted with demographic and lifestyle data. Some of it may be contributed or collected for specific partners. In financial services, this extends to transaction data (such as on credit cards).

Relationship between prospective partners

This includes strategic agreements to meet other objectives, and of course trust.

Why bother? A reminder

Data sharing is just a means to an end. As we stressed in the Introduction, managing consumers to meet the needs of both consumers and supplier depends on understanding and aligning their haloes. This means that the main reason for sharing is that consumers and businesses can see a clear, shared benefit. If an organization is genuinely aiming to do the best it can for consumers, sharing data should be done only if it helps to achieve that.

LOYALTY SCHEMES

Store loyalty cards were widely developed during the mid-1990s, with retailers aiming to develop closer, long-term relationships with consumers.[1] However, Pressey and Mathews[2] emphasize that despite the recent use of loyalty cards and database marketing techniques by UK retailers, most transactions are 'discrete, short-term, one-off acts'. Retailing is becoming more competitive, so retailers have sought different ways of improving sales and profits. They are adopting more transformational relationship marketing and loyalty schemes which aim to build greater customer loyalty and retention, and develop methods of creating longer-term relationships, with the aim of improving profits.[3] Loyalty schemes are just one of many initiatives used to supplement the traditional weapons of brand, customer service, price, merchandise range, product promotions and location. Today, there is a strong focus on the end-to-end shopping experience, on winning and keeping customers and improving the share of selected consumers' business. IBM research[4] shows that:

- increasingly discerning consumers are demanding more services and information;
- heightened competition in mature, saturated markets is making it more difficult for retailers to sustain differentiated brands and value propositions;
- the rapid evolution and adoption of new technologies present both opportunities and risks.

Why bother with loyalty schemes

Specific insights into the consumer loyalty that retailers hope to reinforce by loyalty schemes come from Ogilvy's Loyalty Index programme, including its BRANDZ brand equity consumer research study. This shows a very strong link between emotional loyalty and financial value. 'Emotional' is the key word. It refers not to discount or other temporary loyalty, but to a belief by the consumer in the retailer and its products, value and service. However, retailing is special in that location can skew behavioural loyalty strongly. So even if a consumer has a strong loyalty to a particular retail brand (particularly for convenience shopping goods such as grocery foods), shopping patterns will still be dominated by access. Also, social trends show increasing consumer desire for autonomy and special experiences in relation to the store and the brand. Many additional benefits (including relevant promotions) offered by retailers may be satisfiers rather than differentiators. As consumers become more aware and educated, striving to differentiate could add to retail marketing costs. Still, those not offering these benefits might lose market share. All this places a limit on what can be achieved by a retail loyalty scheme, although most retailers argue that their loyalty schemes help concentrate spend with them, for consumers who have choice of where to shop.

Consumers most strongly bonded to a brand, whether a retail store, consumer product or service, can be worth up to 20 times more than other consumers. Brand leaders have more customers who are bonded to them. In the UK, two out of the top 10 bonding brands were retailers (Boots and Tesco). The relationship between bonding and market share in retailing is given in Figure 8.1. Loyalty needs to be managed, but can it be managed cost-effectively? In the UK, store loyalty schemes that focus just on financial measures of loyalty – up-sell, cross-sell, frequency of visit, even customer retention – tend to fall into disfavour and get replaced. Those focusing on (or forming part of an initiative focusing on) transforming marketing and customer management tend to work better and last longer.

The choice facing retailers

Running a loyalty scheme is a big managerial task. What the consumer sees – a card, a statement, coupons, bonus points – is the tip of the iceberg. Behind this lies a managerial and logistics operation involving card issuing, database management, call centres, statementing, negotiation with partners in the scheme and suppliers of bonus merchandise, and so on. The options are summarized in Table 8.2.

Generally, the lower down the table, the more complex the systems, process and managerial infrastructure, but the greater the economies of scale, particularly in systems, database management, customer communication and negotiation of partnerships with suppliers of benefit offers.

The benefits and costs of customer loyalty schemes

These are summarized in Table 8.3.

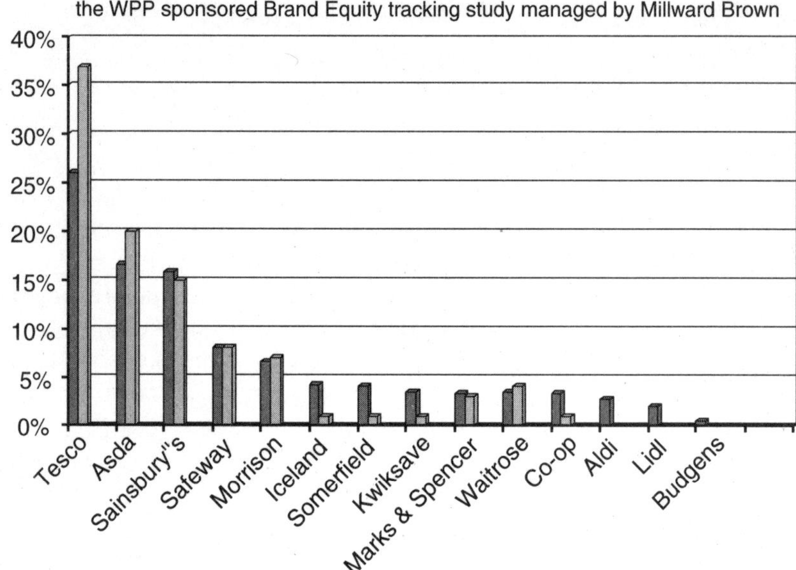

Source: OgilvyOne and Millward Brown

Figure 8.1 *Relationship of bonding and market share: grocery stores – UK*

The mixed history

In the UK, there has been a mixed history of schemes. Around 80 per cent of UK households participate in at least one customer loyalty scheme. The average consumer participates in three schemes. In the grocery market, Tesco claims a 'first mover advantage' - not in the sense of having a scheme but in the sense of being the first where the scheme is a strong part of a transformed marketing approach. Boots is part-way there. Other schemes were stopped for various reasons. Safeway's was stopped mainly because as a second-tier player the scheme had to give too large a discount to get a response from consumers. Sainsbury's Reward Card was transferred to the Nectar scheme, along with similar schemes from Barclaycard and BP. One of the prime issues for Nectar is whether some participants joined just to reduce costs. However, whether schemes are continuing or discontinued, the net effect has been to raise the expectations of many consumers about being rewarded.

The reason that some of the schemes do not continue is that they do not follow some simple rules of loyalty management, which we summarize as follows:

Table 8.2 *Scheme options*

Scheme type	Main characteristics	Example
None	No loyalty scheme. Promotion by in-store price cuts, couponning, etc. Store credit card may be used as way to give service benefits (eg cardholder evenings)	Asda, John Lewis Partnership, Waitrose, Wilkinson, Marks & Spencer (at time of writing)
Solus	Own scheme (may give as benefits offers from partner companies)	Tesco (in origin), Boots, Homebase, new Somerfield scheme, Safeway (discontinued)
Shared	Companies with own schemes share some aspects	Previous Somerfield scheme (with BP and others) Tesco scheme now shared with limited number of other retail partners, eg Allders.
Consortium	Third party sets up and runs scheme	Nectar

- **Know how customer relationship management (CRM) makes money.** Assess which value drivers are in scope. Ensure all CRM activities are targeted at driving value. Omit activities that do not add value.
- **Manage and use data as a strategic asset.** Data is the lifeblood of any CRM programme. Be 'hands on' in gathering and using data. Know it inside out and learn how to use it.
- **Segment consumers.** Understand what behaviours drive value and the Pareto effect. Track changes over time to predict changes in behaviour. Anticipate and act.
- **Create an indispensable/simple value proposition.** Consumers must see value to engage. The best propositions either enable consumers' lives and/or are related to their personal interests.
- **Leverage the brand.** A strong, well-liked brand with the right attributes for the target market is a valuable asset.
- **Carry out continuous testing.** Learn which offers work with which target audiences, and how this changes over time. Do more of what works; stop doing what does not.

Table 8.3 *Benefits and costs of different approaches*

Solus scheme		**Additional with shared scheme**
Customer benefits	▪ Discount. ▪ Promotional offers. ▪ Awareness of products and services. ▪ Basis for information exchange and even relationship, if the consumer wants it. ▪ Consumers feel more positive about reward, thanking or treating aspects of schemes than about discounts. Some enjoy the 'game' of accumulating points through offers to get the rewards or treats they want. ▪ Benefit from buying power of scheme organizer to get third-party offers which consumers could not otherwise afford.	▪ Easier points accumulation. ▪ Wider choice of benefits.
Company benefits	▪ Better insight of actual and potential customer value, behaviour and consumer needs, providing a quantified, measurable basis for determining and implementing efficient policies on customer acquisition, retention, development (up-sell, cross-sell). ▪ Provision of actionable data, ie in a form that can support operational decisions and effective measurement. These include new product, development targeting for new product launches (eg to early adopters), linking with suppliers for product development and targeted marketing activity, allowing offers to meet local needs, development of store formats according to local consumer needs. ▪ Consumer insight for use by other parts of marketing and of the company – for some companies it is the first time they get a clear view of how their business affects individual consumers; associated segmentation and other benefits. ▪ Creating focus – bringing many disparate promotional efforts together with consumers as the focus.	▪ Cross-sell broadening. ▪ Shared learning. ▪ Economies of scale in communication and rewards negotiation. ▪ Delegation of decisions/management focus. ▪ Added branding strength (if partners are carefully chosen to add to rather than detract from the overall branding of the proposition).

Table 8.3 *Continued*

	■ The ability to get quicker learning from launches, other trial activities and marketing activity in general. ■ Improved pricing management and its balance with promotional activity. ■ Prioritizing investment decisions about the overall offer, ie between price, promotions, space and range, environment, customer services, customer communications, product development, format types. ■ Informing trade-offs between different marketing vehicles, by providing common datasets for evaluation (the impact on specific consumers is known). ■ Allows brand strength to be extended and deepened though use of more targeted communication and (in some cases) service differentiation. ■ Allows outsourcing of complex marketing tasks which demand a different management model (based on direct marketing and individual customer communication) from the conventional retail marketing model (broadly based on mass and store-level communication).	
Company costs	■ The discount. ■ The added complexity of data management (gathering, hosting, interpretation, use). ■ Absorption of management attention. ■ Possible confusion caused by complexity.	■ May not be incremental discount – possibly less. ■ Possibly even saved promotional costs. ■ If not used properly, a shared scheme is worse than no scheme.
Issues	■ Value model – does the scheme pay, does it fit with the retailer's overall business model, do individual activities within the scheme pay?	■ Possible increased complexity of data management. If a company wants to use insight persuasively it must control data structures, so partner schemes become additions to the core

(continued)

Table 8.3 *Continued*

Solus scheme	Additional with shared scheme
	rather than a real shared data approach. ■ Sharing of data complex to manage, invoking issues of trust and data protection.* ■ Sharing of strategy – explicit and implicit.

Note:*For more on the problems involved here, see Stone, M and Condron, K (2001) Sharing customer data in the value chain, *Journal of Database Marketing*, **9** (2), pp 119–31.

- **Make investment decisions in the long-term context.** Understand/ decide which capabilities to develop and where investment will be needed over time. This is a journey, not a destination.
- **Deliver the promise consistently across touch points.** Process, technology and people must integrate seamlessly across all channels. Failure in the promise will turn consumers off.
- **Measure.** Successful CRM programmes continuously, consistently and clearly measure their impact. Invest effort in measuring the true financial impact of CRM activities.
- **Develop a new people and organizational framework.** CRM requires new roles and responsibilities and a shift in mindset and behaviour. Plan the organizational change thoroughly.
- **Keep the scheme as simple as possible, given the often complex aspirations for it.**

The reasons why companies cannot observe these rules is that it is hard to do so. Let us see why.

WHAT CUSTOMER LOYALTY SCHEMES INVOLVE MANAGERIALLY

Loyalty schemes involve change in all the areas below:

- processes;
- marketing management;

- consumer-facing IT;
- card management systems;
- database management;
- HR;
- customer service centres;
- internal communications;
- in-store promotion;
- gathering and using consumer data across channels – store, call centre, Web, mobile;
- applied analysis of consumer data;
- segmentation and targeting;
- communication;
- campaigns;
- channels;
- differential pricing/benefits;
- partnership management;
- outsourced supplier management;
- integration with strategy.

Let us examine some of these areas in detail.

Applied analysis of consumer data[5]

The key area here is analysis of transaction data to predict future purchases. Targeted campaign activity based on communication preferences can be tested to check the accuracy of the prediction model. Fundamental to this is the need for continual testing, and for analytical processes to determine the learning from each campaign activity, and to apply them to the next communication activities. This requires a shift in mindset for traditional category/brand/product marketers towards understanding the role that the category/brand/product plays in consumers' lives. The contention between different marketing offers needs to be managed to avoid making competing and inappropriate offers or being restricted to providing discount vouchers at the point of sale. Consumers must be assessed for total spend, not just that currently spent on a specific retailer.

It also requires a shift in mindset for business managers towards accepting that the pursuit of loyalty is a journey, not a destination, with much learning along the way. Not everything will work right first time. Mistakes will be made and money will be lost, particularly in the early part of the journey. Risk money must be set aside to facilitate data-driven marketing 'research and development' (for example, modifying the design of data assets to accommodate new channels and new variables, and experimenting with new data sources).

There is a change in how data on consumer preferences is captured – a move away from market research, with data now used to support extrapolation across the database. Behavioural data about consumers is used to target 'look-alikes' (people with similar profiles to groups of individual consumers). Using a prospect file for a retail catchment area, it is possible to locate individuals within post codes and predict the likelihood that they will respond to a particular offer.

The understanding of what data are needed to support loyalty schemes is weak. There are two main reasons for this. First, marketers cannot articulate their requirements for data to support their marketing activity because they do not understand information management. Second, practitioners often think that data (and technology) is just too complex to grasp, and should be simplified so that it becomes easy to grasp.

An appropriate and sufficient business architecture

The average mass-market retailer has tens of thousands of products and has a weekly footfall of millions of consumers, so lots of data are available. The marketer must understand which data elements indicate current and historical loyalty behaviour, and what level of summarization is most appropriate to support marketing decision-making processes and operational processes at each consumer touch point – either in-store or across multiple channels. Managers must define what they need and consider how it should be managed. Changes are also required in processes and possibly in the technology platform.

The customer service centre (CSC)

A sophisticated customer loyalty scheme involves several different parties, such as the loyalty scheme management, external partners, financial partners and of course, the members. Each involves different information, tasks, types of communication and so on. This complex system must be organized efficiently and in an appropriate structure. One of the best ways to do this is to set up the organization around a central loyalty scheme CSC. In most cases the CSC is either closely linked to, or even partially identical with loyalty scheme management, so that the responsibilities are also of a managerial nature. The CSC coordinates, oversees and organizes the everyday business of the loyalty scheme. Loyalty scheme management is more involved in developing and managing the overall concept, adjusting and improving it. In some cases scheme management gets involved in daily management, and may become part of the CSC. This at least ensures that it is in touch with its realities, but can weaken its focus on strategic development.

Should the CSC be handled internally or by an outside service provider? A loyalty scheme works well, produces good results and transmits its ideas to consumers if it is at least partly run by the company that sponsors it. The company's people are more involved and do not see it as 'another job', and the members are seen and treated more as customers rather than as callers. It is also easier (though not necessarily cheaper) to integrate the scheme with the company's marketing and service policy. But outside help can mean reduced cost, special expertise and so on. One determining factor is the desired neutrality of the CSC, which manages relationships between internal clients, suppliers and business partners. Some companies might find this neutrality difficult to maintain with an in-house CSC. Regardless of whether the loyalty scheme is kept in-house or partly outsourced, loyalty scheme management should always be closely involved in the scheme's daily procedures, not only to control operations but also to get input needed to improve the scheme concept.

Database and analysis

A well-organized database is critical to a loyalty scheme's success, not only because the loyalty scheme itself can be managed more efficiently, but also because the whole company can benefit more from the customer loyalty scheme if it has a database. The database technology must be able to handle large amounts of data quickly, reliably and efficiently. It should be expandable and compatible with other systems and programs (such as analytical software and dealer network support systems). It should allow analysis to be presented in a very customized and flexible way, depending on which department requests the information. The operational systems of the CSC should interface with the database, so that customer service representatives can extract or add data while they are on the phone with a member or in a similar situation. Finally, data quality must be maintained, as failure here can lead to a very high volume of customer queries.

Integrating the loyalty scheme into the sponsoring company

The more independently the customer loyalty scheme can be managed, the more effective it will be. This does not mean neglecting other company divisions, since of course their goals need to be considered as well. It means that the loyalty scheme management should have the authority to make decisions on how to run the loyalty scheme, how to organize it and which benefits to offer, without having to confer with outside parties. This shows how similar loyalty scheme management is to product management. In both areas the responsible managers have to be able to make fast and independent decisions concerning the loyalty scheme or product for which they are responsible. If situations arise that require a quick decision, such as unanticipated price reductions by a major competitor or the introduction of a new loyalty scheme by another major player in the industry, this independence is of particular importance.

Loyalty schemes and the consumer insight they produce can lead to significant changes in how a retailer markets, as shown in Table 8.4. Many retailers need help with the changes entailed by loyalty schemes because they are cannot cope with the speed of change imposed on them by their competitors, by technology or by consumer behaviour.[6] A loyalty scheme focuses so strongly on these three areas, in an accountable way, that it can be the catalyst for transformation, or indeed be the transformation itself. Unless senior managers have not only 'bought in' but actively developed, promoted and resourced the new customer-focused way of doing business, this transformation might not occur. Participation in a shared scheme can accelerate change, mainly because a well-run shared scheme gives access not only to advanced skills and techniques and economies of scale, but also because if the retailer works closely with scheme management, the retailer can learn quickly how to change its own marketing. However, if there are trust issues (such as worries about the security of shared data) or political issues (a version of the 'not invented here syndrome'), then a shared scheme can be weaker than a solus scheme in terms of its potential to create change.

A loyalty scheme encourages transformation in the general direction of CRM. This applies particularly to:

- the marketing planning process;
- communication management – channels used, coordination and focus of communication;
- how information is created, analysed, interpreted, shared and used to manage customers and partners;
- the proposition to all consumers, or certain segments, to improve success in customer recruitment, retention and development, and management of problems;
- how the organization is focused, accountabilities and so on;
- planning and implementation processes.

Table 8.4 *Loyalty schemes and marketing change in retailing – some examples*

Area of marketing to be transformed	Type of transformation
Product/range management	By changing the focus from what sells well in stores today to what further products and services consumers could buy tomorrow, whether physically in the store or as a result of a visit to the store (ie that they could take the brochure for and buy later)
Focus and strategy	Moving from focus on product and sales volume to focus on consumers and on customer value
Customer data management	Move from poor quality (and possibly poor compliance with privacy or data protection laws) of customer data management across different functions (marketing, customer service) to a situation where customer data is managed and exploited well
Analysis, targeting and measurement	Move from tactical focus of analysis and targeting (typically optimizing individual campaigns) to strategic customer management focus, with the result that it is possible to measure the overall effect of different customer management initiatives (and indeed the effect on consumers of any sales, marketing or service initiative)
Store location	Locating stores based on the full potential of consumers in the area, not just what they currently buy within the range currently supplied by the retailer
Customer service	Focus on improving service to the best customers (while giving good service to all)
Competitive strategy	Deliberate attack to win certain consumers away from competitors – either absolutely or in terms of share of business – and defend certain customers from competitive inroads
Supply chain	Streamline number of suppliers by identifying which suppliers best meet the needs of priority customers
	Optimize the number and structure of stock-keeping units (SKUs) by allowing the deletion of SKUs which, although they provide some profit, play no significant role in attracting or retaining more valuable customers
Promotional management	Focus on adding value, to prevent the loyalty card from being used as a discount card rather than influencing shopping destination and driving consumer footfall and share of wallet that consumers spend with the retailer

(continued)

Table 8.4 *Continued*

Area of marketing to be transformed	Type of transformation
Communication management	Much stronger focus on personalized communication, and measuring its impact across all channels
Multi-channel communication	Move to use the loyalty card across multiple customer touch points (eg Web site, call centre and store) and in leveraging customer data across these touch points (do you know who is your most valuable customer across all channels?)
	Integrate data from these different channels to produce a uniform view of how a consumer is behaving, and what offers/ rewards can be given, through which channel, to gain maximum response/greatest efficiency (plus joined-up, consistent processes underpinning this)
IT strategy	Change to focus on managing the consumer
Human resources	A more customer-oriented, value-oriented HR-strategy
	Empower front-line staff with better information (ie at the cash register, client information pops up and allows a personalized comment)
	Provide a more professional and accountable context for managing marketing staff
Overall marketing efficiency	Understand which activities work best and channel funds to them
	Focus marketing activity more strongly on retaining and developing existing customers

HOW SOME LEADING RETAILERS ARE MANAGING THEIR LOYALTY SCHEMES

The Tesco Clubcard – an astute combination of outsourcing and insourcing

Tesco Clubcard's success is part of a wider success. Launched in 1995, it has been part of a transformation of Tesco's marketing that extends beyond its traditional retail product range into personal financial services (2.5 million customers and £40 million annual profit) and Internet ordering. Tesco.com is one of the few grocery e-tailers to make an operating profit and is the world's largest. The Clubcard also paved the way for

Tesco's market share growth in non-food items. Managing such a card involves very large numbers of people (such as 500 manning a hotline). Tesco mails its members every three months with their discount vouchers and coupons, and the call centre gets thousands of calls from customers who want to know when they will get their mailing. The analysis that provides the insight to enable the targeting of promotions is outsourced to dunnhumby, the design of mailings to EHS Brann, and the mailing to Polestar. The Clubcard magazine has a run of nearly 9 million four times a year. Forward Publishing, a specialist in customer magazines and contract publishing, produces it. The general verdict of retail commentators is that Tesco's Clubcard is one of the most successful schemes in the world precisely because it is part of a retail transformation, and the reason that so many of its competitors are trying to follow in its footsteps.[7]

Jigsaw – a loyalty case study in consumer goods

The Jigsaw Consortium, a joint venture between Cadbury Trebor Bassett, Kimberly-Clark and Unilever, was founded in 1997 and includes Cadbury Trebor Bassett, Kimberly-Clark and three Unilever companies: Birds Eye Wall's, Lever Faberge and Unilever Bestfoods. The companies in the Jigsaw Consortium share insight and experience across the consortium because they are broadly non-competitive. Indeed, two of the three (Unilever and Kimberly-Clark) share a very strong common competitor, Procter & Gamble.

The core of Jigsaw's activities is the database, now one of the largest in the UK, which it has created combining data from the partner companies plus new data collected by Jigsaw. Partner companies use the information it provides to create relationship marketing activities across their brand portfolios, and to understand consumer behaviours and attitudes. The consortium appointed OgilvyOne (London) in early 2003 as a new partner in an agreement designed to exploit the full potential of the Jigsaw database and extend the quality of services that Jigsaw offers. The Jigsaw Consortium operating companies now have access to additional expertise and resources to build on the successes that Jigsaw has already achieved. OgilvyOne service supports the implementation of high-quality communication programmes, and includes the provision of support services such as data acquisition and maintenance, database management, data analytics, insight management and evaluation. The OgilvyOne team also provides insights and analyses in support of brand and category management objectives, and manages several third-party supplier relationships in areas like database management and data provision.

The Nectar scheme – another example of outsourcing

Nectar is a coalition loyalty scheme in the UK developed by Keith Mills, the founder of Air Miles, and his company Loyalty Management UK. It was launched in autumn 2002. Nectar brought together leading UK retailers – Sainsbury's and Debenhams, Barclaycard, the largest UK credit card provider, and BP, the leading auto fuel supplier. Sainsbury's had its own solus scheme before, and merged it into Nectar. It was keen to join Nectar because Tesco, helped by its card, had been making steady inroads into Sainsbury's customer base for years, overtaking it to become the UK's number one grocery retailer.

Nectar claims it can achieve all the promotional objectives of its partners and more, at significantly lower costs. In other countries, Mills has shown that partners in his schemes achieved significant growth in market share and profit, reductions in advertising spend and in the size of marketing departments, and sustained this growth even while closing branches. Recently the scheme expanded to include Ford, Vodafone and others. The Nectar launch was its parent company's most successful ever, in terms of the proportion of households in the country joining its scheme two months after programme launch (nearly 40 per cent in the UK). Nectar maintains that one of the major benefits to its partners is customer recruitment (from each others' customer bases), but the long-term benefits come mainly through outsourced marketing, as in the Jigsaw case. Interestingly, Nectar itself is an astute user of outsourcing, with many best-of-breed specialist suppliers contracted to it. In addition Nectar provides expertise in marketing insight to each of its coalition members.

Sainsbury's in Nectar

Since 1999 Sainsbury's has collected data on all loyalty card members. With millions of customers and a data warehouse that provides only raw transactional data, the challenge is to enhance this with demographics (including age, gender, number of children), lifestyle data, mailing history, product IDs and more. The loyalty card data makes transaction data specific to customers and to buying patterns, such as what people buy, when they buy it and how frequently they come into the store. It also covers whether the product was on promotion, how customers paid, any vouchers issued and redeemed, and so on. The data is used for two main work streams. One, called 'broadcast', is about the main variables in the store: pricing, promotions, where products are stocked in the store, and product quality – the shopping experience; and the second is 'personalized,' where communication is with individuals depending on their behavior.

A 'spend-stretch' campaign aims to increase basket size and frequency, using analytics to examine transaction behavior, basket size, spend and shopping frequency. Customers are segmented into groups, and trial mailings carried out. Post-campaign analysis examines the profitability of the offer and how it varies by segment. Models are used to understand and optimize the maximum sales possible and the maximum profit. To optimize individual campaigns, Sainsbury's calculates the return on investment for customers or groups, taking into account factors such as mailing costs, profit margins and any supplier funding. In post-campaign analysis the results are scrutinized, quantifying the size of the 'prize' and showing how both profitability and incremental sales may vary with the size of the mailing. In campaign planning and relationship building, Sainsbury's can measure all programmes and compare results, determine gaps and clashes, and personalize communications. Using this knowledge, business rules can be built that include the payback period for a campaign, the profitability of response for groups or individuals, the time of year and so on.

After the honeymoon – the hard work begins

Partnership schemes have a mixed history. There are also many management difficulties. Some partners might put in more effort than others. Disputes might arise over promotional affairs. Spur-of-the-moment decisions to run promotions are impossible because all parties must agree – the scheme must have rules. Keeping all partners happy means management costs that can cancel out scale economies. Proving that the schemes make net money is hard. Even solus schemes are partly an act of faith. Tesco is fond of its statistic that Clubcard customers spend twice as much as non-Clubcard customers. It implies that Clubcard delivers more spend, but the link may be the other way – high spenders like Clubcard because absolute discounts are higher.

Consumer insight is the key

Are these schemes really about loyalty? Given the criticisms about points being a low priority for consumers in choosing brands, this is a fair question. Giving rewards for a purchase is an easily copied sales promotion, and most so-called 'loyalty' schemes are just that. So for the partners these schemes are not about points, but about consumer insight. The best at this is Tesco, which analyses its customers to measure their loyalty, their commitment to Tesco, their profitability, and their 'headroom': the difference between what they spend at Tesco and how much they could potentially spend. Tesco has created a series of lifestyle clusters, such as those who like high-value pre-packaged foods; people who shop for basic ingredients and value foods; family convenience buyers, and so on. These are more useful than the life stage or recency/frequency/value approaches that had hitherto dominated. Tesco claims that re-running the new lifestyle clusters against old data showed the new segments to be three or four times more powerful than ones based on simple life stage. Cluster naming is important. While marketers often come up with names like 'young families', these do not evoke ideas in the same way as, say, 'high-spending superstore families' does. You can picture the latter better – it conveys an image that allows creative thinking to solve that family's problems.

How far can partnership schemes acquire the consumer insights of a Tesco? Could they do better, as their data extends across many more categories than grocery? Thus, Nectar could perhaps identify a group: males who shop for family goods in Sainsbury's late in the evening, who buy lots of fuel at BP. Let's call them 'busy male executives'. This looks good on paper, but the Tesco story illustrates that getting there is not easy. Its analysts took years of trial and error to get the data flows and data mining right to allow these insights, but at least Tesco was able to grapple with its data from close up. Can Nectar partners emulate its success when their data is held more remotely? This is a risky business. It puts the capabilities of exploiting Nectar's full potential out of the partners' direct control. There have been reports of some schemes' partners having to wait a long time for analysis of customer data: Tesco and Safeway, with their different outcomes, have illustrated the importance of getting this right. Nectar partners may want to copy Tesco's success in identifying 'price-sensitive' consumers, and saving on margin through targeted discounts. However, many of these 'price sensitives' have that characteristic precisely because they have limited disposable income. In this case, what will be the effect of several partners trying to stimulate more spend simultaneously through discount offers? Complex 'rules of engagement' are needed, but who would fix them?

CONCLUSIONS

Perhaps the most significant change induced by a loyalty scheme is how far a retailer manages its business based on insights into consumers and their behaviour and needs. This will not occur if a retailer has a loyalty scheme that yields insights into consumer behaviour, but is managed so separately that these insights are not incorporated into normal marketing, sales and service decision making, but rather only used for one-off initiatives such as individual sales promotions. For this to change, marketing roles and responsibilities will also need to change. New skills may be needed, for instance in data interpretation and use. Planning and implementation processes will need to be changed to ensure they use consumer insights.

The UK experience shows that the schemes that have the greatest impact do so by either transforming the marketing of their retail participants, or being part of such a transformation. In fact, they probably *must* transform the marketing of their partner companies to survive. Otherwise they risk becoming an expensive promotional device that absorbs management attention and budget, distracting companies from more productive ways of investing management time. However, measuring the effect of such transformation is harder than measuring the effect of a loyalty scheme in terms of customer recruitment, up-sell, cross-sell and customer retention. This is probably why such measures are preferred by analysts, and perhaps even by finance directors. Still, finance directors who only count current numbers have been shown wanting all over the world, if these numbers conceal the strategic direction (good or bad!).

The Jigsaw example above prompts the question whether a packaged consumer goods supplier is best served by being a strategic partner of a retail loyalty scheme, buying insights from a retailer and using its data to create offers targeted to consumers, or by spending money as part of a scheme such as Jigsaw, or some combination of both. Our view is that a product supplier must either let the scheme transform its marketing, or not bother. Retailers can show that their own loyalty schemes can be a rational way of doing normal retail promotion, while a Jigsaw approach adds direct contact when before there was none or little. The expertise to manage consumer contacts through various direct media – including now the Web and mobile – is possessed by very few packaged goods suppliers (Cadbury is said to be one of the great exceptions).

NOTES

1 Pressey, A and Mathews, B (1998) Relationship marketing and retailing: comfortable bedfellows? *International Journal of Customer Relationship Management*, **1** (1), pp 39–52.
2 Pressey, A and Mathews, B (2000) Barriers to relationship marketing in consumer retailing, *Journal of Services Marketing*, **14** (3), pp 272–86.
3 See Gilbert, D (2003) *Retail Marketing Management*, Prentice-Hall, Englewood Cliffs, NJ, for a full description of the strategies retailers use.
4 Chu, J and Morrison, G P (2003) Enhancing the customer shopping experience: IBM/National Retail Federation 'Store of the Future' survey, IBM Institute for Business Value, London.

5 The material in this and the next two sections was condensed from Butscher, S A (2002) *Customer Loyalty Programmes and Clubs: A practical guide*, 2nd edition, Gower, Aldershot, UK.

6 This is confirmed by assessments of retailers carried out using the Customer Management Assessment Tool, provided by Ogilvy One's subsidiary QCi Ltd. The results of research using this tool are documented in Stone, M, Woodcock, N and Foss, B (2002) *The Customer Management Scorecard*, Kogan Page, London. In one assessment using this tool, the client had very poor insight of all the customer data it was collecting. Even defining loyalty and retention is problematic for some companies – for more on this see Stone, M, Aspinall, E and Nancarrow, C (2001) The meaning and measurement of customer retention, *Journal of Targeting, Measurement and Analysis for Marketing*, **10** (1), pp 79–87.

7 For a comprehensive history and evaluation of the Tesco scheme, see Humby, C and Hunt, T with Phillips, T (2003) *Scoring Points: How Tesco is winning customer loyalty*, Kogan Page, London.

9 Privacy, risk, and good and bad consumers

Merlin Stone, Bryan Foss, Alison Bond, Martin Hickley and Nick Orsman

INTRODUCTION

Technology and data sources now make it possible for companies of all sizes (not just large companies) and government organizations to differentiate between 'good' and 'bad' individuals and groups. These developments also make it much easier to predict likely 'goodness' or 'badness' using various indicators. Where use of these indicators is forbidden for some reason, surrogates may be sought. Following this approach requires an organization to define what it means by 'good' or 'bad', and to keep this definition under review according to the performance of individuals and evolving law and regulation.

WHO GOOD CONSUMERS ARE

Of course, 'good' and 'bad' are relative terms. Their definition changes with time, with laws and with the strategies and target marketing of companies. We also need to distinguish between character and behaviour. A consumer who might naturally be 'bad' for a company might be constrained to be 'good' by product design or service management. Social and economic factors (the economy, neighbourhood) combine with an individual's characteristics to determine goodness and badness. In the private sector, good individuals are broadly defined as a mixture of some or all of the characteristics below. However, companies can specialize in dealing with consumers who are 'not good' for other companies, turning them into 'good' customers. Thus, some store credit cards are targeted at consumers who are less creditworthy, possibly because of imprudence, or simply low income. So this should be taken more as an example of the spectrum.

- **Good net value.** They yield more value to the supplier than it costs to service them, taking into account all costs. Consider the consumer who keeps a reasonable bank current account balance, never goes into debt without permission, and rarely goes to the branch, but uses cash machines. This consumer is of higher net value than one with the same average balance who constantly moves into a small but free overdraft and uses branch services. Even though the latter might pay higher bank charges, these may not compensate for the extra costs of staff constantly checking to see whether the overdraft will be paid off. Although the bank might try to raise charges to the latter to make the account profitable, it might not succeed.
- **Moral (that is, not fraudulent).** They stay on the right side of the law in dealings with the company. Some companies do well by meeting the needs of consumers who would be considered immoral by most, but stick to the law while interacting with the company: for instance, casinos or betting shops are used to launder money in ways that do not breach company rules.
- **Prudent.** They live their lives within the resources available to them. Note that some companies make a very good living out of the imprudent, even if it does necessitate charging usurious interest rates!
- **Punctual.** These customers pay bills on time, arrive for flights in time, are at home for service appointments.
- **Responsive in a relevant way to communication.** They respond to marketing communications that are relevant to them (in the sense that they are likely to lead these consumers to evaluate seriously the possibility of buying the product or service). However, they do not respond to ones that are not.
- **Responsive to other initiatives:** for instance, willing to try new products.
- **Happy to give relevant and truthful information** to the organization and to update information previously given. This allows the organization to determine the appropriate 'treatment' for the individual, but also to save resources by not offering inappropriate treatment. This also applies to complaints (see below).
- **Healthy** in habits (for instance, moderate drinking, not smoking) and perhaps even in genes.
- **Safe**, for instance in driving and as a pedestrian, and perhaps in sporting habits.
- **Observing rights and responsibilities:** for example, prepared to learn

to work with the organization for mutual benefit, such as installing security devices, looking after credit cards, following a healthy lifestyle.

- **Complaining only when 'justified',** allowing the organization to improve its service and reduce later complaints.
- **Prepared to recommend** the organization to other individuals if the service or product is good.
- **Persistent:** that is, not switching between suppliers – although this depends on the product. Persistent consumers for undertakers are rare (although if the family is the decision-making unit, persistence can exist). Persistent consumers for wedding wear might also be persistent consumers for lawyers, because they can afford to be, and hence possibly good consumers for financial services advisors!
- **Stable or predictable.** Consumers can be good in one domain and bad in another. It is the stability of this pattern, and perhaps more important the stability of individuals as members of groups, which allows organizations to trade with them profitably. Although in theory all risks can be managed via insurance, when it comes to the balance of risk and value, stability may be the key. For example, a high street retailer setting up a new store might reckon on a particular level of abuse (credit default, shop theft, staff fraud), based on experience with similar stores, as well as a particular level of trade. If each new store displays the same pattern, the loss level is acceptable, and standard control procedures can be deployed. If a new store displays different patterns, new approaches to management may be needed.

Again, we stress that these are examples of characteristics that indicate 'goodness' for many companies, but might also be counter-indications for other companies. In some cases, the combination of attributes is important, rather than the possession of individual attributes.

WHO BAD CONSUMERS ARE

Bad consumers have characteristics largely the opposite of those listed above. For most organizations, a key bad characteristic is current and/or likely future unprofitability, although sometimes unprofitable consumers might be valued, for example as recommenders. Companies may include in their definition of bad consumers debtors, switchers, liars, or those with court judgments against them. However, charities, public sector bodies and private sector bodies acting on behalf of these organizations often focus on such consumers.

Examples of bad consumer behaviour are numerous. Some are politically incorrect! Despite this, it is important that management (and government) understands the origins of 'bad' consumer behaviour, as solutions cannot always be found at an individual level. For example, many immigrant communities in Western nations are effectively economic or political refugees. They come from developing or poorer countries where to survive they had to 'look after their own', hiding as much from the government as they could, because they were targeted for 'special attention' by the state. It might take generations before members of these ethnic or national groups adapt their behaviour to the more equitable treatment they should in theory receive from the government of their adoptive state. So they might be reluctant to give personal information, for fear of it being exploited by state or company to their disadvantage. They might also conceal income from tax authorities.

As companies seek to manage consumers more as individuals – but remotely – so some bad consumers learn to exploit this tendency. This is most visible in the areas of credit and debit cards and the Internet, but also in insurance and banking. Bad consumers learn very quickly because the incentive is large (the potential gain), and in some cases transfer their learning very quickly (often to other individuals within an organized criminal network, but sometimes also within their ethnic or professional group or geographical locality). For example, government benefit frauds are often organized within ethnic groups or families. Tampering with utility meters often spreads geographically. In one London borough the utility company could not understand why so many of its meters had rusted. After replacing over a hundred it decided to do some undercover investigation. It discovered that the someone had made a mould of the coin required for the meter and sold it many local residents. This mould was filled with water and frozen, and the pieces of ice were used to feed the meters. This method no longer works as meters have been adapted to prevent it.

Some consumers target particular types of organization. Government and utilities are often regarded as 'fair game' by individuals across the economic spectrum. In the UK, privatized companies (such as utilities and rail companies), whose directors were labelled as 'fat cats' by the government when they profited from big increases in salary or from selling shares at great profit, became a 'legitimate target'.

Certain industries always have relatively high risk/value ratios at the level of the individual consumer. These are mostly those with a large insurance, credit or consequential liability element. They include:

- insurance itself;
- any industry where maintenance contracts are sold;
- all pure credit industries, such as bank loans and credit cards;

- any continuous supply which takes place under credit terms, such as utilities and industrial supplies;
- any situation in which claims are hard to validate;
- products where failure or misuse can cause significant damage to the consumers, leading to a high incidence of product liability claims.

However, other areas of high risk include:

- service industries where complainers - having taken service - often ask for reimbursement of full value;
- products or services where the costs the organization has to incur to serve the consumer after the initial purchase may greatly outweigh the revenues if the consumer behaves in a certain way, for example cherry picks all the high-cost, low or zero revenue parts of the service;
- situations where entitlement documentation can be forged.

To give the reader an idea of the extent and variety of 'bad consumer' situations, and their typical correlates, here are a few examples that differ from the usual ones given.

- Certain clothes shoppers (mostly women - because they are the majority of clothing shoppers) buy merchandise knowing that they are going to wear it once, before taking it back to the shop the next day to exploit the shop's liberal returns policy. Shops develop strategies to deal with this, typically taking the merchandise to the back office and smelling it for signs of body odour, deodorant, perfume and the like - sure indicators of the garment having been worn for an extended period. If this is suspected, management is called in and the consumer is challenged.
- A very high percentage of claims on holiday insurance policies are fraudulent, particularly those involving claims of lost cash. Insurers are dealing with this by developing databases of frequent claimers and by using lie detectors.
- Certain flyers forge airline boarding passes to obtain frequent flyer points. One airline found that there was a correlation between forging and choosing ethnic meals.
- Certain utility users always pay at the very last minute, when they are about to be disconnected or have a prepayment meter fitted. One utility found this to be correlated with ethnic grouping.
- Certain consumers make a habit of claiming that different types of cleaning and washing fluids damage the item being cleaned - or of course their skin! They are traced by keeping properly computerized records of complainers' identities.

Companies can design products for bad consumers (tamper-proof electricity meters and phone booths, insurance products excluding specific risks, service products with prepayment tariffs). However, slack product or service design can turn good consumers into bad consumers, indeed whole markets from good to bad. For example, the recruitment of consumers for cable telephony or motor insurance irrespective of their propensity to pay their bills or to switch on price led to many more consumers turning bad.

The case study below shows how license evaders can be managed using consumer insight-based techniques.

HOUSEHOLD TELEVISION LICENSES

The collection of television licence fees was a very complex operation, made up of lots of different elements and carried out by a number of different parties. OgilvyOne was asked to try to increase the net licence fee income via a more integrated and targeted approach to marketing and communications planning.

The starting point for segmentation was OgilvyOne's Evader Score Model, which scores every postcode in the country on the propensity of households in that area to be unlicensed. To this was added a wide range of lifestyle (including media), geodemographic and financial data to provide a rounded picture of different population segments beyond simply their television licence payment status. The most robust solution to emerge from cluster analysis involved seven segments (see Figures 9.1 to 9.3). The data used to determine segments were a random sample of 50,000 postcodes, weighted by licensable addresses, enhanced by demographic and lifestyle date from several sources.

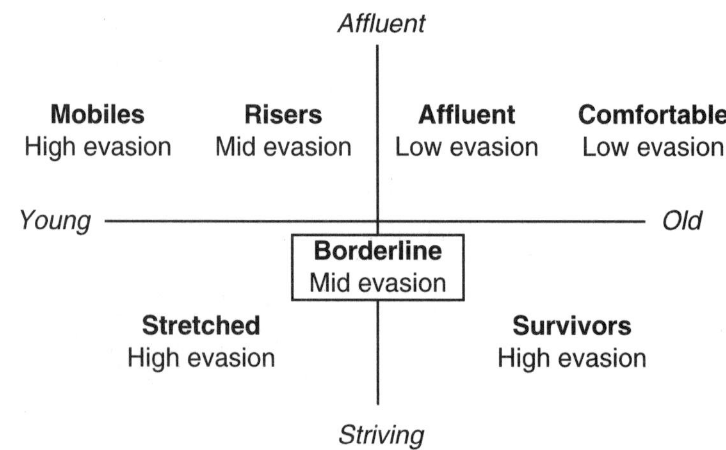

Figure 9.1 *The television licence population: segments by age and wealth*

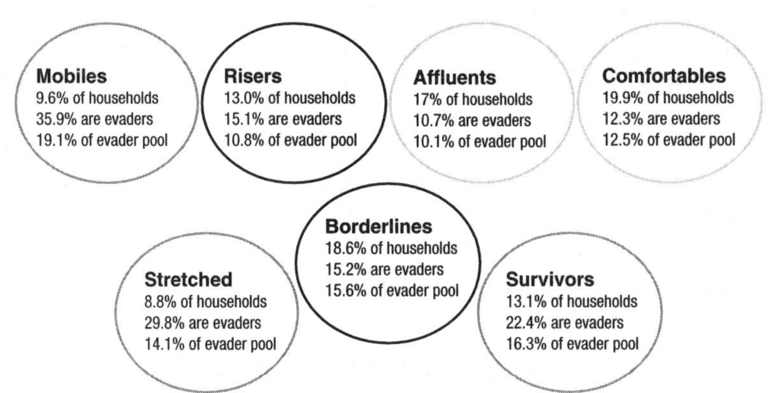

Figure 9.2 *Television licences: main evasion statistics*

The fields used in segmentation were age, marital status, home ownership, length of residence, number and age of children, household size, income and newspaper readership. This allowed these questions to be answered:

- What is the most appropriate/productive way to contact them?
- How can we maximize/maintain the deterrent effect among them?
- What is the appropriate payment channel approach?

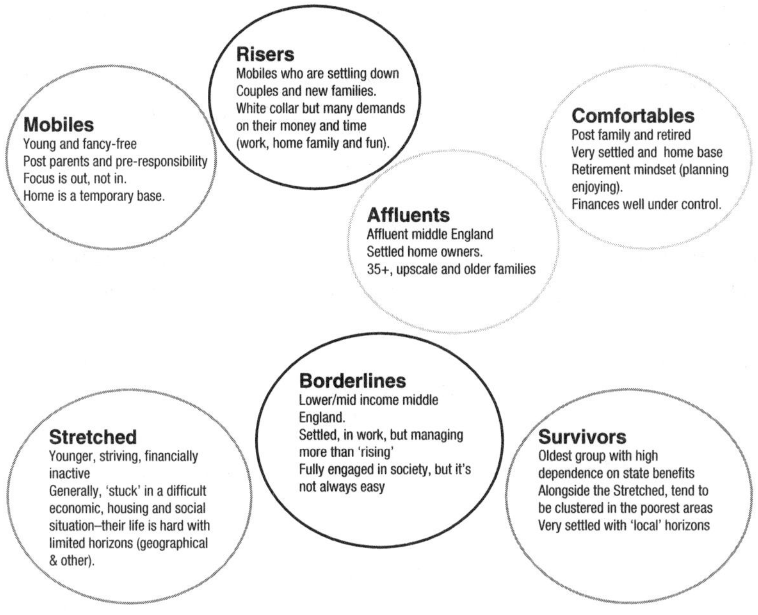

Figure 9.3 *The television licence population: segment 'micro-profiles'*

> Direct marketing and Web techniques were used to make evaders aware that their payment was sought, and to make it easy for them to pay, resulting in a large rise in collection rates for the segments where research and data analysis had shown that customers were most likely to be responsive to efforts to make them pay.

PREDICTION OF GOOD AND BAD

Risk and worth change over time, but companies are faced today with decisions that involve accepting consumers (or not) based on predicted value or risk. A good example of this is a typical student, who is currently high risk and low worth, yet courted expensively by all high street banks because of assumed future value. So a critical factor that affects how organizations deal with good and bad consumers is their need to predict performance rather than observe it in retrospect. In particular, organizations are increasingly keen to use advanced information technology to check the status of an individual not just during their relationship with him or her, but before the relationship is entered into, and predict any likely changes in value or status – especially from good to bad. This allows the organization to price the relationship (for example, in insurance or banking), change its terms (such as requesting prepayment for utility bills), or to refuse to enter into it.

Once the relationship begins, organizations find it harder to change price or terms, and typically accept the risk for the duration of the contract. If the consumer proves more risky than anticipated, the consumer may be trapped into receiving supply from the original organization simply because knowledge of this higher level of risk means that no other organization will offer the relationship. Here, the incidence may include an insurance claim, bad debt, crime, or even making several sales enquiries but never buying. The knowledge of past patterns of risk is vital for organizations trying to reduce risk, so they are keen to obtain and use this data as early as possible – ideally before they open a dialogue with prospective consumers. Here, de-marketing can take the form of selecting apparently risky consumers out of marketing campaigns.

The above demonstrates a general point, that for a particular organization to be able to define badness, let alone identify individual bad consumers, it must do one of two things: either acquire data on apparent badness from other organizations, or accept enough apparently bad consumers and observe/measure their behaviour, so that the organization can learn to recognize them, and avoid most of them in the future.

Note that as patterns of badness change, an organization needs to refresh its knowledge. The organization needs also to have enough good consumers (at least one at any time!) to enable it to define good too! Another general point is illustrated by the insurance example. To manage (and avoid or control) bad consumers, companies seek indicators not only of which consumers are likely to be bad already, but also which ones are turning from good to bad. For credit card companies, this might be a growing outstanding balance with no corresponding increase in monthly repayment. For a commercial consumer, this might mean extended periods before invoice settlement. However, indicators might occur in other domains to which a company has no access, such as payments to other companies - hence the importance of sharing data about creditworthiness or insurance risk.

THE PORTFOLIO APPROACH

In marketing, one of the principal issues at play is the balance between risk and consumer value. Companies can see their market as a consumer portfolio rather than as a set of product revenues. This leads to a focus on which kinds of consumer a company should aim to recruit or retain. The ideal is to develop a portfolio of consumers, with value and risk balanced - either within or between consumers. However, the two might be associated (for instance, consumers with large houses might be more likely to be burgled). Indeed, those with more wealth at risk might be tempted to make fraudulent declarations so as to obtain insurance cover at lower prices.

Good consumers are not necessarily high value always. Good value is a net outcome over several years of buying behaviour. Some organizations develop predictive models, not only to identify whether an individual who was not previously known to the organization *is* good or bad, but also to predict future states - in particular state changes. For example, a good individual turning bad exposes the organization to risk. 'Knowing the consumer' is what small businesses have always done. The use of information on individual consumers has helped large organizations recover from the disadvantage of being large! They have been helped in doing this by companies dedicated to supplying this data and helping organizations use it.

The larger a company becomes, and the more its commercial strategy pushes it in the direction of 'volume marketing', the more problematic the ideas of 'redlining' (avoiding completely certain categories of consumers) and 'cherry-picking' (being very selective about which consumers to recruit) become. Many large companies cannot afford to cherry-pick, as their business strategy is to focus on mass markets. They may not be able to 'redline', if their target consumers demand a simple, standard proposition.

Controlling risk

Together with statistical methods for focusing on good consumers and managing bad consumers come the usual strategies for controlling risk once bad consumers have been accepted. In insurance fraud, frequency and size of claim are both issues. There are well-established procedures for identifying likely sinners. The inflation of valid claims used to be harder to detect and/or manage, but many companies have specific strategies, such as appointing their own repairers (as in the case of automotive crash damage). However, for areas such as fraudulent holiday claims, specialist loss adjusters use various formal and informal techniques to assess whether a claim is likely to be fraudulent, and therefore whether to take investigation further.

A first step is always to see whether a given consumer keeps appearing on the 'bad' side of the consumer balance sheet. For example, frequent complainers about delayed rail journeys are identifiable once identities are checked and complaints properly logged. This has enabled companies to check whether the train that was claimed to be late actually was.

Most markets define an acceptable level of moral hazard. Insurers have commonly accepted an estimated 10 per cent fraudulent claim level, similar to the 'shrinkage' deemed acceptable in retail stocks (half of which is normally attributable to staff theft!). However, in some cases this level exists because the company has not legitimized to its staff the idea that consumers may be hazardous, but instead confined it to one department (such as claims management, credit control or complaints management).

Choosing consumers for positive – and negative – treatment

Not every supplier can choose consumers. For example, public utilities and even retailers are usually under pressure to do business with any consumer, no matter how problematic or litigious. However, the issue is not just what consumers can do (in terms of giving or destroying value) if they want to. Rather, it is a question of which consumers are most encouraged to buy, and which not. Through branding, marketing communications, store layout, pricing, product range and all the other items of the marketing mix, particular kinds of consumer can be attracted, while others can be deterred. For example, retail consumers requiring a close relationship may understand from the layout and staffing of a self-service store and the absence of any loyalty or store card scheme that they are unlikely to get their required relationship. In a department store, the layout and numbers of assistants and the existence of a combined store card and loyalty scheme gives a different message.

Making the decision about acceptable exposure and missed opportunity

In theory, the more information about consumers a company has access to, the more accurately the company can assess consumers' current goodness or badness, and predict future values. The decisions companies have to make range from the simple binary choice (whether to offer a specific product to a specific consumer) to more complex decisions (which product to offer to which consumers, and what terms to supply them under). However, there are diminishing returns to data, particularly as each data item collected has to be maintained (although of course there are diminishing returns to data maintenance as well). Where valuable consumers are rare, the returns to collecting the data that indicate likely future value can be high. However, to establish how much data needs to be collected – and then maintained – companies need to estimate the link between the costs of data collection and maintenance and the benefits – not only overall but for each data item. 'Classic' direct marketing companies with long histories of consumer management can usually estimate the returns to using particular data items, but most companies simply do not have the stable data and analytical framework to achieve this.

A company's knowledge about the consumer becomes firmer after consumer acquisition, when a consumer's pattern of transactions, payments, complaints, queries and so on becomes clear. Of course, the pattern is one thing; knowing the pattern is another – hence the deployment of advanced analytical techniques such as data mining.

SOCIAL, POLITICAL AND LEGAL ISSUES

The data usage practices of large organizations have attracted the attention of governments, social scientists, moral philosophers and others concerned with the ethics of organizational behaviour. The issues emerging in this area can be grouped broadly under the headings of, first, organizational issues (how can the organization achieve its objectives by using consumer data?) and second, public policy issues – what are the consequences of organizations doing this, and should governments constrain organizations' use of data, and if so, how?

Public issues take on particular significance in specific situations. In particular they apply where the government has a direct influence on industry structure, as a supplier or regulator (for example health care provision, public or private utilities, financial services) and where there are significant ethical or social issues (such as the use of genetic data in life and medical insurance, and the emergence of a category of uninsurable individuals or unbankable ethnic businesses that are 'redlined' by suppliers).

In the United States, 'redlining' by insurance companies (for example, for health insurance) caused the government to identify 'pools' of uninsurables. Larger companies were forced to insure people from these pools at reasonable rates, taking them on in proportion to their market share. This made it even more profitable for niche 'cherry-pickers' to operate against the large companies, as it forced the larger companies to charge higher rates to cover the additional risk. This shows why heavy-handed government intervention can change industry behaviour to the disadvantage of 'good' consumers.

In general, companies must use all available data, or else they will be subject to cherry-picking of their 'good' consumers by competitors, leaving them just with 'bad' consumers. In addition, bad customers will seek out suppliers who cannot use data about their badness – the problem of 'adverse selection'.

In the many situations in which individual consumer data is being used, there appears to be an emerging inconsistency of practice. For example, direct genetic data is not generally allowed to be used in the health and life insurance industry, either for red-lining reasons or because some adverse medical conditions that are genetically correlated are also ethnically correlated, and ethnic bias is unacceptable. However, the use of indirect data (obtained by asking about relatives' medical conditions) is acceptable. In other financial services sectors (such as motor insurance, and banking for small businesses and consumers), it is common practice to note the ethnic bias in certain risks and use it to determine consumer recruitment policies and individual consumer pricing and risk management.

ETHICAL ISSUES

Conventionally, discrimination between individual consumers took two main forms. The first was the creation of different offers according to affordability, so consumers could elect for different treatment according to their desire to spend money. The second was vetting – for creditworthiness, fraud, previous claims and the like – which led to the exclusion of certain consumers because of their predicted likely costs (whether legitimate or not!).

The sheer variety of the effects of the widespread use of data on good and bad consumers has caused those concerned with the societal effects of this data usage to think very hard about the right direction. One reaction has been to try to ban a variety of policies. The most obvious is the attempt to ban the use of data about an individual when the individual has not expressly consented to its use for the purpose in question. This idea underlies the drive towards a stronger data protection regime. This idea can be considered either very ethical, or totalitarian! The truth is that governments use data all the time for controlling 'bad consumers' – not necessarily criminals. For example, profiles of 'problem cases' are often developed and then applied in analysing a large number of cases to identify those likely to be problematic – a very different matter. This is the same approach that insurers apply – and would like to apply to identify whether a consumer has a genetic predisposition to certain illnesses. They – like governments – are simply interested in probabilities, as these are the key to reducing (not removing) risk.

This brings us to the banning of the use of data for probabilistic purposes. The genetic issue is a good example. However, capitalism lives on probabilities and risk, rarely on certainties. Owners of buildings thought to be more fireproof gathered together 400 years ago to form mutual fire insurance organizations. Excluding the use of probabilistic genetic data might lead to the same. The central problem is that data collected for one purpose, such as to try to improve the health of an individual, or under one set of rules, is often very useful for another, such as insuring people fairly. This is a theme that recurs throughout marketing, as with the use of credit data used to include/exclude consumers from marketing campaigns, or to predict crime.

Behind some attempts to restrict the use of consumer data is the view that those who hold the data cannot entirely be trusted to use it only for permitted purposes. Putting it simply, some are suspicious of the ethics of companies. (For instance, are honest managers honest data users? Are retail staff more likely to abuse data?) Another source of criticism comes from those who know that 'bad' consumers (as defined by many companies) are biased towards certain ethnic or religious groups, social classes, geographical areas or even gender. As much political emphasis is placed on reducing bias, the use of data that would lead to the exclusion of certain consumer types from particular benefits is seen as back-door discrimination, to be discouraged. A less radical view is that bias is built into society. Forcing companies not to use data to identify biases that affect them commercially will lead to other strategies that might be more insidious, such as 'redlining' of geographical areas because they contain high proportions of risky consumers, even though the use of consumer data and advanced risk assessment techniques would allow many consumers in the area to be treated as low risk and welcomed as customers.

Unrestricted use of consumer data can lead to the emergence of categories of uninsurables and untradables. These consumers would not be able to receive a variety of products and services, would not receive certain communications (they would be subject to de-marketing), and might be confronted by outright refusal to supply, or be charged higher prices. However, despite this, one can ask whether these problems are resolved just by legislation banning use of certain data types. If risk is correlated with certain data items, and use of these items is denied, smart capitalists will find good surrogates – as they do already.

THE INTERNET, TRUST AND ALL THAT

The Internet has brought new focus to the issues surrounding the protection of data. Never before has there been such freedom of access to an immense amount of personal information on a global scale. Countries such as the United States that value their open society and personal freedoms, and find any bent towards totalitarianism deplorable, are being forced to rethink how to deal with the balance between privacy and freedom of information.

The success of a business depends upon the trust of its consumers. Individuals will not choose to do business with companies they do not trust. Trust cannot be won unless privacy is respected and security is assured. Respecting privacy and protecting personal data mean much more than mere adherence to laws and regulations. A company must put in place the standards and disciplines required to meet consumer expectations; it must practise the art of self-regulation. Those companies that harness their understanding of their consumers' data protection requirements will demonstrate integrity to their consumers. Their consumers will have confidence that their privacy is protected and their transactions are secure. Treating people the way they want to be treated can give companies a significant competitive edge.

Opting in separately to all possible uses of consumer information would be virtually impossible. This makes it important to be a trustworthy business. No matter what a company promises, if it deceives consumers or uses information about them incompetently, it pays in the court of public opinion and eventually in revenue and profit.

HOW CONSUMERS FEEL ABOUT THESE ISSUES

Privacy is clearly an issue for some consumers, with physical privacy (the intrusion of direct marketing into their homes) representing an annoyance, and information privacy (relating to the information available on consumers) representing a more substantial worry. In terms of the latter, respondents' level of knowledge varies substantially. People react in different ways. For example, some are pragmatic and recognize that the provision of personal details may improve targeting. However, those who feel particularly strongly attempt to minimize the information held on them, and rarely, if ever, provide direct marketers with personal details or request communications from them.

Interestingly, privacy concerns feature most strongly when respondents perceive that they are targeted with irrelevant marketing communications. The emotive response to this can vary from a general annoyance to overt concern, and the strongest reaction is to actively withdraw from direct marketing communications. Direct mailers do not like the term 'junk mail'. It applies to mail that is perceived by the recipient as being uninteresting or irrelevant.

WHAT THE LAW SAYS

The kind of questions consumer might ask about the use of their data relate to:

- which organizations have what data about them;
- what use those organizations are making of that data;
- whether the data is correct;
- how the use of the data is likely to affect the consumer;
- whether data from different databases have been merged;
- who did that merging and why;
- whether consumers will they be told about the use to which data which relates to them has been put, even if they are not affected directly;
- whether others will get rich from the sale, resale and acquisition of data about them;
- whether they will get a royalty or some other reward for data they give, and if not, why not.

Privacy and data protection legislation and practice, and industry codes of practice, aim to provide answers to some of these questions, or to make it unnecessary to ask some of them. Many industries have their own code of practice (as does banking). These aim to ensure that companies follow good practice, pre-empting government intervention and ensuring that consumers are not dissatisfied by how they are treated. The problem with self-regulation is that it relies on goodwill. The risk is that companies will observe the regulations superficially, but in practice disregard them. Self-regulation that fails might be worse than waiting for the government to act, because consumers have in the interim been lulled into a false sense of security.

This is not the place to cover specific laws and regulations, as they vary from country to country, change over time, relate both to data and to the media used to contact consumers (including e-mail and mobile messaging), and are susceptible to varied and changing interpretation. Readers are referred to the government bodies dealing with data protection and privacy and their Web sites, to the code of practice of the market research association in their country (for the UK code, see page 266), and of course to their own legal advisers.

IMPROVING THE QUALITY OF CONSUMER DATA MANAGEMENT SO AS TO COMPLY WITH REQUIREMENTS

While many legal and administrative issues surrounding data protection directives are unclear, we do know what requirements they place on consumer information management. Companies need to:

- Provide accurate, complete and consistent client information to their business systems. Without this, compliance with data protection directives will prove difficult and costly.
- Provide accurate information on relationships. For example key relationships such as legal guardian, spouse and parent, are important as they determine who is entitled to access personal information.
- Provide complete and accurate information on what services and products a client has purchased. For example a client's credit might be withheld because of an inaccurate account balance.
- Ensure that operational business systems have a common enterprise view of the client and that any updates to client information are reflected across the whole enterprise.
- Ensure that rules relating to creating new consumer information are applied consistently. This might include enforcing the capture of certain mandatory information such as privacy and non-solicitation status.

- Ensure that new consumer data is captured, accessed and updated consistently, and used properly.
- Understand what personal information is captured, why it is captured, and who can create, update and delete it.
- Be able to demonstrate compliance with data protection directives to the relevant statutory bodies.

GUIDELINES FOR DATA PROTECTION

Here are some guidelines to follow. They might not be legally required in all countries, but we would argue that they constitute good practice:

- Treat manual records like computer records, particularly concerning consumer access.
- Check all manual records for compliance with regulations.
- Check all forms on which personal data are obtained to ensure that they contain the necessary consent notices, particularly in relation to any sensitive data. At source, the data must be collected fairly. Make it clear to the consumer what it is going to be used for.
- Use data according to the business purpose for which it has been collected, which should also be the one explained clearly to consumers at or before the time of collection.
- Clarify to consumers how data is intended to be used within the organization, for example for cross-selling.
- Ensure legal advisors are closely involved in reviewing existing practice and any changes in practice. Ensure they understand the business purposes and can therefore advise on what the organization can do, not just what it cannot do!
- Extend existing systems for giving access to computerized data to word-processed and manual data. Where the data is really essential, it might be better to computerize it to ease access (for example through text search engines) and provide higher-quality processing.
- Ensure all processing of personal data is based only on one of the allowed grounds, including those for sensitive data. The data must always be processed fairly. For example, is it fair for an individual to be grouped with neighbours (or indeed any other individuals) for the purposes of credit assessment?
- Do not continue old practices without thinking. Ask whether old processes comply with current law. If not, can the same objective be achieved in a different way?
- Check that procedures meet all requirements for informing consumers when obtaining or disclosing data.

- Ensure consumer access procedures conform to access requirements. Ensure they can service high volumes of requests.
- Any automated systems that use personal data should be especially carefully checked for compliance. In particular, can the reasoning behind the processing be explained 'manually'?
- Network and Web site infrastructure should be checked to ensure that any personal data given to or posted on the system is processed according to the regulations.
- Check that any data the organization allows to be viewed by a third party, or transfers to a third party, receives adequate protection. Check for contractual safeguards.
- Keep up to date with advice and practice.
- Always provide opt-out boxes to allow consumers to refuse to let their data be used for additional purposes. If the organization wants to be really certain of where it stands, it should use opt-in boxes.

CONCLUSIONS

Consumers have a right to expect companies to manage their data professionally. This is not just a marketing question – financial issues are at stake too. Companies should review how far their own practices match best practice, and establish strategies and targets to improve their practice. In a world where identification and management of good consumers brings rich rewards, try to follow these guidelines:

- Define good and bad consumers, recognizing that most consumers are a mix of good and bad attributes.
- Remember, bad consumers often occur in groups, might work together, might collude with your staff, and get better at being bad if you let them (they learn from experience). So do not assume the situation is static.
- Don't be afraid to 'think the unthinkable', in terms of how 'badness' may be distributed, but make sure that you base your analyses on hard evidence, not prejudice, and that you stay clearly within the terms of the various laws that determine what you can do. These include laws covering data protection, racial and other types of discrimination, employment, and specific industry regulations.
- Ensure that your databases and data sources allow you to identify good and bad consumers.
- If you can, measure the performance of your business in terms of the net value you obtain from each consumer – including all exposures

and not just routine costs. Where you do not have individual consumer revenues and costs, use research-based estimates.

- Estimate your net exposure to bad consumers, and calculate if it is worth investing in reducing exposure.
- If it is worthwhile, make sure that your systems at the point of contact with consumers allow you to identify bad consumers, and also predict whether a new consumer will be good or bad.
- Where the data you need to do this is somewhere else, obtain it, and if possible, develop relationships with your competitors that allow you to identify bad consumers and warn each other about them – subject to the provisions of the Data Protection Act and any special industry regulation.
- Develop, test and refine different strategies to deal with bad consumers, combining limits to exposure or refusal to deal, with techniques to reduce exposure to bad consumers who have 'got through'.

10 Consumer insight systems

Merlin Stone, Julie Abbott, Bryan Foss, Paul McDaid and Doug Morrison

THE HISTORY

In many ways, the drive towards the use of IT in marketing and sales was intuitive, rushed and generally poorly focused. There was little understanding of the critical success factors for bringing different customer management technologies together under new management processes. Symptoms of failure included:

- tactical solutions (possibly) meeting today's requirements, but making tomorrow hard to manage;
- poor choice of applications and technology because users' needs were not really understood, so that the resulting system performs poorly for the business and in some cases not at all;
- difficulties in convincing users of the benefits of the technology;
- over-spend and over-specification, normally because there was no clear focus, so it was decided to try to cover all possible requirements, with the result that few requirements were met fully.

One of the main causes of failure – poor communication and integration between IT and marketing functions – is being remedied in some companies, as their IT and marketing communities are learning new ways of working together. This includes involvement in each other's strategic planning processes, joint training and combined project management. There is some debate about whether the so-called 'legacy systems' are a major part of the problem, or whether it rests in failure to consider how systems can be adapted to improve performance, as opposed to how systems can be radically redesigned to achieve perfect performance.

Some companies have been optimistic about how far a single customer database can cope with all the operational, marketing and strategic needs of a business. Others recognize that systems development and integration in this area will be a series of compromises for many years to come. However, most expect to give increasing emphasis to integration of marketing and service applications, with the big database engines behind them increasingly required to perform as database servers for these multi-channel customer management applications, and optimized for this purpose. In addition, older systems can be effectively combined, migrated or updated over time. This is often the best way for established businesses to introduce consumer relationship management (CRM). Having a clear strategy separating out transactional from analytical needs allows companies to hold data at different levels for different purposes, yet to integrate them into a closed-loop business process. This ensures good performance for consumers, while allowing sophisticated segmentation and measurement. Early thinking that one could run all aspects of a business on a single database has been replaced by a view that transaction and analysis systems should be separate, but linked.

More recently there has been increased understanding that operational management requires a more integrated approach to systems, such that the different types of systems that hold consumer data should be accessible (with varying degrees of ease) by operating functions such as sales, service and transaction processing. In particular a full customer management cycle data architecture is required. This means collecting the main data needed to manage the full cycle and using it for planning, decision, action, measurement and so forth. Data quality is key in fuelling and managing this cycle. It is necessary for the organization to ensure that it recognizes existing customers when it is recruiting new ones (de-duplication). It must also collect valid data about events. Examples of this include:

- which campaign consumers responded to;
- through which channel;
- what follow-up was requested;
- what modes of contact the consumer prefers;
- the key events (eg life stage) that segment customers for targeting, timing, the offer and so on.

In the case studies below, we give two examples, one private sector, one charitable, of how an organization's systems work together to improve customer management.

US AUTOMOTIVE COMPANY

A US automotive manufacturer is using a new analytics platform, built using SAS Customer Relationship Management Solutions, to provide data mining, predictive modelling and information analysis to support CRM applications and help ensure high customer satisfaction levels for its customers around the world. Extracting data from the existing warehouse, new analytics functions include reporting, trending, segmentation, customer scoring, predictive modelling and customer life cycle analysis, supporting key CRM activities and campaign management. The company believes that one of the biggest challenges for any company marketing to consumers is to apply these models more and more effectively.

Its marketers use predictive models to target the right customers for hundreds of marketing campaigns every year. These models examine millions of customer records and select the best households to target for each campaign. The company realized that predictive modelling is a complex collaborative effort between data experts, data modellers, brand managers and advertising agencies. Modelling efforts are minimized when there is a clear vision for data management. This requires an understanding of data, data environment and data structures.

The company's data warehouse contains several terabytes of data on millions of customers, including warranty information, survey results, retail sales feeds, finance records and more. Its scoring process analyses customers at the household level and automatically applies predictive models to each household in the database, then sends that information back to the data warehouse. This gives the company's marketing teams easy access to a variety of up-to-date customer scores, which they use to manage outbound marketing campaigns and inbound traffic at the customer call centre.

AMERICAN HEART ASSOCIATION

The American Heart Association (AHA) is a non-profit organization dedicated to reducing disability and death from heart attacks, strokes and related cardiovascular disorders. It funds medical research, develops and communicates consumer health information, and advocates public health policy. The AHA has volunteers and staff in every state and most communities in the United States.

One of the AHA's major initiatives is to expand and enhance its activities by better use of information technology. As part of this, the

AHA implements systems that will improve the efficiency and effectiveness of interactions with individual donors, volunteers, schools and businesses that represent its 'customers'. Previously, staff at different regional offices used various database and spreadsheet systems to manage customer information. These different systems led to inefficiencies and inconsistencies in how various offices contacted individuals and organizations, designed programmes, and cultivated opportunities and relationships over time. For example, offices around the country used many different prizes to reward participants in school fund-raising activities. This inconsistent approach cost more than buying prizes in bulk and establishing a standard prize structure nationwide. In addition, lack of a central, multi-channel system for managing customer information led to repetition of effort and missed opportunities. Two staff members at the same office, for example, might end up contacting the same individual for the same reason. Staff at regional offices lacked access to information on individuals' histories of donations and involvement in other parts of the country. Even the operators staffing the AHA's toll-free call centre had a limited view of individual and organizational profiles and records of activities.

The AHA deployed Siebel Sales, Service, and Analytics to standardize and enhance its interactions with its 'customers.' This improved efficiency in outreach and fund-raising programmes, responsiveness, service levels and the ability to cultivate lasting and productive customer relationships. The AHA has consolidated all customer information into a single, centralized repository that can be accessed and leveraged by staff across all regional offices and communication channels.

First, the AHA standardized its system across several core business units, including Schoolsite, which enlists schools to help the AHA raise money and awareness; Corporate Relations, which manages outreach to businesses and the media; Donor Management, which interacts with nearly 3 million individual donors; and Advocacy, which recruits volunteers and works with legislators to advance public policy in the area of health. Then it deployed analytic dashboards for monitoring and analysing customer data. Across business units, the AHA uses information captured in the system to measure the effectiveness of campaigns and events. The analytics module focuses on opportunity management, income management and activity management, enabling managers to view and evaluate the results of outreach activities. For example, the organization can now monitor in a comprehensive way the dollar contributions secured by activities at various schools and businesses. If it becomes apparent that a school or business is falling short of goals, the organization can more quickly realign resources to make the effort a success.

A SENSE OF PERSPECTIVE

Many of today's most successful customer management technologies were pioneered in the 1980s and before. The pioneer industries were either direct marketers, such as mail order and publishing, users of large sales forces, such as business equipment, or combinations of the two, such as a few financial services companies. Some of them managed to change their focus from products to consumers. Today, many trends have accentuated the need for deployment of the technologies they pioneered. These trends include deregulation, increased competition, globalization, cost pressures (particularly headcount reductions) forced by economic conditions, channel diversification, the consumer's desire for service that is personal, low cost and direct, and of course the falling price of computing and telecommunications technology.

Technology is no longer the main constraint – if it ever was. However, data often is, which is why there is an increasing tendency for companies to regard data as an asset, not a cost. There are still many problems with the processes for using information systems and data. Many processes are slow, expensive and cumbersome. Many organizations are still 'command and control' oriented – focusing more on controlling the impact of the consumer in the organization than allowing the consumer to obtain better service from the company. This creates a barrier between the customer and the company, which the company then tries to fix, often using even more control. Distribution channels and processes that were stars 20 years ago (such as the sales force or the branch network) become dogs for the mass-market business or consumer. Still, the culture of operations, not consumer acquisition and retention, dominates many organizations. At the same time, many new entrants found that their life was made much easier by the 'it'll never work' scepticism of existing suppliers.

However, a realistic technological perspective is apparent in most companies today. There is an acceptance that one never arrives at the chosen destination but that a continuous stream of benefits is gained along the way. Meanwhile, having a map is critical, because it tells you the right direction. There are always new challenges, and the settle-down state is an illusion. Also, investment never stops.

Perhaps the key point about technology is that a stable approach to deploying it in managing consumers works the best. There needs to be a clear model of customer management (acquisition, retention, and development), and a clear IT model to support this. However, marketing staff are often on the look-out for the next job, and the average tenure in the chief information officer position is less than two years in the United States. So it is not surprising to find that while 50 per cent of all IT projects fail, 80 per cent of IT projects in sales and marketing fail to meet their objectives.

Stability in approach does not necessarily mean a fixed strategy with a clear end point. Rather, it means a journey in a consistent general direction, but with recognition that the speed of progress and precise direction at any one time will depend on a range of factors, such as current business priorities and tactical market opportunities. It is the consistency of general direction that helps companies avoid conflicting, often tactical, actions. One of the main consequences of non-strategic, tactical management of this area is severe failure in data quality and in delivery of data to the point of usage. Often, the last thing to be considered is how the data that will be used to manage consumers will be maintained and updated, and how its quality will be ensured. Over-ambitious data collection, maintenance and delivery requirements resulting from unrealistic customer management models lead to poor, expensive performance of customer management systems and poor consumer service.

One approach is what is called a 'layered approach'. This involves bringing the records in to what is called a system of record (a store of assured business data). Then a distribution database is used to deliver (sometimes copies of) the data to the required functional areas. In this way the data flows can be understood and the system designed to handle them. For data to be accessible at the point of sale is all about the relevant information being delivered to it, in a timely and up-to-date manner.

HOW TECHNOLOGY OPENS UP NEW OPPORTUNITIES

Many companies face strong competitive pressures, and are seeking ways to maintain the quality and reach of their interface with consumers while reducing costs. Consumers' expectations continue to rise – they want more, faster, better, cheaper. Whether or not consumers ask for it, competitors will provide it – so companies feel under pressure to innovate. So, most companies are exploring new technologies. However the size, scope and complexity of their interface with consumers means that changing it is expensive, so most confine themselves to experiments and pilots. Improvement in consumer management achieved by these systems may simply lead to increased cost if technologies are not also used to expand business or reduce the cost of managing the consumer at different stages of the relationship (recruitment, retention, development and so on).

Much progress has been made in computerization at the consumer interface – the point of sale or service. Examples include kiosks and

Internet and extranet pages – to provide a full shop window in limited space, including all the information enquirers need and instant ability to 'buy', including online credit checking. These ensure not only that consumers find it easier to be recruited or serviced, but that more consumer data are available to the supplier. The problem often lies in the failure to use this data subsequently to achieve higher standards of customer management. This includes recognition of existing consumers, which is strongest is telemarketing environments, but generally weak in counter service and similar situations. In retailing, this is based mainly on card technology (magnetic stripe or smart card). Updating of data from different sources (such as transaction/billing, campaign response, consumer service) is still a problem for many companies.

Consumers also want access to information about offers, about their previous and current transactions and about the state of their relationship with the supplier. However, consumers' expectations that data about them will be available at all points of contact with them and used constructively is causing improved consumer recognition, consumer data availability and associated multi-channel processes to be built into a new generation of system specifications. Today, though, few consumer contact systems can display a full and relevant customer record quickly (that is, so fast that the consumer barely notices the delay). Most companies realize the need for improvement here, and many are working on improving information flows to and from consumer-facing systems, and helping operators (sometimes the consumer) to navigate systems, as the following case shows.

ALBERTA TREASURY BRANCHES

In Canada, the bank Alberta Treasury Branches (ATB) needed a more efficient way to service customers. The company sought software to enable its contact centre representatives to give a better service than its competitors, and allow its sales team to find and exploit new opportunities. ATB's cumbersome contact centre system lacked the functionality to service customers quickly. Often customers who thought they were phoning a local branch office had their calls redirected to the central contact centre. The agent who answered had no way of knowing who the caller was, his or her history with the bank, or what the call was about. The first minutes of the conversation were typically spent resolving confusion on both sides. Then to find the answers the customer needed, the contact centre representative would bring up one of several different screens, another laborious process.

ATB's field sales force, or relationship managers, had the same disadvantage. Almost none of the tools so crucial to effective management of a sales organization, such as account profiles, product and service information, call tracking, and sales management calendars, were in place. Most reports were on paper.

ATB had worked with IBM on previous projects, and used IBM as the systems integrator to implement Siebel eFinance, to allow it to engage in dialogue with customers. Whether at an ATM, an interactive voice response unit, the Internet or a branch office, customer interactions are now captured across all touch points and made available to assist representatives in the next interaction. When a call comes into the contact centre, the customer's profile pops up, giving the representative information about who the customer is, the customer's address, a listing of the customer's holdings, and a description of the customer's last contact with the bank.

Most companies realize the continuing need to train consumer-facing staff, for whatever 'expertise' there is in the system, there is a continuing need for the human factor. In fact, it can be argued that using smart systems to liberate the operator to become 'human' again is a key to competitive service advantage. Customers can spot a script and other techniques like diffusion of anger practised with customers who complain.

In inbound telemarketing, many companies expect to make most progress with intelligent systems that manage the script according to consumers' responses, supplementing information already on the database. Most companies expect their use of computer telephony integration will increase rapidly, with information exchange and consumer recognition becoming more common. This will lead to enhanced segmentation strategies for customer management, with calling triggered by segment needs. Also, the triggering of calls by key events is likely to increase – for example, what we call 'intensive care' calls triggered by service problems or changing decision-making units. Contact centre/field sales teamwork will also become essential, as it often is in service or technical support environments.

This will apply even in mixed or hybrid channel marketing – in which a company addresses a given set of consumers via a variety of channels, which might appear to conflict with each other but actually meet different need sets. Communications can even today be converted between various channels so that the consumer can choose an appropriate channel at any time. For example e-mails can be read over voice connections or vice versa. At the same time, many companies will continue to make the error of thinking that advanced telephony is a substitute for strategic thinking. An advanced contact centre working to the wrong brief is like a powerful army marching very fast in the wrong direction!

Many companies have found that using a customer database as part of the service improvement process has been an important justification for investment. Doing the simple things right – writing or calling the right consumers, getting their details right at the point of contact, and following up by handling consumers quickly, efficiently and professionally – seems to be the key here. This is demonstrated in the following case study.

AMERICAN CANCER SOCIETY

The American Cancer Society is a nationwide voluntary health organization dedicated to eliminating cancer as a major health problem by supporting research, education, advocacy and volunteer service. Headquartered in Atlanta, Georgia, it is the largest source of private non-profit cancer research funds in the United States. To support its mission, it must perform well in three key areas. First, it must give its constituents – over 2 million volunteers, patients and donors – the best information available on prevention, detection and treatment of cancer. Second, it must demonstrate that it does well with funds entrusted to it by the public. Third, it must get donations of time and money from its constituents. Its success is directly related to giving excellent information and service, as well as to having an integrated view of its relationship with constituents.

The Society's information technology had hindered its ability to provide the best information and service to its constituents. It had too many versions of constituent records and supporting applications. Lack of integration between systems meant that cancer specialists could not draw instantly on its own and other cancer databases when serving callers. It was not easy to give callers all the information they needed. Lack of integration between systems also hindered agents' ability to identify opportunities to develop a constituent's relationship with the Society. Call centre agents did not know if a caller was both a donor and a volunteer, or if a caller was volunteering for the Society in several ways. This fragmented view made it hard for Society representatives to deliver personalized service and make informed recommendations regarding other opportunities in the Society that might interest a caller.

To improve its ability to serve constituents, the Society implemented an integrated computer system. Critical to its success was consolidating information from various databases across the organization to provide a single view of constituents and all information required to serve them. The Society implemented Siebel eBusiness Applications, focusing first on its Planned Giving Group, which served donors who might expand their charitable efforts to include planned giving (gifts of assets rather than outright income). The Society's donor base included many who, through their wills or other financial instruments, could make substantial contributions. They are targeted as a specific group for fund-raising. The success of planned giving depends also on current donors referring the Society to prospective donors, and the new system helps with this. The system also gives better access to the Society's cancer information database as well as to various other databases and information sources that its specialists use. The system also enables Society staff to identify more easily donors who might be interested in becoming volunteers and vice versa.

However, there is a strong tendency to over-complicate the matter – from both a systems and process perspective. This leads to what we would regard as over-specified systems, and processes that take too long to deliver (or that may never be delivered). Here, the key is to view things from the consumer's perspective, and to avoid investing in approaches that make no significant difference to the way the consumer is handled.

One way companies over-complicate their decision making in this area is by trying to impose a spurious rationality on the process by which consumers are managed. The commonest form of this is trying to allocate different consumer types to different distribution channels or different communications media. Today, consumers want to be managed and to manage their suppliers through many distribution and communication channels. In this world of 'hybrid marketing', new technologies and channels are used in a complementary rather than competitive manner, to reduce costs and recruit, develop and retain consumers more effectively. So electronic commerce is often very effective in combination with other communication methods in managing existing consumers, but often less effective in consumer recruitment, where the contact centre can be very strong. Unless this more flexible approach is taken, new technologies such as contact centres and electronic commerce can add cost and create conflict.

DATA WAREHOUSING, DECISION SCIENCE AND DATA ANALYSIS

Data warehousing (the aggregation of all consumer and supplementary data into one dedicated analytical database) is becoming more popular, although few companies have done it fully. Its advantage is that it allows the design of marketing and sales systems to be optimized for handling transactions and for the company's particular organization structure, working across the boundaries of business silos. Analysis issues can be resolved separately according to different priorities, for example to provide customer management-based scorecards and profit models, or to identify particular groups of consumers requiring different treatment across the enterprise. Of course, data warehousing and data mining are not an end in themselves, but should support the development of more competitive strategies or operations.

Data-mining techniques and practices have evolved rapidly, with evidence of really strong gains, for example, in reducing unnecessary activities (such as through better targeted mailings) or achieving stronger focus on higher-value consumers – especially higher future value consumers. But there is still much to be done to make a more professional and rapid approach to quantification, analysis and subsequent action a stronger part of the marketing process, rather than something that is done afterwards to find out what worked, if at all. Warehousing and then mining of consumer data is most effective when it is enterprise-wide, allowing the company to gain a single view of the consumer and business profitability. This contrasts with the approach where only one aspect of the consumer's relationship with the company is warehoused and mined – that aspect often being based on a particular organizational interpretation of the relationship, such as a single product or channel.

Analysing data about consumers over a long period can lead to complete reinterpretation of a company's success or failure in managing consumers. For example, what was seen as a problem in selling a new product might be seen as a problem of recruiting consumers new to the segment or category. It can also lead to quicker identification of where competitors are making inroads into the business, and also where new opportunities lie for the organization's own competitive activity. The following two case studies show how two leading airlines have developed and used data warehouses to improve their insight and CRM.

CATHAY PACIFIC

Cathay Pacific Airways carries passengers and cargo to many destinations globally. Its subsidiaries provide in-flight catering, aircraft maintenance engineering, cargo handling and related services at the airline's Hong Kong hub. In 1996 the airline identified 38 'islands of information' containing customer data. It was impossible to gain a consistent, consolidated view of customer behaviour or business performance.

Working in partnership with IBM, Cathay implemented a customer information system (CIS), including an enterprise-wide data warehouse and rich customer data analysis tools, including a purpose-built customer segmentation tool. By predicting customer behaviour, personalizing service and targeting marketing campaigns better, Cathay

Pacific got a 300 per cent return on investment on its data warehouse investment between 1998 and 2000. As well as consolidating the different stores of customer data, IBM assisted Cathay Pacific to achieve better-informed decision support, more personalized customer service and improved target marketing.

Cathay Pacific has improved decision support by extracting information from the data warehouse to supply analytical and reporting applications in different areas. The data warehouse enables Cathay Pacific staff to obtain key performance indicators, such as booking patterns, travel agency performance, customer satisfaction scores and customer service levels, which can then be 'sliced and diced' in order to identify trends or drive segmentation. The airline has used behavioural insight derived from analysis to deliver differentiated and personalized service to its customers.

Cathay Pacific has also greatly improved returns from its targeted marketing initiatives by use of a campaign management system, called CDMS. Cathay Pacific reports that CDMS allows it to run over 150 campaigns a year with a staff of only three, and has delivered a 50 per cent increase in return on investment for the company. The system allows the airline to maintain and monitor a control group to measure the value of its marketing initiatives. As a result of greater revenue per campaign and the greater ease of running campaigns, the airline has generated a 200 per cent increase in incremental revenue from its campaigns to members of its Asia Miles frequent flyer programme.

UNITED AIRLINES

With heightened security at airports and the unavoidable effects this has had on air travellers, airlines are focused on doing a better job of minimizing delays and improving the customer experience. To sustain continued business from their best passengers – their frequent flyers – carriers such as United Airlines (UAL) are trying harder than ever to minimize delayed flights, baggage losses and other inconveniences. To do so, UAL is embarking on a new plan to optimize operations and provide better CRM for the around 40 million members of its Mileage Plus frequent-flyer programme.

UAL maintains many systems for managing its customer accounts, operations and planning. Realizing that it could improve its flight operations and CRM systems by using data from these separate systems, UAL decided to develop a data warehouse to make its data available for enterprise-wide analysis and applications. The goal was to keep passengers satisfied by providing excellent service, and doing a better job of reaching out to customers when service interruptions occur.

United Airlines uses its IBM data warehouse to minimize inconveniences to customers and to improve its CRM, as well as to make operational improvements and to allow better planning. The database serves hundreds of business users who access it over an intranet. The data are exploited through a high-availability infrastructure, with the reservation centre and the Web site providing access to thousands of end-users.

While UAL had the ability to interact with broad segments of frequent flyers, it was not able to respond on an individual basis. For example, if a frequent-flyer passenger's baggage had been lost or the passenger had been on several delayed flights, the airline lacked the insight to be able to quickly and proactively make amends. UAL has now implemented a programme enabling it to generate letters when a customer receives poor service. By combining data from airport and flight operations with planning and customer data, UAL has improved its capacity planning operations and continues to raise its standard of customer service.

INTEGRATION

In most CRM programmes, different methods, tools and techniques are used to integrate CRM and legacy systems, so as to link the channels, administration and analytics required for closed-loop business processing. As a result the full benefits of integration stay out of reach for many companies. Integration does not happen overnight, but if a company does not work to a consistent view of how it will be achieved over time, using common approaches at each programme stage, it will fail.

To get the 'right data to the right place at the right time' to support the defined CRM activities, data needs to be moved and restructured in one of three ways.

Batch

This is used where the data can be moved overnight, usually in large quantities, and is still timely for the business activity. It is usually achieved using various extract, transform and load (ETL) tools. The choice of batch movement of data is usually for one of these reasons:

- The data are not required by the business user/process to be updated in a more immediate manner (for example quarterly or annual regulatory reporting).
- The data sources are not updated more frequently than this (for example data updates are only received from some intermediaries on a daily, weekly or monthly basis).

- The costs or complexity of other types of data movement outweigh the value of more timely data provision.

Asynchronous

This is used where the data needs to be moved in a timely manner, usually in small quantities. Timeliness may be sub-second, or longer. Implementation is normally achieved using a message switching technology. Examples of when to use this approach include:

- When (like real-time) a process waits on a rapid response, for example when a consumer service representative is entering an address change.
- When a change is propagated to multiple systems: for example a consumer's address change causes multiple systems to be updated. This can be achieved *after* the consumer is informed that the request has been captured and acknowledged.
- When a process requires many transactions to be completed, as a workflow process, over a short or extended time (for example a complete consumer application for an additional product).

Real time

This is used where data must be moved immediately, and the process waits for confirmation of successful movement (as in real-time ordering or any other transaction process with immediate confirmation).

These different methods might be used within a company's own systems, or within the systems of other companies. In practice all three types of integration need to be combined in planning and implementing CRM, whereas they have normally been implemented separately in different CRM-related projects. The same is true for new analytical or administrative systems components within the CRM program. It is best to take a common approach to planning integration needs, so that:

- different build and update techniques can be deployed against the same systems and databases;
- a variety of update techniques can be implemented cooperatively against the same systems and databases;
- update frequency and methods can be more easily changed at a later date when business requirements change or cost – benefit equations change (for example due to the reducing costs of technology over time);
- over time all the disparate systems (legacy, CRM, analytical, external, etc) can be integrated without being thwarted by horrendous

complexity, eventually appearing to be seamless to business users (for instance within a role-based portal or e-workplace) and through unbroken business processes.

E-BUSINESS INFRASTRUCTURE

Over time, research and experience have shown that closed loop integration of complete business processes (e.g. retention) is key to achieving return on investment. Figure 10.1 introduces an updated and more detailed representation of this architecture using financial services as an example.

Analysis (on the right of Figure 10.1), sometimes called analytics or business intelligence (BI), is where the process should start. For example in a retention exercise it is necessary to aggregate holdings to determine which consumers are most valuable, which are most likely to leave, how best to recognize these consumers and predict lapsing, and how best to address their needs to retain them while remaining profitable. This knowledge (the brain) could then be deployed for benefit through the most appropriate consumer touch points (the hands). The analysis area typically contains a common data warehouse (preferably with an industry data model), data extracts and/or views (data-marts) and applications (such as data mining) to analyse and present or prepare data (segments, propositions, reports, interchange tables and so on) for subsequent stages of the closed loop.

Collaborative channels (on the left of Figure 10.1) are more than multi-channel operations. The term implies that there are integrated channels working cooperatively to acquire, retain and develop consumer relationships in the most productive and cost-effective manner. Collaborative channels may be self-service, assisted or business to business (B2B) (including distribution alliances), although these channels often share the same technologies beneath (for instance, e-business, telephone and wireless often reappear in each).

Business operations includes the core systems that will account for business transactions, including product structures, pricing tables and transaction logs. These systems are the core of business operations, wherever they are accessed. They are often referred to as 'legacy systems' as if these are the systems that organizations are stuck with. There is an increasing recognition that the opposite is true, that these systems are valuable assets, often providing the rugged, reliable and scalable characteristics of the business. In fact a recently offered definition of a legacy system was 'any system that had achieved production', highlighting the fact that many new or replacement systems still do not make the grade.

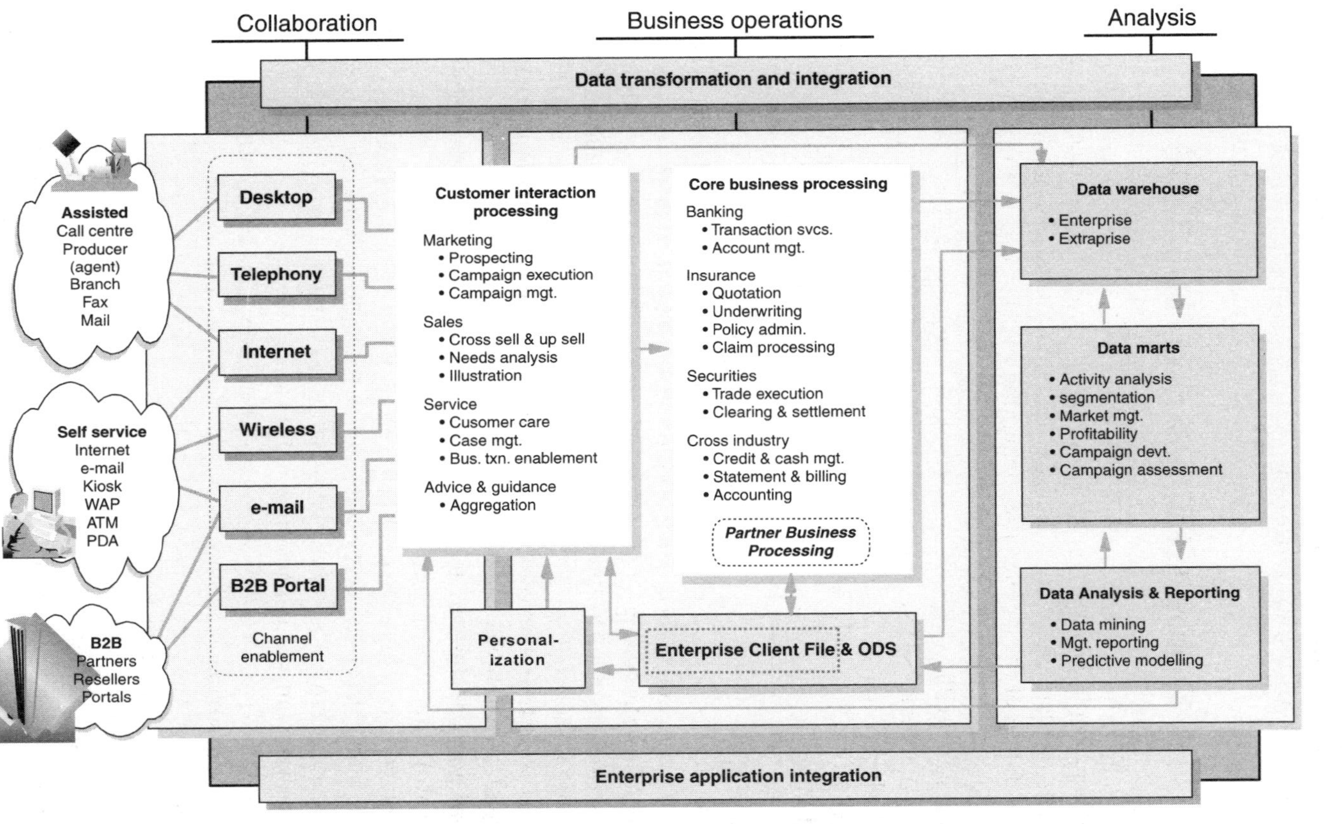

Figure 10.1 *E-business infrastructure, financial services example*

To develop a true collaborative channel approach, which supports consistent consumer knowledge and personalization across all touch points, certain components need to be common across all touch points. These components are the *enterprise customer file* (or operational data store), any real-time *personalization* engines, and the common control of *consumer interaction processing* that assures consistent customer management. Unfortunately most channel-related applications are developed with one or more of these capabilities within the channel, although it is impractical in a large and complex organization to expect that one application or channel technology will meet all current and future needs. Sharing these capabilities across channels, and deploying the common integration methods already outlined, gives an enterprise-wide solution that can be justified and developed in stages, but also allows achievement of the collaborative goal.

Behind and below Figure 10.1 lies the consistent batch, asynchronous and real-time integration required to complete closed-loop processing, to develop aggregated views of consumer relationships, and to deploy this knowledge most effectively across integrated channels and transact using high-performance, reliable and secure systems. While this diagram may look idealized, or seem unrealistic or unachievable, it provides:

- a checklist to assess what components are already in place in the business;
- a checklist for projects underway, including integration dependencies;
- an opportunity to highlight where effort would be better rewarded if it were focused on integration of existing components rather than the additional or more components;
- a map for the long term, which can include past, current and future systems;
- a common language for a cross-enterprise CRM programme;
- a checklist and map for further mergers and acquisitions;
- a checklist for supplier decisions, and/or standard components to be shared across an enterprise;
- a mature and proven approach to delivering RoI from an otherwise disparate application set.

WHAT HAS BEEN LEARNT FROM IMPLEMENTING NEW TECHNOLOGY

Learning from these experiences includes the following:

- Most consumers do not really want to know about the details of new technologies (except of course for the IT departments of consumer companies). However, at the leading edge of an application, segmentation on ability to use a technology may be important in order to get enough users, cost-effectively.

- Ideas are best and most cost-effectively driven forward by pilots and experiments, as these quickly reveal what consumers are prepared to do and want to do, where they want to change their habits and where they do not. They also quickly reveal where the technology really does improve things for consumers. Even beyond the pilot or prototype, the implementation is more likely to be a phased approach than a 'big bang'.
- Companies often treat implementing new technology in customer management as a technological experiment rather than a change to marketing and service technology. Even in productive users of contact centre technology, it is not uncommon for senior marketing management to treat the contact center as a black box, although it is their main location for handling consumers. This means that many opportunities for improving customer management are lost. For example, data on the types of consumers calling and why they calls are often not analysed for their implications for consumer recruitment and retention.
- Technology changes the relationship achieved. The best demonstration of this comes from the direct financial services providers and some utilities, which have succeeded in achieving an openness to consumer contact which has directly improved their market share and consumer retention.
- Mass customization is becoming possible with product and service packaging. With physical products it is harder, because the number of product dimensions that can be varied late in the supply process is limited. Here the best examples are achieved by automotive manufacturers, which have combined ideas of modularity with factory and supplier-facing IT to allow the cost-effective manufacture of many variants. They also use consumer-facing IT to allow consumers to explore and then order from a much larger number of variants. Other examples of this include manufacturers of furniture (particularly of the fitted kind), but also fashion. In service industries - such as financial services - where in principle almost anything can be provided, the key is to manage the cost–benefit and risk–reward profiles for both parties. The use of improved technology allows the capture of more consumer data, producing more suggestions on how consumers can vary the service. It also allows the customized product to be offered back to the consumer without human intervention.
- Improved knowledge of consumers and prospects is allowing companies to increase the cost-effectiveness of managing consumers. Contact

media can be adjusted to find the best combination for each consumer. Improved understanding of consumers allows the best prospects to be targeted for new products. This might produce quicker product launch cycles, as targeted media are used to communicate with the best prospects.

- The increasing use of systems has exposed the slackness with which marketers often use terms such as consumer, prospect and loyalty. Consumers have many kinds of relationships with the companies that supply them, and if they are to be managed according to these relationships, then the latter need to be clearly defined, using criteria based on data that are actually available.
- As the ability to manage data improves, there has been a strong move away from 'snapshot' marketing, which is based on an understanding of consumers as they are now, to 'curriculum marketing'. This is because the supplier has access to more data about the consumer's development over time and about key events in the consumer's buying and overall life cycle. For consumers, there are various family and buying cycles. If companies adopt the halo technique of focusing and targeting, they will be driven by their bigger objectives and understanding of what they really stand for and are offering to the customer.
- Benefits cited by suppliers are usually better consumer knowledge, a more precise knowledge of what levers to pull to improve consumer recruitment, retention and development, and improved profitability of individual marketing initiatives. For some, the technology has opened new ways of managing consumers (that is, new channels). However, the benefit has been across the board, not just in direct channels. For suppliers that achieve high degrees of personalization and customization, a major benefit has been an increase in consumer loyalty, because consumers feel that they are being treated as individuals, and like it.
- For consumers, the benefits are mainly improved access to information, and ease of contacting and dealing with their suppliers. Sometimes, the improved speed (for example, case processing cycle time in financial services) has led to less stress and user cost. Improving the consumer's ability to affect the relationship – even customize it – can put more control in the hands of the consumer, and some consumers like this. In particular, consumers increasingly want to access their suppliers at times and in locations and ways that suit them rather than the supplier. For example, in some cases they want to separate information gathering from decision making, gathering information at leisure over weekends and then making a transaction during the working week.

WHAT THE FUTURE HOLDS

One question an IT director faces is, 'Will the future hold anything qualitatively different, or will it be more (faster, more comprehensive) of the same?' Of course, the answer is, both. However, in terms of what actually works at the interface with the consumer, companies with the best consumer ratings (often what we call the 'new breed directs'), tend to combine tried and tested technologies with innovative marketing and consumer service approaches. They stay away from the 'bleeding edge'. Companies that get involved at the bleeding edge often do so as a substitute for a genuinely consumer-oriented marketing and service policy, or for identifying their halo. New customer management technologies take time to diffuse, and new systems to support them are often in place for 10 years or more, with perhaps a significant update every five years. So the real question for the IT director is not how fast to implement new technologies, but how to ensure that they are used to support genuine initiatives that will improvement customer management, rather than technical experiments as a substitute for improved marketing and service strategies.

11 Organizing and managing consumer insight

Merlin Stone, Bryan Foss, Bryan Hassett, Alison Bond and Ronèl Schoeman

Despite direct marketing's reliance on technique and technology – especially since the arrival of advanced database and customer contact systems and new electronic media – database marketing is still planned and implemented by people. Even when the customer interacts with Web sites, e-mail management systems or interactive television, people are involved in planning and managing the interaction, and of course in handling cases that cannot be handled automatically. So in this chapter, we examine the main jobs done by those who work in database marketing and consumer insight. We start with a case study, which shows how a leading retailer organizes its consumer insight.

RETAILER'S APPROACH TO CONSUMER INSIGHT MANAGEMENT

A UK retailer has worked hard to become more 'customer facing', with many managers and users involved in this success. Its Customer Insight Unit (CIU) has played an important part in this by helping it to achieve its mission 'to focus on our customers and be driven by their needs', using SAS Customer Relationship Management Solutions. The CIU draws together previously fragmented analytical experience in areas such as marketing, sales promotion, customer relationship management, footage assessment and location analysis. This concentration of expertise has enabled cross-pollination of ideas and analytical techniques, providing consumer insights including confirming who the customers are, what they want and perhaps equally importantly, when and why they are tempted to go to the competition.

Data from the charge card system, combined with external sources such as census, demographic and national panel data, tells the retailer much about its customers. Around a hundred explanatory variables are held for each UK household, rising to several hundred for customers with charge cards. Information collected at the point of sale, via cash tills, through its direct marketing channel or the growing number of Web site interactions, is consolidated to tell the retailer what consumers actually buy. Analysis helps in a variety of ways, from corporate branding through to operational decision making within the business units. It enables the company to ensure that the products in a particular store are the ones customers want.

Whereas in the past stores were stocked according to their square footage, now they are increasingly supplied according to a detailed profile analysis of their customers. Detailed segmentation analysis is also driving much-expanded communications and sales promotions activity. Traditional gravity analysis and spatial modelling, which fuses geographical information system functionality, have long supported decisions about when and where to refurbish, redesign or replace stores to attract higher volumes of sales. Footprint analysis enables the retailer to predict the catchment area and any sales volumes of any planned stores. However, these types of analysis usually assume a static, residential customer base, whereas today's strategies often call for a different approach. The company has recently introduced new trading formats such as railway terminal outlets and food-only stores. The resident population around a food store at a city rail terminus was negligible, therefore modelling was geared to predicting sales based on the flow of people through the station rather than the expenditure of local households.

THE PEOPLE INVOLVED IN MANAGING AND USING CONSUMER INSIGHT

The main managers and users are the following.

The direct/database marketing manager

This is the leader of the direct/database marketing organization, usually reporting either to a more senior marketing manager (such as the head of marketing communications or marketing services, marketing director, or marketing and sales director), or rarely (usually in smaller companies) to a non-marketing person. In some companies, particularly smaller ones, direct marketing specialists are more junior, reporting to marketing management (or indeed the only marketing manager). In the smallest companies, there is unlikely to be a direct marketing specialist, and one person will fulfil many of the roles described in this chapter. Some large companies believe that direct marketing is so well integrated into their marketing that there is no need for separate senior responsibility, and that direct marketing skills are essential for all marketers. So instead of having specialists, they train all marketers in direct marketing, and senior marketers are expected to be able to manage direct marketing along with their other responsibilities

CRM manager/director

The development of customer relationship management (CRM) approaches has led to many companies renaming some senior marketing roles and some more junior roles. For example, a senior direct marketer might now be called 'CRM director'. This is not simply a renaming – it usually reflects a broadening of focus, away from campaigning to achieve sales volume objectives, to focusing on recruitment, retention and development of customers – although the focus on sales volumes and revenues is usually still strong.

The direct marketing specialist

This is the most commonly encountered direct marketing type. Often recruited from an agency or another user company, the specialist usually develops and implements campaigns. Companies often put trainees into a junior version of this role, growing them into the specialism by experience and training.

The systems specialist

In smaller companies, much of the systems work is contracted to external suppliers, so they are unlikely to have systems specialists dedicated to database marketing. In larger companies that have their own customer database, there may be many in-house systems specialists involved in database marketing. They are usually assigned to support marketing systems by the IT manager. Some will be only temporarily involved, but in large companies, a permanent team is needed to support marketing systems and develop them further. Systems specialists often help integrate database marketers' work with mainstream marketing, perhaps by drawing customer data from general marketing and sales and administrative systems, and feeding back data gathered from direct marketing campaigns into marketing systems. Alternatively they develop decision support systems that can be used in all marketing contexts (such as management reporting systems).

IT specialists also play an essential role in liaising with external suppliers such as computer bureaux and data suppliers. New media are very IT-intensive, and the IT team does essential work in ensuring that, for example, contact centre systems and the Web are properly connected with other marketing work. Database marketers must communicate well with their IT department, to ensure their requirements are understood. IT departments can easily misinterpret requirements or hold up campaigns, so it is up to the database marketing manager to ensure that everyone understands what his or her role is in a campaign. Good project management also helps.

The media specialist

With an increasing variety of media available, companies that become big users of a particular medium may need to employ specialists in developing and using that medium. This applies particularly to new media. However, other companies take the view that this expertise is best supplied by agencies.

Customer data/customer insight management

As companies have increased the size and complexity of their customer databases, they need managers who specialize in developing and maintaining customer data and deriving knowledge from it – whether for campaign selections or for developing new customer management strategies. In some companies, customer information from all sources (not just marketing data, but also, for example, market research and customer service data) is brought together under a new type of manager, who is expected to be familiar with how all these sources should be managed and combined to create customer insight. In some companies, a consumer or customer insight department has been created. This includes database marketing and market research specialists. The department's job is to provide insight to all users. Roles might be allocated according to target segments, as well as to specialisms. The insight role might be interpreted very proactively, with insights extended beyond consumer characteristics and behaviour into the policy area. The insight team might be part of a larger marketing team focused on a particular large segment. For example, some banks have split their retail marketing into business and consumer, and have an insight team attached to each segment.

The statistician, data analyst or modeller

If you are in the early stages of using database marketing, your statistical or analytical expertise is likely to be supplied as part of a package deal with your direct marketing agency, which carries out (or uses specialist suppliers to carry out) any statistical analyses needed. These analyses are likely to be quite simple, for example comparing results of different tests, or analysing the performance of different selections within a campaign.

As the organization gets more sophisticated in its use of data – particularly if it develops its own database – it might need to use advanced statistical techniques such as data mining to analyse customers and group them into categories likely to be more responsive to different offers. The strategic advantage gained from using these techniques may make policy in this area a sensitive competitive issue. There might be worries about using external suppliers. Also, the depth of the analysis required means that there are real gains in having internal experts. They know the company, the customers, the strategies and the data. They should know their business well enough to identify opportunities from the data. However, many companies have found that this approach does not work in practice, and that it is better to have a close relationship with a specialist analysis company, whose only job is to turn analysis into money. Attracting and retaining top quantitative people can be easier for such specialist companies, which can also ensure high levels of utilization to keep them intellectually challenged, and more importantly to ensure that they are used cost-effectively.

Good statisticians/analysts are rare birds. They do not require great skills in statistical manipulation, which is the job of sophisticated computer packages – which even tell them what is worth analysing. However, they must of course be able to understand perfectly the output of statistical packages. Most importantly, they must have insight and creativity. They are not statistical purists. They must be prepared to live by the central rule of database marketing – what works, works. Most database marketing statistics are 'dirty statistics'. They do not observe nice theoretical pure statistical rules, which are designed to provide near-scientific degrees of certainty in making predictions. Rather, they aim to find patterns that can be shown to continue (or not!) by testing. Findings have to be actionable and not just nice to know. So statisticians/analysts must be happy working with live, imperfect data. They must know how to cope with its shortcomings. They must understand how to fill gaps in data, perhaps using third-party data. They need to be able to build and test models, and to interpret trends, while keeping in mind external influences that could change trends and make previous models invalid. This includes creating control cells and interpreting test results against control cells.

It is important to get input from statisticians in the area of database design. Database design must support analysis as well as customer interaction. If data are missing, or if relationships between data entities are incorrectly specified, analysis cannot be deployed. In practice, a key role of statisticians and analysts is 'data engineering' - getting the data into a state where it can yield business conclusions.

Market researchers

Market researchers may use data generated by or recruited for database marketing to reach research conclusions for use in the wider marketing organization. They are also providers of data for customer insight - particularly qualitative research designed to probe more deeply the characteristics of segments identified on the customer database. As mentioned above, some research teams have been merged with customer database teams into insight departments.

Users/internal customers

Users are responsible for putting together campaigns. They may be specialists (direct marketers) or generalists. The latter are marketers with other accountabilities such as product, brand, category, area or segment management, but today they often are involved in database marketing. Increasingly tools are available that put the ownership and updating of business rules and campaigns directly into their hands.

Support staff

These provide various support functions needed by users and internal customers. They include specialists in print, data analysis systems support (who help marketing staff operate database and campaign management systems) and database management. Often these are shared resources.

Senior marketing management

These are the individuals who secure funding, create direction and manage resources. They are in a sense the ultimate internal customers for insight. When they are distant from insight, their understanding of customers' needs and behaviour tends to be weak, and they may steer the organization in the wrong direction. Their halo is likely to diverge from their customers' halo.

MANAGING CONSUMER INSIGHT STAFF

Consumer insight is a new way of looking at disciplines that have been around for some time. Managing insight staff well is more important to companies as they base their strategies increasingly on knowledge derived from insights. However, this also produces new requirements for professional management of consumer insight, as it becomes more critical to the organization, as the following case study shows.

MANAGING CONSUMER INSIGHT IN FINANCIAL SERVICES – STAFF AND KNOWLEDGE RETENTION

A large consumer financial services company invested in a customer insight project, using IBM consultants and services, to address the very high lapse rates of new life policies. After six months of a data mining and discovery exercise, the core project team of three all left the company within a few weeks of each other. Despite the project materials still being available for further use, the early successes were never followed through to retain likely lapsers.

Two years later the company decided to revisit the retention topic as the situation had not improved. When reminded of the previous project they were able to analyse which predicted lapsers had now left the company – due to no corrective action being taken. The results were stunning for the current directors. The majority of predicted lapsers had in fact cancelled their policies. This increased marketing costs as new customers had to be found to replace those who had been lost.

This example demonstrates that new knowledge of consumers and capabilities, not yet formalized within operational processes, can be most valuable yet most easily lost when staff move or leave the company.

The commitment to quality is illustrated in the next case study.

INSURANCE COMPANY NEEDS ANALYTICAL SKILLS

This company is one of the leading home and auto insurers in the United States, and one of the nation's leading life insurers. As it expands its financial services product line, it has recently focused on improving the quality of marketing analytics and decision support. It relies on SAS analytics to identify business opportunities among the middle-aged, middle-income market, as well as to analyse the performance of intermediaries who sell its products and services.

The company aims to profile its customer base, to understand who is in the market and to gauge the effectiveness of the programmes it executes on a day-to-day basis. Frequency distributions and cross-tabulations of customers who have purchased financial products before are used to describe who these customers are by segment and channel, as well as see who sold which products to whom. The project team then sets out to establish a premise for executing effective marketing campaigns, based on the knowledge derived from the analysis of existing relationships. There are distinct differences in the kind of customer that buys through the various channels. By being able to delineate these differences, the company has the intelligence to determine which product will best fit which channel, and can give this information to the product development and distribution organizations.

There are significant differences between the available channels (banks, brokerages and so on), and the kinds of people attracted to each channel vary dramatically. Being able to recognize the differences supports many of the customer management product design and management functions that are delivered. The company believes that if you really want to move the business, you must hire the most highly skilled people. A few highly skilled analysts are preferred to many less skilled staff.

Required skills and capabilities

The main skills, insight and capabilities required for data-based customer management are:

- strategic analysis/planning/audit/review of customer management activity;
- strategic IT planning for customer management;
- consumer data analysis – for all purposes from understanding the customer base to analysing results;
- determining data requirements for customer management;
- customer information management systems selection and implementation;
- gathering consumer data from non-transactional sources such as questionnaires and guarantee data;
- extracting consumer information from client transactional sources;
- campaign planning;

- selection management;
- media planning – including new media;
- outbound communications management;
- response handling and fulfilment.

These tend to be resident in the following types of company:

- data analysis houses;
- lifestyle data suppliers;
- list brokers;
- database management bureaux;
- direct marketing agencies;
- response handling and fulfilment agencies;
- IT hardware suppliers;
- IT systems integrators;
- software suppliers;
- management consultancies;
- client direct/database marketing departments (or similar) – often including insight staff;
- client IT departments.

Using external suppliers

The important points to understand about the third parties are the nature of their core skills/insight/capabilities, and their main business model(s): that is, how they make their money (for example through sale of staff time, software, data access or service usage). The main choice facing the client is the management advantage of reducing the number of suppliers, against the advantage of using the best of breed for each task. However, in some cases this problem is dealt with by outsourcing customer management activities to one or more companies, leaving them to select partners for the provision of specialist skills, insight or capability. Given the complexity of the above, many companies have realized that selecting suppliers to help in customer management is a critical decision, to be handled as a coordinated supplier selection process, rather than as a series of one-off decisions.

The mistake many companies make is to assume that the choice of customer management system is the most important choice. Good systems working with poor data, processes and implementation programmes usually lead to very expensive ways of managing customers that do not please the finance director! The practical implication of all this is that where a company is considering involving a third party in any area of customer management, and particularly where that involvement may lead to intense inter-working with other suppliers or to data cooperation with peer companies, a key selection criterion should be a strong track record of working professionally and (usually) quickly within a wider team.

The decision whether to contract out consumer insight

Most companies routinely contract out market research. One reason is that codes of practice usually require that the respondent's identity be kept from the client. With consumer information from databases, the opposite is true. A database of existing customers, and even some databases of prospects, must in most cases by law consist of individuals who have given permission for their name to be used by the client company. This means that they can be managed in-house. However, scarcity of the required database and statistical skills, combined with the fact that outsourced suppliers have fine-tuned their policies and processes and their own partnership relationships (such as with suppliers of statistical and analytical tools), means that many companies still outsource some or all of their database analysis. This means that market research agencies increasingly need to work alongside other suppliers. One difference between them is that while market researchers are used to analysing relatively small and deep databases, consumer database analysts are used to analysing very large and relatively shallow databases. Different statistical skills and knowledge are required for these two. However, some suppliers have realized this and have established consumer insight agencies which are used to working alongside market research agencies.

Whichever option a company chooses, the strategic importance of consumer insight is such that most companies opt for a strategic rather than a tactical relationship with the suppliers they choose to help them, continuously considering how to transform and improve marketing processes rather than simply operate them. Suppliers need to work with each other over many campaigns. This necessitates close teamwork between suppliers themselves, and between the suppliers and the various internal departments involved. On each project or campaign, the team should be brought together at as early a stage as possible, in order to agree the work programme and sort out any potential problems. Many inter-supplier problems are caused by centralization of communication. In practice, it is best if suppliers work closely with each other according to a tight brief from the client (see Chapter 4). This is much better than their having to rely on the client being at the centre of a network of communication.

Selection of consumer insight suppliers

Selection of suppliers is an important first step. Some criteria for selecting suppliers are:

- **Creativity** – do they provide that extra spark, but one which fits the brief? For agencies, this may depend on the quality of the creative brief as well as on the quality of creative staff.
- **Quality** – is their work of a consistently high standard, and is this high standard a result of good management rather than chance?
- **Reliability** – can they be relied upon to perform well every time?
- **Ability to observe deadlines** – do they meet all their deadlines? If there are problems, do they inform the client quickly enough, or try to hide the problems?
- **Ability to understand client needs**.
- **Openness** – are they honest with clients?
- **Ability to take criticism** and bounce back with better solutions.
- **Price** – do they give good value for money? This does not mean being cheap. Can they account properly for the money that clients pay them?
- **Ability to work with others** (the client and other suppliers). Do they enter into the team spirit, and not try to look good at others' expense? Do they accept problems as team problems?
- **Ability to add value** – do they execute briefs and instructions blindly, or do they help achieve more by identifying weaknesses in the brief and remedying them?
- **Awareness of the client's industry** –which must be kept updated.
- **Ability to match the solution to the client's needs**.

Managing the strategic relationship with suppliers

Increasingly companies use suppliers or business alliances to carry out what they consider as non-core (for their own internal business model) activities. Campaigns are outsourced, with the relevant fulfilment involving sales, delivery and even some aspects of service. For example promotional programmes have been implemented where the supplier (or alliance) provides not only consumer insight, data management and campaign resources, but also contact centres and other follow-through actions, within the complete sales process. In addition physical fulfilment can include the mailing of brochures and price lists on request, delivery of ordered goods and acceptance of returns. In such cases it is important to agree how responsibility for consumer insight and data is shared between the partners. This should be well documented, in a 'document of understanding' or 'service level agreement'. Substantial risk sharing and far more flexible cost and service models (sometimes called 'on demand') normally result from well-chosen relationships. Given the additional effort involved, few companies would embark on such alliances unless the gains from each were expected to be exceptional.

Distribution networks may be managed by an alliance partner, enabling much more of the market to be addressed than by the initial supplier's traditional channels alone. In many countries grocery and other retailers are playing to their strengths as general purpose distributors, moving into telecoms, financial services, electronic goods and other areas of profitable distribution. As businesses continue to focus on their core product and/or consumer management capabilities, the trend to outsource even more non-essential business components to alliances and suppliers will continue to develop at an increasingly rapid rate. While these are general trends, evidenced in the most forward-thinking companies, many are still struggling with the contractual management of traditional supplier relationships.

TWO CASE STUDIES OF PARTNERSHIP

Brittany Ferries

Brittany Ferries is one of Europe's leading ferry operating services, known for its route network, high levels of onboard service and a wide range of self-drive holidays to France and Spain. Brittany Ferries partnered with the Database Group (DbG) in an effort to maximize customer retention, promote repeat purchase and improve the effectiveness of its direct marketing (DM), which is a core element of its business.

DbG built a marketing database capable of supporting Brittany Ferries' DM campaign activity and analysis. The database holds customers (bookers), enquirers and prospects, and is updated from Brittany Ferries' booking and reservations systems, so it contains full transactional details. DbG applies predictive technology and data enhancement techniques to allow Brittany Ferries to target its campaigns more effectively. The database is updated monthly via feeds from several sources. The update files hold information on new bookings and enquiries made over the phone or Web, and amendments to existing records. Brittany Ferries has access to the database. The secure online connection to the database enables Brittany Ferries to perform counts and analysis to aid campaign planning.

Targeting has improved following a customer modelling exercise carried out by DbG. This identified the characteristics of customers with the highest propensity to respond to campaigns or make bookings.

Brittany Ferries also uses a particular analytical and selection software tool which allows it to visualize segments by accessing and analysing their database remotely.

UIA

UIA is a specialist affinity insurer that provides general insurance products to members and supporters of not-for-profit organizations such as trade unions, charities and associations. The general insurance market is characterized by its maturity and competitiveness, and UIA relies heavily on direct marketing to grow its business. The quality and accuracy of data and a thorough understanding of customers is crucial for producing cost-effective targeted campaigns.

The Database Group (DbG) hosts, manages and develops UIA's marketing database, and provides support for its customer management activity for both customer and prospect direct mail. Working with various data sources, including UIA's own data, third-party product providers and affinity partners, DbG provides UIA with a single view of its customers and prospects, and remote access to the database, and holds a complete record of contact history for acquisition and retention programmes.

To achieve this, DbG consolidated data and, in conjunction with UIA, designed a marketing database of several million live records. Data is cleansed on input with DbG's full suppression suite applied to remove duplicates, gone-aways and bereavements. DbG designed a bespoke visualization tool, 'Dataminer' to UIA's specific requirements, allowing the UIA marketing team to view and amend the live database remotely. To increase the effectiveness of targeted DM activity, DbG has worked with UIA to load a number of segmentation models based on recency, frequency and value (RFV) and lifestyle into the database. The database allows complex selections for DM activity, and the customized front end provides UIA with access to data on all customers and prospects. The database allows UIA to data mine with ease, manage its customer communications strategy, and ultimately enhance campaign effectiveness.

In our final case study, we show how consumer insight management, when managed by a specialist supplier, can transform the profitability of a business.

UK INTERNET SERVICES PROVIDER (ISP)

The explosion of the Internet has made the UK ISP market very competitive. All the major players found it hard to match the pace of change. With the advent of broadband, the usual complexity of ISP management was compounded by the need to meet tough revenue and cost targets for the enhanced capability, while achieving high rates of conversion from narrowband to broadband, quickly followed by strong retention rates. This ISP, one of the UK's leading providers, decided to outsource much of its customer management and insight function, to ensure achievement of the best results, to Digital Data Analysis Ltd (DDA), a leading UK customer data engineering and insight company.

As in most telecommunications and similar organizations, the client's IT systems had been developed piecemeal as required operationally, and without regard to any overall customer or information strategy. The client found itself data rich but knowledge poor, but recognized this and the innate difficulties any large corporate has in managing such situations, and decided to outsource.

Through innovative application of tried and tested technology, DDA almost immediately identified and implemented several quick wins. Key to this was cleaning and transforming the various customer data sources and system logs into a form where they provided useful transactional information at a customer level. The Internet, like most communication networks, is a shared service that relies on everyone not wanting to use it at the same time. As in most cases a fixed monthly fee is charged, the customer's usage can be thought of as a cost. DDA built a net value profile of the customer base. This highlighted that the most significant skew was a small but highly significant segment of unprofitable customers.

A major part of the problem was that the customer journey depended on and was described by various bits of information scattered throughout the ISP's systems and departments. The inefficiencies and problems caused by this fragmentation were not the clear responsibility of any one person or department. Outsourcing helped here, because as a third party DDA found it easier to move between the divisions within the business, bypassing and even breaking down organizational barriers. A staged approach was taken to developing the required consolidated analysis database. Each dataset and project was justified on its own merits before proceeding, but all the while a consolidated data view was being constructed, the value of which far exceeded the sum of its parts.

Figure 11.1 shows a simple view of the customer management cycle. For the acquisition phase DDA built a series of propensity models, enabling it to target potentially higher-value customers. This helped cut the cost per acquisition by over 40 per cent. DDA integrated transactional and customer data with third-party data, and embarked on an insight journey, starting with a profile of unprofitable customers.

DDA used this to advise the client how to stop targeting them, as they were damaging overall profitability because of the high cost of service, even though they had a low cost of acquisition. DDA used operational data sources to identify customers who experienced problems or issues during set-up. A trigger-based communication strategy was used to keep these customers warm until their service was activated.

Given resource constraints, the welcome call strategy was prioritized according to potential customer value. During the 'welcome' phase additional, attitudinal and needs-based customer information was captured, to allow the customer segmentation to be refined further, and to identify additional opportunities for growth via cross-sell and up-sell. The results from this demonstrated that customers who were contacted were one-third less likely to churn during early life than the control cell. Significant increases in the frequency of usage of the service were also observed. The number of additional services subsequently purchased in early life was significantly increased. Brand perceptions were also positively influenced. In the 'early life' phase, data captured at 'welcome', combined with market research data, was modelled to identify the most appropriate up-sell and cross-sell strategies for next best product.

At this stage, DDA was also able to enhance the understanding of customers with high potential and of those that could damage profitability. A key area where profit was damaged was the cost of customer service. Through root cause analysis of customer complaint and support data, DDA identified the issue as a combination of product performance, ambiguous customer communications, back-end processes and systems misalignment. The business addressed these issues and turned these non-profitable customers into customers contributing value. DDA also identified these customers in advance. They were intercepted at their first point of contact and handled differently.

Speed as ever is an issue, yet rushing data management is often the cause of problems. DDA's solution has been to create its own data-handling environment where services run, rather than applications. FIDO (flexible integrated data object) is a DDA service that sits behind a secure firewall, waiting for data to arrive. Depending on the characteristics of the data set, FIDO sets in motion a variety of activities, from performing physical audit checks on the data to sending e-mails to various team members, informing them that the data has arrived. From there, provided the data passes quality control, FIDO starts to process the data in anticipation of updating a variety of databases. For example, if data arrives on a Friday evening, then much of the required processing will already have taken place by the opening of work on Monday morning. The smart use of technology enables DDA to keep up with the demands from the client, freeing people from boring and error-prone work. It gives

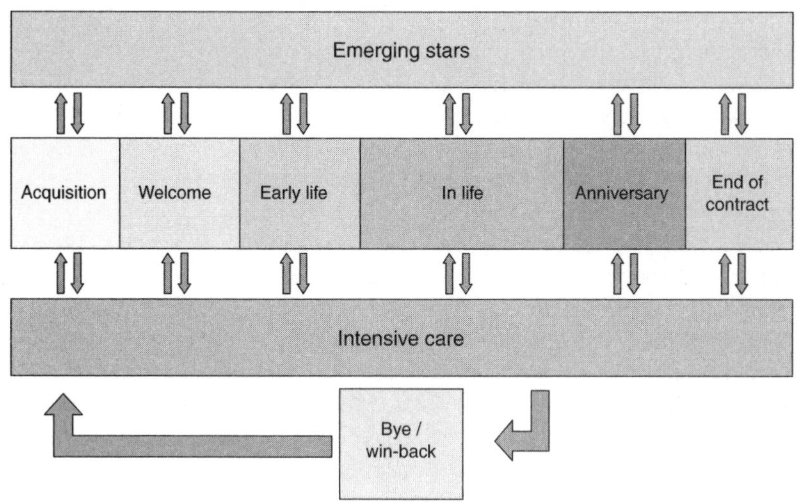

Figure 11.1 *DDA customer management life cycle overview*

them the opportunity to really understand the data they are working with, allowing them to focus on spotting problems early in the process.

At the 'in life' stage, DDA combined enhanced needs segmentation and potential value modelling to implement a differentiated cross-sell and up-sell strategy. Customers at risk of churn were identified by combining predictive modelling and behaviour-based triggers such as downturn in usage, customer complaints and account tenure. They were placed into an intensive care programme until the risk of churn was significantly reduced, then reintegrated into the main life cycle programme. Likewise customers with exceptional potential for growth were identified and given VIP treatment. Specific propositions were developed and tested for tenure stages where customers were displaying the greatest risk of churn, such as end of contract. The learning from these tests was also applied in a specialized customer care team. This resulted in a significant rise in long-term retention. Underpinning the entire programme was the aim to match desired customer behaviour as described by the propensity models and market research with actual customer behaviour observed later. This enabled DDA to further enhance and evaluate the model, and to research the methodology used.

As the broadband market continues to grow rapidly, so has the cost of providing help desks to cope with customer enquiries. Help desk logs provide more useful data. The accuracy of the logs, taken from an outsourced system with limited access to other operational systems, was improved by strengthening the feedback loop between the call centre and the client's internal systems via the CRM database. The help desk life cycle of a customer can be very different from the usage life cycle, so DDA developed models demonstrating strong relationships between patterns of help desk usage and churn behaviour. This enabled the help desk to be more proactive. Thus, customers with patterns of failed usage after a recent install were targeted for care calls, to help them successfully install the product.

The planning and execution of such campaigns demanded a broad skill set, requiring knowledge of the ISP's marketing/business domains together with advanced technical expertise. Underpinning DDA's efforts was the automation of transfer, processing and loading of tens of millions of rows of data daily. The client found that the traditional distinction between technical and account handling staff was rather blurred at DDA. DDA consultants were well-rounded knowledge workers, well placed to provide consultancy as well as hands-on support to the client operation. Over time the ISP took on secondment several DDA consultants, greatly promoting the efficiency of the relationship and knowledge transfer.

Another nice surprise for the ISP was that DDA combined a profound understanding of technology with a healthy disrespect for it. Technology was seen in context, as a tool for satisfying a business need, not an exercise in technical brilliance or excellence. DDA was also aware of the dangers of bleeding-edge technology, and the preferred approach was to harness the power of stable and established technologies in innovative ways. Marketing is communication, so it is an important part of the customer journey. It is so easy to forget, when producing a 'customer centric' view of a business, that it is the business's products, services and customers that are of primary concern. Thus DDA fostered close links not just with the marketing department but also with the product and operational divisions.

In delivering significant gains for the ISP, DDA clearly demonstrated the soundness of its approach to the role of information. DDA champions the view that information is a continuum. It is not solid, it is ethereal and can change as it passes from one system to another, from one person to another. Customer information must be engineered differently from classic engineering. A hybrid approach is needed, taking account of the fact that designing is for information and people, not concrete, steel or silicon. This hybrid approach requires more nonlinear input than technical people on their own can provide, thus the need to move closer to the marketing and business functions of a company, bringing both teams closer together. As DDA puts it, 'databases are the sands on which the footprints of the customer journey can be seen'.

CONCLUSIONS

This book has described the emerging discipline of consumer insight management. Although the discipline is considered to be new, it is effectively a combination of consumer database analysis and market research. It is not at such a stage of maturity that we are able to say, to do consumer insight you need to do X. Instead, to manage consumer insight well you need to draw upon the two source disciplines to achieve the combination that suits your own company. We hope that this book helps you do it.

Appendix: The Market Research Society Code of Conduct

INTRODUCTION

The Market Research Society

With over 8,000 members in more than 50 countries, The Market Research Society (MRS) is the world's largest international membership organization for professional researchers and others engaged in (or interested in) marketing, social or opinion research.

It has a diverse membership of individual researchers within agencies, independent consultancies, client-side organizations, and the academic community, and from all levels of seniority and job functions.

All members agree to comply with the MRS Code of Conduct, which is supported by the Codeline advisory service and a range of specialist guidelines on best practice.

MRS offers various qualifications and membership grades, as well as training and professional development resources to support these. It is the official awarding body in the UK for vocational qualifications in market research.

MRS is a major supplier of publications and information services, conferences and seminars and many other meeting and networking opportunities for researchers.

MRS is 'the voice of the profession' in its media relations and public affairs activities on behalf of professional research practitioners, and aims to achieve the most favourable climate of opinions and legislative environment for research.

The purpose of the 'Code of Conduct'

This edition of the Code of Conduct was agreed by The Market Research Society to be operative from July 1999. It is a fully revised version of a self-regulatory code which has been in existence since 1954. This Code is based upon and fully compatible with the ICC/ESOMAR International Code of Marketing and Social Research Practice. The Code of Conduct is designed to support all those engaged in marketing or social research in maintaining professional standards. It applies to all members of The Market Research Society, whether they are engaged in consumer, business to business, social, opinion or any other type of confidential survey research. It applies to all quantitative and qualitative methods for data gathering. Assurance that research is conducted in an ethical manner is needed to create confidence in, and to encourage cooperation among, the business community, the general public, regulators and others.

The Code of Conduct does not take precedence over national law. Members responsible for international research shall take its provisions as a minimum requirement and fulfil any other responsibilities set down in law or by nationally agreed standards.

The purpose of Guidelines

MRS Guidelines exist or are being developed in many of these areas in order to provide a more comprehensive framework of interpretation. These guidelines have been written in recognition of the increasingly diverse activities of the Society's members, some of which are not covered in detail by the Code of Conduct. A full list of guidelines appears on the Society's Web site, and is also available from the Society's Standards Manager.

One particular guideline covers the use of databases containing personal details of respondents or potential respondents, both for purposes associated with confidential survey research and in cases where respondent details are passed to a third party for marketing or other purposes. This guideline has been formally accepted by the Society, following extensive consultation with members and with the Data Protection Registrar/Commissioner.

Relationship with data protection legislation

Adherence to the Code of Conduct and the database Guidelines will help to ensure that research is conducted in accordance with the principles of data protection legislation. In the UK this is encompassed by the Data Protection Act 1998.

Data Protection Definitions

Personal Data means data which relates to a living individual who can be identified

- from the data, or
- from the data and other information in the possession of, or likely to come into the possession of, the data controller

and includes any expression of opinion about the individual and any indication of the intentions of the data controller or any other person in respect of the individual.

Processing means obtaining, recording or holding the information or data or carrying out any operation or set of operations on the information or data, including

- organization, adaptation or alteration
- retrieval, consultation or use
- disclosure by transmission, dissemination or otherwise making available
- alignment, combination, blocking, erasure or destruction.

It is a requirement of membership that researchers must ensure that their conduct follows the letter and spirit of the principles of Data Protection legislation from the Act. In the UK the eight data protection principles are:

- **The First Principle**
  Personal data shall be processed fairly and lawfully.
- **The Second Principle**
  Personal data shall be obtained only for one or more specified and lawful purposes, and shall not be further processed in any manner incompatible with that purpose or those purposes.
- **The Third Principle**
  Personal data shall be adequate, relevant and not excessive in relation to the purpose or purposes for which they are processed.
- **The Fourth Principle**
  Personal data shall be accurate and, where necessary, kept up to date.
- **The Fifth Principle**
  Personal data processed for any purpose or purposes shall not be kept longer than is necessary for that purpose or those purposes.

- **The Sixth Principle**
  Personal data shall be processed in accordance with the rights of data subjects under this Act.
- **The Seventh Principle**
  Appropriate technical and organiszational measures shall be taken against unauthorized or unlawful processing of personal data and against accidental loss or destruction of, or damage to, personal data.
- **The Eighth Principle**
  Personal data shall not be transferred to a country or territory outside the European Economic Area, unless that country or territory ensures an adequate level of protection for the rights and freedoms of data subjects in relation to the processing of personal data.

Exemption for Research Purposes

Where personal data processed for research, statistical or historical purposes are not processed to support decisions affecting particular individuals, or in such a way as likely to cause substantial damage or distress to any data subject, such processing will not breach the Second Principle and the data may be retained indefinitely despite the Fifth Principle.

As long as the results of the research are not published in a form, which identifies any data subject, there is no right of subject access to the data.

Code Definitions

- **Research**
  Research is the collection and analysis of data from a sample of individuals or organizations relating to their characteristics, behaviour, attitudes, opinions or possessions. It includes all forms of marketing and social research such as consumer and industrial surveys, psychological investigations, observational and panel studies.
- **Respondent**
  A respondent is any individual or organization from whom any information is sought by the researcher for the purpose of a marketing or social research project. The term covers cases where information is to be obtained by verbal interviewing techniques, postal and other self-completion questionnaires, mechanical or electonic equipment, observation and any other method where the identity of the provider of the information may be recorded or otherwise traceable. This includes those approached for research purposes whether or not substantive information is obtained from them and includes those who decline to participate or withdraw at any stage from the research.

- **Interview**
  An interview is any form of contact intended to provide information from a respondent.
- **Identity**
  The identity of a respondent includes, as well as his/her name and/or address, any other information which offers a reasonable chance that he/she can be identified by any of the recipients of the information.
- **Children**
  For the Purpose of the Code, children and young people are defined as those aged under 18. The intention of the provisions regarding age is to protect potentially vulnerable members of society, whatever the source of their vulnerability, and to strengthen the principle of public trust. Consent of a parent or responsible adult should be obtained for interviews with children under 16. Consent must be obtained under the following circumstances:
  - In home/at home (face-to-face and telephone interviewing)
  - Group discussions/depth interviews
  - Where interviewer and child are alone together.

Interviews being conducted in public places, such as in-street/in-store/central locations, with 14 and 15 years olds may take place without consent if a parent or responsible adult is not accompanying the child. In these situations an explanatory thank you note must be given to the child.

Under special circumstances, a survey may waive parental consent but only with the prior approval of the Professional Standards Committee.

- **Records**
  The term records includes anything containing information relating to a research project and covers all data collection and data processing documents, audio and visual recordings. Primary records are the most comprehensive record of information on which a project is based; they include not only the original data records themselves, but also anything needed to evaluate those records, such as quality control documents. Secondary records are any other records about the Respondent.
- **Client**
  Client includes any individual, organization, department or division, including any belonging to the same organization as the research agency which is responsible for commissioning a research project.
- **Agency**
  Agency includes any individual, organization, department or division, including any belonging to the same organization as the client which is responsible for, or acts as, a supplier on all or part of a research project.

- **Professional Body**
  Professional body refers to The Market Research Society.
- **Public Place**
  A 'public place' is one to which the public has access (where admission has been gained with or without a charge) and where an individual could reasonably expect to be observed and/or overheard by other people, for example in a shop, in the street or in a place of entertainment.

PRINCIPLES

Research is founded upon the willing cooperation of the public and of business organizations. It depends upon their confidence that it is conducted honestly, objectively, without unwelcome intrusion and without harm to respondents. Its purpose is to collect and analyse information, and not directly to create sales nor to influence the opinions of anyone participating in it. It is in this spirit that the Code of Conduct has been devised.

The general public and other interested parties shall be entitled to complete assurance that every research project is carried out strictly in accordance with this Code, and that their rights of privacy are respected. In particular, they must be assured that no information which could be used to identify them will be made available without their agreement to anyone outside the agency responsible for conducting the research. They must also be assured that the information they supply will not be used for any purposes other than research and that they will not be adversely affected or embarrassed as a direct result of their participation in a research project.

Wherever possible respondents must be informed as to the purpose of the research and the likely length of time necessary for the collection of the information. Finally, the research findings themselves must always be reported accurately and never used to mislead anyone, in any way.

RULES

A. Conditions of Membership and Professional Responsibilities

A.1 Membership of the professional body is granted to individuals who are believed, on the basis of the information they have given, to have such qualifications as are specified from time to time by the professional body and who have undertaken to accept this Code of Conduct. Membership may be withdrawn if this information is found to be inaccurate.

General Responsibilities

A.2 Members shall at all times act honestly in dealings with respondents, clients (actual or potential), employers, employees, subcontractors and the general public.

A.3 Members shall at all times seek to avoid conflicts of interest with clients or employers and shall make prior voluntary and full disclosure to all parties concerned of all matters that might give rise to such conflict.

A.4 The use of letters after an individual's name to indicate membership of The Market Research Society is permitted in the case of Fellows (FMRS) and Full Members (MMRS). All members may point out, where relevant, that they belong to the appropriate category of the professional body.

A.5 Members shall not imply in any statement that they are speaking on behalf of the professional body unless they have the written authority of Council or of some duly delegated individual or committee.

Working Practices

A.6 Members shall ensure that the people (including clients, colleagues and sub-contractors) with whom they work are sufficiently familiar with this Code of Conduct and that working arrangements are such that the Code is unlikely to be breached through ignorance of its provisions.

A.7 Members shall not knowingly take advantage, without permission, of the unpublished work of a fellow member which is the property of that member. Specifically, members shall not carry out or commission work based on proposals prepared by a member in another organization unless permission has been obtained from that organization.

A.8 All written or oral assurances made by anyone involved in commissioning of conducting projects must be factually correct and honoured.

Responsibilities to Other Members

A.9 Members shall not place other members in a position in which they might unwittingly breach any part of this Code of Conduct.

Responsibilities of Clients to Agencies

A.10 Clients should not normally invite more than four agencies to tender in writing for a project. If they do so, they should disclose how many invitations to tender they are seeking.

A.11 Unless paid for by the client, a specification for a project drawn up by one research agency is the property of that agency and may not be passed on to another agency without the permission of the originating research agency.

Confidential Survey Research and Other Activities

(apply B.15 and Notes to B.15)

A.12 Members shall only use the term *confidential survey research* to describe research projects which are based upon respondent anonymity and do not involve the divulgence of identities or personal details of respondents to others except for research purposes.

A.13 If any of the following activities are involved in, or form part of, a project then the project lies outside the scope of confidential survey research and must not be described or presented as such:

- (a) enquiries whose objectives include obtaining personal information about private individuals per se, whether for legal, political, supervisory (e.g. job performance), private or other purposes:
- (b) the acquisition of information for use by credit-rating or similar purposes;
- (c) the compilation, updating or enhancement of lists, registers or databases which are not exclusively for research purpose (e.g. which will be used for direct or relationship marketing);
- (d) industrial, commercial or any other form of espionage;
- (e) sales or promotional responses to individual respondents;
- (f) the collection of debts;
- (g) fund raising;
- (h) direct or indirect attempts, including the framing of questions, to influence a respondent's opinions or attitudes on any issue other than for experimental purposes which are identified in any report or publication of the results.

A.14 Where any such activities referred to by paragraph A.13 are carried out by a member, the member must clearly differentiate such activities by:

- (a) not describing them to anyone as confidential survey research and
- (b) making it clear to respondents at the start of any data collection exercise what the purposes of the activity are and that the activity is not confidential survey research.

Scope of Code

A.15 When undertaking confidential survey research based on respondent anonymity, members shall abide by the ICC/ESOMAR International Code of Conduct which constitutes Section B of this Code.

A.16 MRS Guidelines issued, other than those published as consultative drafts, are binding on members where they indicate that actions or procedures *shall* or *must* be adhered to by members. Breaches of these conditions will be treated as breaches of the Code and may be subject to disciplinary action.

A.17 Recommendations within such guidelines that members should behave in certain ways are advisory only.

A.18 It is the responsibility of members to keep themselves updated on changes or amendments to any part of this Code which are published from time to time and announced in publications and on the Web pages of the Society. If in doubt about the interpretation of the Code, members may consult the Professional Standards Committee or its Codeline Service set up to deal with Code enquiries.

Disciplinary Action

A.19 Complaints regarding breaches of the Code of Conduct by those in membership of the MRS must be made to The Market Research Society.

A.20 Membership may be withdrawn, or other disciplinary action taken, if, on investigation of a complaint, it is found that in the opinion of the professional body, any part of the member's research work or behaviour breaches this Code of Conduct.

A.21 Members must make available the necessary information as and when requested by the Professional Standards Committee and Disciplinary Committee in the course of an enquiry.

A.22 Membership may be withdrawn, or other disciplinary action taken, if a member is deemed guilty of unprofessional conduct. This is defined as a member:

(a) being guilty of any act or conduct which in the opinion of a body appointed by Council might bring discredit on the profession, the professional body or its members;

(b) being guilty of any breach of the Code of Conduct set out in this document;

(c) knowingly being in breach of any other regulations laid down from time to time by the Council of the professional body;

(d) failing without good reason to assist the professional body in the investigation of a complaint;
(e) having a receiving order made against him/her or making any arrangement or composition with his/her creditors;
(f) being found to be in breach of the Data Protection Act by the Data Protection Registrar.

A.23 No member will have his/her membership withdrawn, demoted or suspended under this Code without an opportunity of a hearing before a tribunal, of which s/he will have at least one month's notice.

A.24 Normally, the MRS will publish the names of members who have their membership withdrawn, demoted or are suspended or have other disciplinary action taken with the reasons for the decision.

A.25 If a member subject to a complaint resigns his/her membership of the Society whilst the case is unresolved, then such resignation shall be published and in the event of re-admission to membership the member shall be required to cooperate in the completion of any outstanding disciplinary process.

B. ICC/ESOMAR Code of Marketing and Social Research Practice

General

B.1 Marketing research must always be carried out objectively and in accordance with established scientific principles.

B.2 Marketing research must always conform to the national and international legislation which applies in those countries involved in a given research project.

The Rights of Respondents

B.3 Respondents' cooperation in a marketing research project is entirely voluntary at all stages. They must not be misled when being asked for cooperation.

B.4 Respondents' anonymity must be strictly preserved. If the Respondent on request from the Researcher has given permission for data to be passed on in a form which allows that respondent to be identified personally:

(a) the Respondent must first have been told to whom the information would be supplied and the purposes for which it will be used, and also

(b) the Respondent must ensure that the information will not be used for any non-research purpose and that the recipient of the information has agreed to conform to the requirements of the Code.

B.5 The Researcher must take all reasonable precautions to ensure that Respondents are in no way directly harmed or adversely affected as a result of their participation in a marketing research project.

B.6 The Researcher must take special care when interviewing children and young people. The informed consent of the parent or responsible adult must first be obtained for interviews with children.

B.7 Respondents must be told (normally at the beginning of the interview) if observation techniques or recording equipment are used, except where these are used in a public place. If a respondent so wishes, the record or relevant section of it must be destroyed or deleted. Respondents' anonymity must not be infringed by the use of such methods.

B.8 Respondents must be enabled to check without difficulty the identity and bona fides of the Researcher.

The Professional Responsibilities of Researchers

B.9 Researchers must not, whether knowingly or negligently, act in any way which could bring discredit on the marketing research profession or lead to a loss of public confidence in it.

B.10 Researchers must not make false claims about their skills and experience or about those of their organization.

B.11 Researchers must not unjustifiably criticize or disparage other Researchers.

B.12 Researchers must always strive to design research which is cost-efficient and of adequate quality, and then to carry this out to the specification agreed with the Client.

B.13 Researchers must ensure the security of all research records in their possession.

B.14 Researchers must not knowingly allow the dissemination of conclusions from a marketing research project which are not adequately supported by the data. They must always be prepared to make available the technical information necessary to assess the validity of any published findings.

B.15 When acting in their capacity as Researchers the latter must not undertake any non-research activities, for example database marketing involving data about individuals which will be used for direct marketing and promotional activities. Any such non-research activities must always, in the way they are organized and carried out, be clearly differentiated from marketing research activities.

Mutual Rights and Responsibilities of Researchers and Clients

B.16 These rights and responsibilities will normally be governed by a written Contract between the Researcher and the Client. The parties may amend the provisions of rules B.19–B.23 below if they have agreed this in writing beforehand; but the other requirements of this Code may not be altered in this way. Marketing research must also always be conducted according to the principles of fair competition, as generally understood and accepted.

B.17 The Researcher must inform the Client if the work to be carried out for that Client is to be combined or syndicated in the same project with work for other Clients but must not disclose the identity of such clients without their permission.

B.18 The Researcher must inform the Client as soon as possible in advance when any part of the work for that Client is to be subcontracted outside the Researcher's own organization (including the use of any outside consultants). On request the Client must be told the identity of any such subcontractor.

B.19 The Client does not have the right, without prior agreement between the parties involved, to exclusive use of the Researcher's services or those of his organization, whether in whole or in part. In carrying out work for different clients, however, the Researcher must endeavour to avoid possible clashes of interest between the services provided to those clients.

B.20 The following Records remain the property of the Client and must not be disclosed by the Researcher to any third party without the Client's permission:

(a) marketing research briefs, specifications and other information provided by the Client;

(b) the research data and findings from a marketing research project (except in the case of syndicated or multi-client projects or services where the same data are available to more than one client).

The Client has, however, no right to know the names or addresses of Respondents unless the latter's explicit permission for this has first been obtained by the Researcher (this particular requirement cannot be altered under Rule B.16).

B.21 Unless it is specifically agreed to the contrary, the following Records remain the property of the Researcher:

(a) marketing research proposals and cost quotations (unless these have been paid for by the Client). They must not be disclosed by the Client to any third party, other than to a consultant working for the Client on that project (with the exception of any consultant working also for a competitor of the Researcher). In particular, they must not be used by the Client to influence research proposals or cost quotations from other Researchers.

(b) the contents of a report in the case of syndicated research and/or multi-client projects or services when the same data are available to more than one client and where it is clearly understood that the resulting reports are available for general purchase or subscription. The Client may not disclose the findings of such research to any third party (other than his own consultants and advisors for use in connection with his business) without the permission of the Researcher.

(c) all other research Records prepared by the Researcher (with the exception in the case of non-syndicated projects of the report to the Client, and also the research design and questionnaire where the costs of developing these are covered by the charges paid by the Client).

B.22 The Researcher must conform to current agreed professional practice relating to the keeping of such records for an appropriate period of time after the end of the project. On request the Researcher must supply the Client with duplicate copies of such records provided that such dupliates do not breach anonymity and confidentiality requirements (Rule B.4); that the request is made within the agreed time limit for keeping the Records; and that the Client pays the reasonable costs of providing the duplicates.

B.23 The Researcher must not disclose the identity of the Client (provided there is no legal obligation to do so) or any confidential information about the latter's business, to any third party without the Client's permission.

B.24 The Researcher must, on request, allow the Client to arrange for checks on the quality of fieldwork and data preparation provided that the Client pays any additional costs involved in this. Any such checks must conform to the requirements of Rule B.4.

B.25 The Researcher must provide the Client with all appropriate technical details of any research project carried out for that Client.

B.26 When reporting on the results of a marketing research project the Researcher must make a clear distinction between the findings as such, the Researcher's interpretation of these and any recommendations based on them.

B.27 Where any of the findings of a research project are published by the Client, the latter has a responsibility to ensure that these are not misleading. The Researcher must be consulted and agree in advance the form and content of publication, and must take action to correct any misleading statements about the research and its findings.

B.28 Researchers must not allow their names to be used in connection with any research project as an assurance that the latter has been carried out in conformity with this Code unless they are confident that the project has in all respects met the Code's requirements.

B.29 Researchers must ensure that Clients are aware of the existence of this Code and of the need to comply with its requirements.

NOTES

How the ICC/ESOMAR International Code of Marketing and Social Research Practice should be Applied

These general notes published by ICC/ESOMAR apply to the interpretation of Section B of this Code in the absence of any specific interpretation which may be found in the MRS Definitions, in Part A of the MRS Code or in Guidelines published by the MRS. MRS members who are also members of ESOMAR will in addition be subject to requirements of the guidelines published by ESOMAR.

These Notes are intended to help users of the Code to interpret and apply it in practice.

The Notes, and the Guidelines referred to in them, will be reviewed and reissued from time to time. Any query or problem about how to apply the Code in a specific situation should be addressed to the Secretariat of MRS.

The Rights of Respondents

All Respondents are entitled to be sure that when they agree to cooperate in any marketing research project they are fully protected by the provisions of this Code and that the Researcher will conform to its requirements. This applies equally to Respondents interviewed as private individuals and to those interviewed as representatives of organizations of different kinds.

Note on Rule B.3 Researcher and those working on their behalf (eg interviewers) must not, in order to secure Respondents' cooperation, make statements or promises which are knowingly misleading or incorrect – for example, about the likely length of the interview or about the possibilities of being re-interviewed on a later occasion. Any such statements and assurances given to Respondents must be fully honoured.

Respondents are entitled to withdraw from an interview at any stage and to refuse to cooperate further in the research project. Any or all of the information collected from or about them must be destroyed without delay if the Respondents so request.

Note on Rule B.4 All indications of the identity of Respondents should be physically separated from the records of the information they have provided as soon as possible after the completion of any necessary fieldwork quality checks. The Researcher must ensure that any information which might identify Respondents is stored securely, and separately from the other information they have provided; and that access to such material is restricted to authorized research personnel within the Researcher's own organization for specific research purposes (eg field administration, data processing, panel or 'longitudinal' studies or other forms of research involving recall interviews).

To preserve Respondents' anonymity not only their names and addresses but also any other information provided by or about them which could in practice identify them (eg their Company and job title) must be safeguarded.

These anonymity requirements may be relaxed only under the following safeguards:

(a) Where the Respondent has given explicit permission for this under the conditions of 'informed consent' summarized in Rule 4 (a) and (b).
(b) where disclosure of names to a third party (eg a Subcontractor) is essential for any research purpose such as data processing or further interview (eg an independent fieldwork quality check) or for further follow-up research. The original Researcher is responsible for ensuring that any such third party agrees to observe the requirements of this Code, in writing, if the third party has not already formally subscribed to the Code.

It must be noted that even these limited relaxations may not be permissible in certain countries. The definition of 'non-research activity', referred to in Rule 4(b), is dealt with in connection with Rule I5.

Note on Rule B.5 The Researcher must explicitly agree with the Client arrangements regarding the responsibilities for product safety and for dealing with any complaints or damage arising from faulty products or product misuse. Such responsibilities will normally rest with the Client, but the Researcher must ensure that products are correctly stored and handled while in the Researcher's charge and that Respondents are given appropriate instructions for their use. More generally, Researchers should avoid interviewing at inappropriate or inconvenient times. They should also avoid the use of unnecessarily long interviews; and the asking of personal questions which may worry or annoy Respondents, unless the information is essential to the purposes of the study and the reasons for needing it are explained to the Respondent.

Note on Rule B.6 The definitions of 'children' and 'young people' may vary by country but if not otherwise specified locally should be taken as 'under 14 years' and '14–17 years' (under 16, and 16–17 respectively in the UK).

Note on Rule B.7 The Respondent should be told at the beginning of the interview that recording techniques are to be used unless this knowledge might bias the Respondent's subsequent behaviour: in such cases the Respondent must be told about the recording at the end of the interview and be given the opportunity to see or hear the relevant section of the record and, if they so wish, to have this destroyed. A 'public place' is defined as one to which the public has free access and where an individual could reasonably expect to be observed and/or overheard by other people present, for example in a shop or in the street.

Note on Rule B.8 The name and address/telephone number of the Researcher must normally be made available to the Respondent at the time of interview. In cases where an accommodation address or 'cover name' are used for data collection purposes arrangements must be made to enable Respondents subsequently to find without difficulty or avoidable expense the name and address of the Researcher. Wherever possible 'Freephone' or similar facilities should be provided so that Respondents can check the Researcher's bona fides without cost to themselves.

The Professional Responsibilities of Researchers

This Code is not intended to restrict the rights of Researchers to undertake any legitimate marketing research activity and to operate competitively in so doing. However, it is essential that in pursuing these objectives the general public's confidence in the integrity of marketing research is not undermined in any way This Section sets out the responsibilities which the Researcher has towards the public at large and towards the marketing research profession and other members of this.

Note on Rule B.14 The kinds of technical information which should on request be made available include those listed in the Notes to Rule B.25.

The Researcher must not however disclose information which is confidential to the Client's business, nor need he/she disclose information relating to parts of the survey which were not published.

Note on Rule B.15 The kinds of non-research activity which must not be associated in any way with the carrying out of marketing research include: enquiries whose objectives are to obtain personal information about private individuals *per se*, whether for legal, political supervisory (eg job performance), private or other purposes; the acquisition of information for use for credit-rating or similar purposes; the compilation, updating or enhancement of lists, registers or databases which are not exclusively for research purposes (eg which will be used for direct marketing); industrial, commercial or any other form of espionage; sales or promotional attempts to individual Respondents; the collection of debts; fund-raising; direct or indirect attempts, including by the design of the questionnaire, to influence a Respondent's opinions, attitudes or behaviour on any issue.

Certain of these activities – in particular the collection of information for databases for subsequent use in direct marketing and similar operations – are legitimate marketing activities in their own right. Researchers (especially those working within a client company) may often be involved with such activities, directly or indirectly. In such cases it is essential that a clear distinction is made between these activities and marketing research since by definition marketing research anonymity rules cannot be applied to them.

Situations may arise where a Researcher wishes, quite legitimately, to become involved with marketing database work for direct marketing (as distinct from marketing research) purposes: such work must not be carried out under the name of marketing research or of a marketing research Organization as such.

The Mutual Rights and Responsibilities of Researchers and Clients

This Code is not intended to regulate the details of business relationships between Researchers and Clients except in so far as these may involve principles of general interest and concern. Most such matters should be regulated by the individual business. It is clearly vital that such Contracts are based on an adequate understanding and consideration of the issues involved.

Note on Rule B.18 Although it is usually known in advance what subcontractors will be used, occasions do arise during the project where subcontractors need to be brought in, or changed, at very short notice. In such cases, rather than cause delays to the project in order to inform the Client it will usually be sensible and acceptable to let the Client know as quickly as possible after the decision has been taken.

Note on Rule B.22 The period of time for which research Records should be kept by the Researcher will vary with the nature of the project (eg ad hoc, panel, repetitive) and the possible requirements for follow-up research or further analysis. It will normally be longer for the stored research data resulting from a survey (tabulations, discs, tapes etc.) than for primary field records (the original completed questionnaires and similar basic records). The period must be disclosed to, and agreed by, the Client in advance. In default of any agreement to the contrary, in the case of ad hoc surveys the normal period for which the primary field records should be retained is one year after completion of the fieldwork while the research data should be stored for possible further analysis for at least two years. The Researcher should take suitable precautions to guard against any accidental loss of the information, whether stored physically or electronically, during the agreed storage period.

Note on Rule B.24 On request the Client, or his mutually acceptable representative, may observe a limited number of interviews for this purpose. In certain cases, such as panels or in situations where a Respondent might be known to (or be in subsequent contact with) the Client, this may require the previous agreement of the Respondent. Any such observer must agree to be bound by the provisions of this Code, especially Rule B.4.

The Researcher is entitled to be recompensed for any delays and increased fieldwork costs which may result from such a request. The Client must be informed if the observation of interviews may mean that the results of such interviews will need to be excluded from the overall survey analysis because they are no longer methodologically comparable.

In the case of multi-client studies the Researcher may require that any such observer is independent of any of the Clients.

Where an independent check on the quality of the fieldwork is to be carried out by a different research agency the latter must conform in all respects to the requirements of this Code. In particular, the anonymity of the original Respondents must be fully safeguarded and their names and addresses used exclusively for the purposes of back-checks, not being disclosed to the Client. Similar considerations apply where the Client wishes to carry out checks on the quality of data preparation work.

Notes on Rule B.25 The Client is entitled to the following information about any marketing research project to which he has subscribed:

(1) **Background**

- for whom the study was conducted
- the purpose of the study
- names of subcontractors and consultants performing any substantial part of the work

(2) **Sample**

- a description of the intended and actual universe covered
- the size, nature and geographical distribution of the sample (both planned and achieved); and where relevant, the extent to which any of the data collected were obtained from only part of the sample
- details of the sampling method and any weighting methods used
- where technically relevant, a statement of response rates and a discussion of any possible bias due to non-response

(3) **Data Collection**

- a description of the method by which the information was collected
- a description of the field staff, briefing and field quality control methods used
- the method of recruiting Respondents; and the general nature of any incentives offered to secure their cooperation
- when the fieldwork was carried out
- (in the case of 'desk research') a clear statement of the sources of the information and their likely reliability

(4) **Presentation of Results**

- the relevant factual findings obtained
- bases of percentages (both weighted and unweighted)
- general indications of the probable statistical margins of error to be attached to the main findings, and the levels of statistical significance of differences between key figures
- the questionnaire and other relevant documents and materials used (or, in the case of a shared project, that portion relating to the matter reported on).

The Report on a project should normally cover the above points or provide a reference to a readily available document which contains the information.

Note on Rule B.27 If the Client does not consult and agree in advance the form of publication with the Researcher the latter is entitled to:

(a) refuse permission for his name to be used in connection with the published findings and
(b) publish the appropriate technical details of the project (as listed in the Notes to B.25).

Note on Rule B.29 It is recommended that Researchers specify in their research proposals that they follow the requirements of this Code and that they make a copy available to the Client if the latter does not already have one.

CODELINE

Codeline is a free, confidential answer service to Market Research Society Code of Conduct related queries raised by market researchers, clients, respondents and other interested parties. The aim of Codeline is to provide an immediate, personal and practical interpretation and advice service.

Codeline is directly responsible to the MRS Professional Standards Committee (PSC) to which each query and its response is reported at PSC's next meeting. Queries from enquirers are handled by an individual member of the Codeline panel, drawn from past members of the PSC. As long as contact can be made with the enquirer, queries will be dealt with by Codeline generally within 24 hours. Where necessary, the responding Codeline member can seek further specialist advice.

Codeline's response to enquirers is not intended to be definitive but is the personal interpretation of the individual Codeline member, based on personal Code-related experience. PSC and Codeline panellists may highlight some of the queries and responses for examination and ratification by the PSC, the ultimate arbiter of the Code, at its next meeting. In the event that an individual Codeline response is not accepted by the PSC the enquirer will be notified immediately.

Enquirer details are treated as totally confidential outside the PSC but should 'Research' or any other MRS journal wish to refer to a particularly interesting or relevant query in 'Problem Page' or similar, permission is sought and obtained from the enquirer before anonymous publication and after that query's examination by PSC.

Codeline operates in the firm belief that a wide discussion of the issues arising from queries or anomalies in applying the Code and its associated guidelines within the profession will lead both to better understanding, awareness and application of the Code among members and to a better public appreciation of the ethical standards the market research industry professes and to which it aspires.

How to Use Codeline

Codeline deals with any market research ethical issues. To contact Codeline please phone or fax the MRS Secretariat who will then allocate your query to a Codeline panellist.

If you choose to contact MRS by phone, the MRS Secretariat will ask you to confirm by fax the nature of your query, whether or not the caller is an MRS member or works for an organization which employs an MRS member and a phone number at which you can be contacted. This fax will then be sent to the allocated panellist who will discuss your query directly with you by phone as soon as possible after receipt of your enquiry.

Please forward any queries about the MRS Code of Conduct and Guidelines, in writing to the:

MRS Secretariat, 15 Northburgh Street, London EC1V OJR
Tel: 020 7490 4911 Fax: 020 7490 0608.

Index